BANTUSTANS

A TREK TOWARDS THE FUTURE

BANTUSTANS

A TREK TOWARDS THE FUTURE

BY

PAUL GINIEWSKI

Human & Rousseau

CAPE TOWN

1961

PRINTED BY
CITADEL PRESS · CAPE TOWN
TYPOGRAPHY BY A. J. MALHERBE

ACKNOWLEDGEMENTS

I am indebted to many South Africans for the experiences, the facts, the ideas reported in this book. Some I met in person, others I met through their writings. I am particularly grateful to Garry Allighan, Dr. the Hon. Thomas Boydell, Mr. Justice H. A. Fagan, George Golding, W. van Heerden, C. W. de Kiewiet, J. J. Oberholster, Alan Paton, P. S. Rautenbach, Anton Rupert, J. L. Sadie, A. Schauder, and many more, Bantu, Coloured, Afrikaner and English, who asked me not to mention their names in the report of this inquiry.

The photographs in this book
have been supplied by the Information Office
of the Department
of Bantu Administration and Development
and by the South African Information Service

CONTENTS

Introduction   1

PART I · ANATOMY OF A SMOKESCREEN
Anatomy of a smokescreen   7

PART II · ANATOMY OF THE PROBLEMS
1. History   19
2. South Africa's three million Whites   27
3. Why South Africa is disliked   39
4. Eleven million Bantu   48

PART III · ANATOMY OF A SOLUTION
1. The roots of apartheid   85
2. Bantu Education   98
3. The agricultural development of the Bantu territories   114
4. The industrial development of the Bantu territories   127
5. Self-government   152
6. New frontiers   177
7. How much independence?   182
8. Coloureds and Indians   188
9. South Africa and the wind of change   209
10. The creative withdrawal   220
11. The heavy burden of the white man   246

God always takes the side of the persecuted. If a just man persecutes another
just man, God puts himself on the side
of the persecuted; if a bad man persecutes a just man, God puts himself on
the side of the persecuted; and if a just
man persecutes a bad man, God puts
himself on the side of the persecuted.

VAYIKRA RABBA, 27

INTRODUCTION

I

On the threshold of the last third of the twentieth century, Western civilization is on trial in two different parts of Africa. In Algeria and in South Africa, the "little Europes" at the extremes of the Black continent, Western civilization must prove, through new policies, new trends, "new deals", that it can still adapt itself to the inexorable changes which make up the march of history. World opinion demands generous policies, in line with the true fundamental principles of the West. This challenge is important; the way in which the West meets it, in Algeria as in South Africa, will determine the entire future attitude of the Black continent. If the policy is generous, it may lead to a reconciliation between Africa and a Europe which will have accepted the continuation of its mission, the "heavy burden of the white man" which yesterday meant colonization, and today means the ending of colonial ties. If the policy is selfish and short-sighted, it may consummate the break of Africa's Mediterranean ties and attract it into the orbit of the East, whence come all the political lures, the technicians, the automatic votes against the nations who yesterday were the masters of the Blacks.

This inquiry is concerned with one of the great problems of the African continent. It proposes to throw a candid glance over the shoulders of one of the "dunces" of the White world: South Africa.

Many bad things are said about South Africa; she is judged severely; and she has, indeed, a considerable number of sins on her conscience. But because she is very far away, at the other end of Africa, she is not well known. Sometimes she is misunderstood, and what is known about her is so twisted by propaganda, prejudices, and the ready-made ideas held in 1961 about Blacks and Whites, and about their relationships, that one must fight against a giant tide of false ideas and misconceptions which have beclouded the truth, when one wants simply to recount facts. To get rid of prejudices is not easy.

1

I once had a strict teacher who always asked us to summarize our problems, sometimes in a single word. He claimed that a well-posed problem is always susceptible to such short cuts.

This teacher would have found a perfect example of this in the problems of South Africa, for they can easily be summarized in one word—perhaps one of the most complex words formed in the clash of theories, the word *apartheid*.

Few words have so many meanings, few words contain so many contradictions, few words are making so many rivers of ink flow—and let us pray that there will not also be rivers of blood. The word apartheid and the realities it stands for, are no more for internal consumption in South Africa alone. Africa is today one of the most important theatres where world history is taking shape. This history is written and played in strange languages (in the proper and figurative meaning of this word) almost unknown in the political vocabulary of the European scene; the playwrights and the actors have scarcely made a name for themselves to the north of the twenty-third parallel. This book has a double purpose: 1. to clarify the meaning of apartheid in all its political, social and cultural implications for the readers of Europe; 2. to present a mirror to South Africa, where South Africa, perhaps, will recognize some of her most hidden features. Sometimes, when analysing with a fresh eye, a foreigner is able to uproot the few big trees obstructing a clearer view of the entire forest, and to act as pathfinder . . .

II

By offering solutions to the problems of South Africa with all the audacity of a distant observer, and the irresponsibility of a witness who is not an actor in the drama, I am simplifying an extremely complex matter.

My exacting teacher also wanted the replies to problems to be condensed into one single word.

By offering South Africa a remedy in three syllables, *Bantustans*, as a solution to the three syllables of *apartheid*, I am subscribing to a policy which has, amongst those who are interested in the affairs of Africa, more opponents than supporters. Its detractors try to give it a meaning of division and degradation, but to me it sounds rather like the "Judenstaat", the "Jewish State" of Theodor Herzl, sounded in the ears of the Jews at the end of the nineteenth century. This was a one-word idea, a three-syllables idea.

The word Bantustans, when applied to the Bantu, seems to me of the same psychological texture as the Jewish State of Herzl: a challenge which human nature instinctively wishes to meet, like the rivers we harness in dams, and the peaks we climb to affirm our domination over nature. In the "Judenstaat" also appeared the underlying folly of wishing to turn into a state the human wrecks, the flotsam and jetsam of a nation discriminated against and rejected by mankind, which the entire world thought impossible to regenerate after so many insults.

Yet, when writing on December 3, 1897: "I have founded the Jewish State; if I said it out loud there would be a roar of laughter, but in five years, in fifty years, everybody will admit it," Herzl was only mistaken by a few days, as the decision of the United Nations to create the state of Israel was made on November 29, 1947. Herzl was a prophet in the literal meaning of the word. His political descendants have made a dogma of the conviction that the true realist is he who believes in miracles and in the reality of utopias . . .

III

The word Bantustans has the same utopian quality and merit; it is the same apparent impossibility, the same empty dream, and yet I believe the idea to be as great and as valid as the Zionist utopia, and just as indispensable to the rapid march of humanity towards its better future. This book sides with both factions in the contest, with the Blacks in South Africa and with the Whites in South Africa.

I am strongly convinced that both causes are just and capable of just solutions, although both goals are at the summit of a high peak, and a lot of climbing, a great fatigue awaits both Black and White on this arduous journey.

I believe in the fruits of effort, I believe in the virtue of hard work.

In their magnificent *Martin des Magiciens*, Louis Pauwels and Jacques Bergier say that "the gap has not yet been bridged between the old times of the shotgun and the time of the space-rocket. But people are thinking of a bridge. We write to add to this thinking."

3

Mine is a similar purpose. I believe, as Chesterton put it, that ideas that don't tend to become words are bad ideas, that words that don't tend to become acts are bad words . . .

PART ONE

ANATOMY OF A SMOKESCREEN

ANATOMY OF A SMOKESCREEN

Anton Rupert lifted his glass of South African sherry, called the waiter, and asked him for the bottle. The waiter put it down on the table, and Rupert pushed it towards us.

"You see," he said, pointing to the label, "produce of South Africa . . ."

Rupert finished his sherry, and our little group left the lounge to go up to the private room on the first floor where the table had been laid for eight. A bright wood fire was burning in this room; the flames added red and yellow to the blue Delft tiles.

Dr. Anton Rupert is one of the outstanding industrialists of South Africa. Within a few years he has built up a tobacco company with vast international ramifications. He has given his group, as its coat-of-arms, a self-portrait of Rembrandt, enclosed in an oval frame— an emblem which is turned out by the million from the presses of Stellenbosch. I had gone without much enthusiasm to meet this industrial magnate, for I did not think he would have very much to say to me on my own problem. But from the start, from the first casual sentences, I put away my fountain pen and notebook and looked squarely at him. I was obviously in the presence of a keen, guiding intelligence, not just a voice automatically replying to me. Only occasionally and by chance, anywhere in the world—in ports, in aeroplanes, at international grand hotels—does one meet such patently leading intellects. This is a reward one occasionally has in the dreary round of news-gathering.

"First of all take the name of our country—South Africa. I wonder how much this name 'Africa' is responsible for the picture they have of us abroad, of the Whites, as impostors and intruders in a Black man's country. Does that seem absurd to you? It does not to me. The other day in Hamburg, I was making a little investigation. Now, Hamburg is an intellectual town, and a great port, with an international outlook. I realized then that the idea they have of South

Africa is of a country compounded of jungles, tropical forests, coconuts, bananas and great heat. There are wild animals and snakes everywhere, the people are either excessively lazy or completely primitive, and protected by shields covered with skin they struggle through jungles. Others—and I must emphasize that we are in Hamburg in 1961—conjure up images of great deserts of sand, pyramids and gold and diamonds to be picked up in handfuls. Those who know a little more are convinced that there are only Whites in the towns and that all the Blacks work in the mines or on the farms. The dominant impression is that the Whites treat the Blacks as slaves, and that it is time these Whites went home.

"I did meet one solitary old man who had a vague memory of the Transvaal, the Boer War and of Oom Paul Kruger.

"In the eyes of the world, our international trade-mark is a cute little Black boy, with strings of Zulu beads around his neck, busily stirring his porridge in a big earthenware pot.

"That is the picture they have of Africa, and we can't get rid of it. That is the meaning the word 'Africa' has for them, and it has become our label. We would, perhaps, have done better to have called ourselves Natal or Transvaal or Land of Good Hope. Instead of that, our publicity does the opposite, and we exploit the Africa theme. To attract tourists, we beat drums, we exhibit Bantu pottery and skins; we present ourselves as a country of primitive life, of wild animals roaming around free in our national parks. And, after all that, how the devil can we explain to people that we are the most modern country on the continent, that we have thousands of miles of tarred roads, that we produce more steel than the rest of Africa put together, that we have the biggest wine cellars in the world, the biggest synthetic petrol plant in the world, the most modern air-conditioned mines, and that the Bantu have more than 100,000 motor-cars registered in their names? You just go and tell them that. They won't understand it; and we ourselves are responsible."

II

South Africa today is one of the world's powder-kegs.

Sharpeville (like Little Rock, for completely the opposite reasons) has become a symbol, and people think of it with sympathy, pity and hope, as well as resentment. And so we wait, expecting news of some

8

new Sharpeville, ten times bigger, if that were possible; or for some huge massacre of the Whites after a revolt. We wouldn't really be astonished, and a good many of us wouldn't even be upset. But apart from Sharpville, apart from this vague sense of impending doom in Johannesburg, we have only the faintest idea of the problems of South Africa. Who are the people most actively involved? What is the situation of the Blacks? Who are they? What is being denied them? What is the meaning of this word "apartheid"? What kind of people are the Whites? If we look closer we discover an immense smokescreen, a whole series of smokescreens enveloping this country and its problems. Smokescreens of malicious propaganda put up by the enemies of the Verwoerd Government, smokescreens which systematically distort the more praiseworthy and the more dis-interested aspects of its policy, to emphasize only the dark side; the smokescreens of self-justification, ineffectual because clumsy, put up by this Government; and, worst of all, the smokescreens of routine and comfort which hide from the White people of South Africa that reality which they are so well placed to observe and to control, since they are in the midst of it, and since they create it.

As though we were flying, jolted about in the thick clouds, we see nothing on the other side of the fog. But there is another side—there are many other sides. Beyond the clouds the countryside is visible. Suddenly, through the plane's window we catch a glimpse of clear, sun-bathed land, all the more vivid as the clouds are low.

"Within a few years," added Rupert, "we have lost our greatest ally : distance as expressed in time—and most of us haven't even noticed it. Just think : within three generations it has taken seven months, then seven weeks, then seven days for a letter to reach South Africa from Europe. Soon it will take seven hours : planes which take seven hours already exist. And the age of the postal rocket, when it will take seven minutes, will be tomorrow. The world has shrunk. There are no longer matters which affect Europe and not us. We can not longer claim to be interested only in our own internal affairs, in our own little parish. Since Hiroshima the history of each country is world history. What takes place in one country and in one nation, despite the great variety of po-litical and social systems, will have repercussions in all other coun-tries, and in all nations. All of us, all the peoples of the world, are

9

caught up in a chain reaction of revolutions : the military revolution brought about by nuclear bombs; the scientific revolution of ballistic weapons and the conquest of space; the historical revolution of the Soviet Union as a world power; the industrial revolution of automation which is moving towards the elimination of human work; the political revolution of Africa and Asia, who are freeing themselves. Even here, in our own country, one does not realize that three revolutions are simultaneously disturbing the three layers of South Africa's population : the 'American revolution' of the Afrikaners, who won their War of Independence in 1948 when the Nationalists came to power; the 'industrial revolution' of the English who are busy transforming our country into a Power; the 'French revolution' of the Blacks who want liberty, equality and fraternity. And with all this we are already in a biological revolution which concerns the Lapps as much as the people of Leningrad. At the dawn of our civilization, five thousands years ago, there were twenty million people on the earth. Our annual increase is forty million. At this rate there will be six thousand million people on the planet in the year 2000. In 39 years, to be exact, that is to say in the lifetime of most of us, half of this population will be Chinese and two-thirds will be Asiatic. Whatever may be the degree of civilization and the degree of freedom achieved by this mass of people, we can assume that we shall be living in a second 'medieval' epoch when men can travel without passports and can live freely where they want to.

"This means that international pressure will be brought to bear on all the under-developed countries. And we are, in relation to our immense resources, a completely under-developed country. We will be told : if you do not exploit your wealth, we will do it for you. Perhaps nothing will even be said to us, and our riches will be seized, because people will be hungry, and because we have uncultivated land; because people will be cold, and we have forests; because people will be unemployed and we have unexploited riches. In order to forestall this danger, we must first of all recognize it."

Rupert said all this simply but seriously. He had clearly grasped the anatomy of the smokescreen which clouds the minds of his compatriots and prevents them from seeing what is going on . . .

. . . which prevents them from seeing that they are not alone with their problems; that the whole world is watching them; that this is

10

inevitable; and that if they fail to solve their problems, their most distant neighbours will one day do it for them . . .

III

To illustrate the problems of the Blacks in South Africa, the American example is often used. There was a time in the United States when the Blacks had no rights. The Americans passed laws against segregation and, against all expectations, the Whites accepted them, by and large without a fuss, just as the Parisians (recently) accepted the prohibition of their traditional street noise—the motor hooter. Why not do in South Africa what was done in the United States?

The example of the United States is one of those smokescreens which consistently obscure the real issues in South Africa. Those very people who do not know anything about it, will use the example of Little Rock . . .

Comparison, of course, is ever a paradox. In Israel, for instance, they often say: "We received a million and a half immigrants, and it is just as though France had taken in seventy million in ten years." With such arguments one can prove anything, that is to say, nothing. A thousand workers were necessary to build this bridge in ten years, and so ten thousand workers . . . and so on, and so forth. Logic explains neither reality nor fact: the South African fact is specific, as is the American fact.

And the solutions adopted on one side of the Atlantic cannot be exported to the other end of the world.

But since America is a part of the complex of ideas that constitutes Africa for us, let us come to grips with the fact behind the fiction.

One sees that in America, ignoring legal technicalities, the North is for integration, the South for segregation. This is simply because in the North there are few Blacks, and in the South there are many of them. I think that for this simple reason the integrationists, if they were living in the South, would be segregationists, and *vice-versa*. If integration is today the national policy of the United States, it is because there are 90 per cent Whites and 10 per cent Blacks, and there is no possibility at all of the White population being absorbed by a Black minority . . .

Neither is there in America discriminatory legislation against Blacks. This is because the Blacks, as soon as they had crossed the

11

barriers of a certain number of social conventions, came across not the law, but illegal action of the Whites, "who took the law into their own hands". The shock-absorbers placed in the United States at the precise points where Black expansionism could manifest itself, are the laws of the lynch gang, not the laws of apartheid. If a few hundred Blacks of Harlem took it into their heads to live near Fifth Avenue, they would not hold out for five minutes.

They would be told to buzz off, they would be beaten up, and their houses might even be burnt. The Whites would be on top, because they are 90 per cent of the population.

A parallel could be drawn between the United States and South Africa, but only if the following conditions obtained in America:

If it had a population of twenty million Whites, who would, for example, have French (or rather a dialect of French) as a mother tongue;

If it had fifteen million other Whites who speak English;

If it had 400,000,000 Indians of different tribes, barely emerged from tribalism;

If it had 160,000,000 of these Indians living in their own hunting grounds, and living according to the law of their ancient customs;

If there were another 120,000,000 Indians in the areas of the Whites;

And if there were a further 120,000,000 Indians in the big towns belonging to the Whites, drunk on the new wine of the Western civilization which they had recently assimilated in strong doses, but had not well digested.

In addition to all this, there would have to be 20,000,000 Coloureds, living for the most part grouped around a single town— Boston, for example—and 5,000,000 Asiatics and a few groups and sub-groups of lesser importance, notably the Eskimos.

If 40,000,000 Whites, placed in these conditions, and holding the reins of power, adopted the present-day racial policies of the United States government, then, of course, the comparison would be valid. If then this policy worked smoothly and to the satisfaction of all, the government in Pretoria should, of course, make inquiries in order to apply it at home . . .

"The decision of the United States Supreme Court against racial discrimination in education was more than a statement of principle. It was also a manifestation of security," wrote a South African historian.* This is perfectly true. The Whites of the United States do not feel in danger because they are not in danger.

IV

Another illusion is that the Republic of South Africa is a multi-*racial* state. South Africa is a multi-*national* state in which several nations are rubbing shoulders with one another, a situation which sooner or later must lead to a sharing of the land. In travelling across South Africa one soon realizes that the problem of discrimination as it is seen by liberal opinion is badly conceived. When one visits the Transkei and the Ciskei, fairly compact "reserves" where, because of their traditional attachment to their homelands, a truly national Xhosa community is concentrated, with its own language, its own tribal customs, its hierarchy of chiefs and even a "Parliament" which possesses certain powers, then one realizes that in the heart of South Africa there is a truly homogeneous core in which the national unity, the cultural, and even the economic levels are not inferior to the standards which have given national independence to other groups in Africa, together with all the exterior signs of power, such as a flag and a seat in the United Nations.

The individuality, the homogeneity of the tribal groups in the Northern Transvaal and in the East of South Africa are less accentuated, if only for this simple reason—the lands occupied by the Blacks and the Whites are more inextricably mixed, giving one the confused picture of a map of Germany in 1780 with its duchies, its counties, its margravats and its principalities, like a haphazard mosaic. But one could easily imagine the results of partitioning, of exchanges of territory consolidating the regions of dense African population. One would then have seven or eight national territories, corresponding to the great Bantu "nations" who live side by side today in South Africa, each one of whom could rightfully claim a flag.

One then realizes very quickly that the true problem of South Africa is not the assimilation of the Blacks by the Whites, of the integration of the Blacks in the cultural and economic community of the Whites—who would then certainly be submerged—but the classical problem of decolonization.

In 1652, when the Dutch East India Company established a

*C. W. de Kiewiet : *An Anatomy of South African Misery.*

"refreshment station" for its ships, South Africa was an outpost of the classical type. Since the middle of the eighteenth century she has been an underpopulated colony. Since the diamond and gold booms of the nineteenth century she has been a European country, and since the industrial boom of the past World War she has been an industrial power. South Africa has the unique advantage of colonies in the very heart of the mother country, which saves transport costs of the manufactured products to overseas territories, and transport costs of raw materials to the metropolitan power. That is why South Africa has been one of the richest colonial powers whose riches are irrefutably proved by the standard of living which she enjoys. But at the point of no return which the colonial powers have reached on the road to freeing all their subject peoples, this advantage is turning into a handicap. South Africa cannot carry on a "colonial war" to retard an evolution, because that would be civil war. South Africa cannot free her colonies by purely and simply abandoning another Congo, because that would bring anarchy to the heart of Johannesburg and Durban. One must, therefore, for this singular situation find singular solutions.

This is the aim of the policy of apartheid, officially defined as a policy of "separate development" for the two groups, Black and White, each in its particular sphere.

If this policy is honestly carried out to its logical and necessary conclusion, which is the creation of Bantu states (or Bantustans) corresponding to the different Bantu "nations" then apartheid is just, and must be given all support. Whether these Bantustans enjoy complete independence, or whether they are linked to the Republic by political and economic ties—these are problems for the future.

It is certain that the nationalist aspirations of Africa's march towards "international sovereignty" must be completely realized in South Africa. The Blacks who now carry "passes", which to most of them symbolize their handicaps and the controls to which they are subjected, must instead be given passports which would symbolize sovereignty; and that, they would very quickly learn, is made up more of responsibilities than of liberties: but nothing except complete political emancipation will satisfy them.

If "separate development" effectively leads to this emancipation, we must welcome it wholeheartedly, and we must even accept, as inevitable evils, certain negative measures of apartheid which tend to confine the Blacks in their territories, to use their creative energies in their own national environments, and to raise their political capacities only in the Black communities. These evils are inherent in a process of education, which can never be free from constraint.

But if the policy of apartheid uses its positive content only as a veil of decency to camouflage measures of oppression, and if oppression is being entrenched at the expense of independence, then we must reject the whole comedy, and do our best to force the actors off the stage.

"If the final result", Dr. Verwoerd declared in Parliament in 1959, "is a situation in which there would be Bantu groups and territories (or states, if you would prefer it), I am in agreement." And Thomas Boydell, in an appeal which was widely published in the South African Press on August 10 of the same year, warned the supporters and the opponents of apartheid against "assailing the honesty of purpose of the Government and impugning its integrity. If once the trusting Bantu lose faith by being constantly told they are just being fooled, and that this so-called nation-building is a dishonest trick on the part of the White man, retribution and vengeance will deservedly follow."*

V

When approaching the problems of South Africa, I wanted to know whether the Government was sincere or not, to decide whether I should applaud or accuse, which battle I should invite my readers to join.

I had a very simple idea of things: Three million Whites and eleven million Blacks live side by side within the frontiers of the same state. The Blacks do not take part in the government of the state. They are told that separate states are being prepared for them. If this was true, I was going to approve this policy and help the Government of Dr. Verwoerd. If it was false, I was going to denounce the fraud, and work to modify the policy of this Government: in either case, I was going to write a book to justify my convictions.

I thus tried to see through the smokescreens, to decide who had set them up, or who feeds them their smoke.

Before leaving for South Africa, I must add, I had my "working

*Thomas Boydell : *My Beloved Country.*

15

hypothesis"—innate convictions, strongly felt, but without rational cause.

I think complete justice must be done to the Blacks, as it should be done to any race. But the huge tide of liberation which is sweeping the world, and which is filling us with enthusiasm for the rights of Coloured races and of ex-colonial peoples, has a meaning only if the rights of the White man are not in their turn trampled on—because the White man has great merits, acquired throughout his history, which is the history of human civilization. Has the White man *no* rights? Does the White man need no protection? Is it not the White man who freed the Black man from the jungle, from war, from disease?

Consequently I believe that many of the slogans shouted by newly-independent people are partly false or inevitably facile generalizations, and that "Africa for the Africans" is the prototype of that false slogan, "Europe for the Europeans". However the idea of Europe as an entity may have developed, it does not mean that a Norwegian in Spain or Italy, or in Luxembourg, should have the same rights as he has in his own country.

I do not feel any of these guilt complexes, which seem to imply that the non-White man should be allowed everything: rape in the Congo, the theft of the Suez Canal, the destruction by the Afro-Asian group of the immense hope which the United Nations meant for us after World War II. I think that the White man has the right to defend himself against these abuses of a noisy adolescence, exactly as a non-European is justified in struggling for his rights, and winning them, in the teeth of all who refuse him.

VI

After one leaves Nice in the late afternoon, in the brightness of a summer sun, one sees the season change quickly to winter as one flies south over this truly black continent. In the opaque darkness one builds up a splendid image of the immense virgin stretches with the isolated lights of its aerodromes, and its distantly-spaced cities. One arrives at Johannesburg during the day. In the daylight, after the African night, a veil of mist parts itself to reveal its great golden-coloured minedumps and its skyscrapers.

16

PART TWO

ANATOMY OF THE PROBLEMS

Just and moderate governments are everywhere quiet, everywhere safe. But oppression raises ferments, and makes men struggle to cast off an uneasy and tyrannical yoke . . . Suppose this business of religion were let alone, and that there were some other distinction made between men and men upon account of their different complexions, shapes and features, so that those who have black hair, for example, or grey eyes, should not enjoy the same privileges as other citizens; that they should not be permitted either to buy or sell, or live by their callings; . . . that they should either be excluded from the benefit of the laws, or meet with partial judges: can it be doubted but these persons, thus distinguished from others by the colour of their hair and eyes, and united together by one common persecution, would be as dangerous to the magistrate . . . But there is one thing only which gathers people into seditious commotions, and that is oppression.

John Locke
A LETTER CONCERNING TOLERATION
1667

CHAPTER 1

HISTORY

I

"Why don't they go back to England?"

We are in 1961. Television, press and radio have popularized the most complex ideas. One can follow on the screen the process of history in the making: in the forum of the United Nations, in the streets of Budapest, or in the charnel-houses of the Congo; and one can still hear it said, when the problem of South Africa is discussed, "Why don't they go back to England?"

This is because the problems of South Africa are so badly known, except for sporadic outbursts of violence and discriminatory laws which oppress the Blacks and dishonour the Whites; so that for many people this country is like the Congo or Ghana or the Ivory Coast: let the Whites go back, let independence be given to the Natives, and everything will then be all right.

One cannot compare South Africa with the Congo or with Ghana, or with any of the new Black states of Africa. In the former European colonies the White man was represented by a minority of officials, missionaries, teachers and traders, who came one after the other as temporary residents, and by a layer of colonists who left once they had made their fortunes.

At best, these colonists were rooted there for only a generation. But all of them had a motherland elsewhere. They spoke its language, they carried its passports. They were not of Africa. The colonies were, above all, producers of raw materials, and drew their revenue from the export of natural resources. Most of them were underdeveloped countries.

South Africa has no colonists. Most of her three million Whites have roots which grow back two or three hundred years into the historical soil of this country. They are not officials and traders who return to their own country after serving their time in the colonies. There are some who look to England as the "spiritual fatherland": but they are the minority, and they would not dream of uprooting

19

themselves. The majority, the Afrikaners of Dutch origin and the South Africans of English culture, no longer have any kind of relationship and affinity with the country of their ancestors. South Africa is a sovereign and independent state in the widest sense of the word. She is such a "European" motherland that she is, in her turn, forced to decolonize, to grant independence to those parts of her territory inhabited by "natives". The economy of the country has been built up by these three million Whites. It is industry, and not the export of raw materials, which supplies most of the national revenue—quite the opposite to what happens in the under-developed countries.

Only one attempt at the evacuation of the Whites of South Africa took place: that of the Boers in 1900. The Governor of Arkansas offered five million acres of his state to welcome them. So did Colorado. Wyoming had actually sown 300,000 acres for them.* Not one South African out of a hundred thousand remembers these attempts. Sixty years ago already it would have been impossible.

The rightful claims of the Whites in South Africa are not only rooted in their origins, their total population and their economic success. The Bantu are, indeed, as recent immigrants as the Whites.

When the Whites arrived three hundred years ago there were no Bantu at the Cape. The local population was composed of a few nomadic tribes of Bushmen and Hottentots. *There was not a single Bantu in the whole of the territory of the present Republic of South Africa.* The Bushmen have survived. The Hottentots, very few in number, were almost entirely wiped out by an epidemic of smallpox in 1713. By a curious twist of history, at the very same time when the White man was disembarking at the Cape, the Bantu was crossing the Limpopo, which forms the present northern frontier of the Republic.

South Africa was thus simultaneously "invaded" from the South and the North by two groups of immigrants, who, urged on by the same need for space and grazing, were going to take eighty years before meeting one another. In 1736 a hunting expedition of eleven Whites, led by Hermanus Hubner, was attacked on the Fish River by a hunting party of Xhosas, the most southern group of the Bantu. There is a striking parallel in the destiny of these two groups, and the legitimate rights of the one are the basis of the legitimate rights of the other.

*Evelyn Waugh, *A Tourist in Africa*.

Because if the South African Bantu of today have inalienable rights to their country, the Whites have similar rights. And if we refuse to admit the rights of the Whites, then we deny that the Bantu have any moral basis for their demands. When the Dutch met the Xhosa on the Fish River, it was an encounter between two migratory peoples. The Whites came from Europe, and had landed at the Cape two thousand years after the indecisive voyages of the ancients. The Bantu, who had come from the forest regions of the Gold Coast and from the Great Lakes and who were crossed with Hamitic blood from the North, had begun their migration in the ninth century, and by the seventeenth had reached Bechuanaland to the West, Barotseland, and Natal to the South-East of their primitive cradle.

Further: The legitimate rights of the Whites are also based on "historical moralities". The Whites not only arrived during the same period as the Bantu; their areas of the country have also been developed much better than the areas conquered by the peoples from the North.

The Bushmen and the Hottentots are an example of this. Coming originally, it is believed, from what is now Somaliland, they must have been pushed back little by little by Bantu pressure right down to the South of Africa. In their march, the warlike Bantu tribes massacred and reduced to slavery the weaker tribes. The Zulus under Chaka and Dingaan in Natal, the Matabele under Moselikatse in the Western Transvaal, exterminated whole peoples. Voortrekkers who penetrated the Transvaal and the Orange Free State found huge spaces where the *impis* of the Zulu and Matabele had destroyed everything. Rare survivors of scattered tribes were hiding in the mountains, starving and reduced to cannibalism. In his *History of the Basutos*, Ellenberger estimates "that in 1833, shortly before the arrival of the Voortrekkers in the region between the Orange River, the Drakensberg and the Vaal, there were eight thousand cannibals who had devoured more than 288,000 human beings between 1822 and 1828."[1]

It is certain that the Whites, wherever they penetrated, ended the reign of "hunger, terror and devastation."[2]

[1] Sen. J. H. Grobler, *Africa's Destiny*. The Book of the Month Club, Johannesburg, 1958.
[2] Dr. W. W. M. Eiselen, *Christianity and Religious Life of the Bantu*.

21

The tribes who survived owe this to the arrival of the Whites. A historian of the Bantu Wars, McCall Theal, estimates that one of the Zulu chiefs, Chaka, was alone responsible for the death of two million Bantu. Whites and Bantu thus penetrated simultaneously into a no man's land. They brought with them differing ethics and differing ideas of behaviour. This is not a partisan point of view, but a statement of historical fact.

On the question of legitimate rights, White rights in South Africa must also be briefly compared to White rights in two territories where the circumstances of conquest do have parallels—the United States of America and Australia. These two countries "belong" to the indigenous races in a very different way to South Africa. The Red Indians in North America and the Aborigines of Australia controlled their countries until the arrival of the Whites: these two races have almost completely disappeared. We know what was done to the Red Indians. The history of the conquest in Australia is less known, but giving poisoned food to the Aborigines, a sort of rat hunt, was a general practice amongst the colonists.

L. E. Neame in *White Man's Africa* reminds us that "the Boers who penetrated into the hinterland of the Cape did not—as the Whites did elsewhere in the world—destroy the original inhabitants. When the English and the French began to colonize North America, the Red Indian population probably consisted of about a million people. Today, there are five hundred thousand. In Australia and in New Zealand they have been exterminated. In South Africa the Natives have increased three or four times since their contact with the White man . . ."

II

The discovery of South Africa goes back to 1486, and this honour goes to the Portuguese.

Portugal in the fifteenth century had a flourishing trade with India and China, but the land route taken by the traders in silks and spices was so uncertain, so many robbers preyed on the caravans and so many taxes were levied during the journey, that Portugal had every incentive to establish a direct route.

Bartholemew Diaz sailed round the southern tip of Africa in 1486. Vasco da Gama did the same in 1497. Da Gama even dropped anchor in St. Helena Bay, a little to the north of the Cape. But the

22

Portuguese did not settle in the South of Africa, which gained a sinister reputation after Don Francisco d'Almeida, the Viceroy of the Portuguese Indies, and 65 men, twelve of whom were captains, were massacred by the Hottentots there.

That was in 1510: he had anchored in Table Bay, the present site of Cape Town, to take on water . . . For yet another century the Cape was to remain virgin until its nominal "annexation" in 1620 (the year in which the Mayflower set sail for America) by two English captains, Shillinge and Fitzherbert, who ran up the Union Jack over Saldanha Bay: until 1648 when a Dutch crew spent a year there after a shipwreck. The landing of the Dutch, which was the first stage of the true history of South Africa, took place in 1652. The Dutch had also been driven by economic motives. In 1581 the Union of Spain and Portugal under Philip II had led to the secession of the Low Countries, and to the closing of Lisbon to these ships of the Netherlands Provinces which used to go there to buy spices in bulk, afterwards retailing them throughout Europe. In order to replace this market and to obtain supplies of spices, the Dutch had to navigate on their own account the passage to the East: in 1602 they founded the Dutch East India Company, which had the right to establish colonies, to wage war and make peace, to navigate, to mint money and to exercise sovereign rights wherever they pleased.

It was on the sixth of April, 1652, that the Drommedaris, the Reyger and the Goede Hoop dropped anchor in Table Bay. This small fleet was commanded by Jan van Riebeeck, one of the company's surgeons. His mission was a limited one: to establish a refreshment station for ships almost half-way in their long, ten-month journey between Texel and India, a station which would be able to supply them with fresh water, fresh vegetables (to prevent scurvy) and meat. This undertaking was so free of colonial intent that most of the officials left without their wives. They were going to return home once their mission was over. It was so non-political that Van Riebeeck was told what to do if another nation established a refreshment station at the Cape: "not to pay any attention as long as the place chosen would be beyond the limits that you will have chosen for your own safety and for your stock and your crops". The garrison was to consist of seventy to eighty men. Almost at the same time other Hollanders had reached Manhattan. They had also built a fort in the form of a star, according to the plans drawn up by the same expert from Utrecht. The American Van Riebeeck was called Peter Minuit. Both of them baptized the first street that they had laid the "Heerengracht" . . .

However, within a few years the re-victualling station grew. Growing vegetables, buying them from the native peoples, and selling them to passing ships was not a work for officials. To encourage production—productivity, we would say today—the company in 1657 created "free burghers", who were given land and pasturage. But faithful to the monopoly principle, which governed mercantile thought in the seventeenth and eighteenth centuries, prices and standards were fixed for them. In 1688 there were already some six hundred burghers who had set up villages as far away as Stellenbosch, Drakenstein and Paarl, and who were beginning to murmur against the iron hand with which the company controlled them. They were beginning to claim political rights and to think of moving away in a "trek" to get away from this unsympathetic authority— a very easy matter in this empty and deserted country. This tendency to trek, to escape physically, was born very early. It was going to dominate the whole of the history of South Africa.

All the future problems of South Africa were there in embryo in the Dutch establishment.

When the Hottentots did not bring enough cattle to the Cape, it became essential to send out exploring parties to the hinterland to bring back the Hottentots and their herds to the ships. When the Hottentots could not supply the increasing numbers demanded, there was nothing else for them to do but to go in for stock-breeding themselves. They thus occupied pasture land: they discovered the country. From this developed genuine colonization, and also the conflict with the native peoples, sometimes about rights to cross territory, sometimes on the question of stock-theft, of which both sides were guilty. From these conflicts came the need for a defined frontier to separate the colonists from the Hottentots and to prevent further fighting. In the beginning the company wanted to dig a ditch across the Cape Peninsula to isolate its officials and to avoid trouble. Van Riebeeck was satisfied with planting a hedge of bitter almonds and building three forts whose names reveal a lot about the intention of this Maginot Line. They were *Kijck-uyt* (Look Out), *Keert de Koe* (Stop the Cow) and *Houd den Bul* (Hold the Bull). But as soon as a frontier was set up, natural expansion, the need for more land for crops, and the natural increase of men and cattle, made it ineffective and out of date.

In 1685 the revocation of the Edict of Nantes brought a wave of French immigrants to South Africa. Already under Philip II the expulsion of the Jews and the Protestants had made the Low Countries into a powerful nation, thanks to the capital and the enterprise of the exiles who found refuge there. Louis XIV through another act of intolerance was going to grant to Holland and the new colony of the Cape an infusion of fresh blood.

The frontier was marching irresistibly towards the hinterland. The successive *placaats* of the administration redefined the White and Black territories after each new advance of the trek towards the interior. But these ordinances merely defined an accomplished fact and could neither modify it nor prevent future developments. The whole history of South Africa is the history of a frontier on the march, and of ordinances which could not stop it . . .

When London conquered the Dutch colony at the Cape in the Napoleonic Wars, the "Boers" again fled farther to the interior in the great historical Trek of 1838. They were fleeing from the new laws that the English had imposed: the controlled sale of residential land which deprived farmers whose ideal was never to see the smoke from a neighbour's chimney, of free and unlimited land; the abolition of slavery in 1835, which ruined them; the reforms which introduced between master and servant an equality which was a scandal in their eyes.

They fled so far that they finished by setting up, far from the Cape, their own republics in the Transvaal, in the Orange Free State and in Natal. And the "Voortrekkers"—literally "those who go ahead"— fled with such obstinacy, that they acquired during their trek, as did the people of Moses in the Sinai Desert, the characteristics of a new nation. This was the Afrikaner nation, with its language and its will to be; *Afrikanerdom*, so deeply rooted in its desire for independence that the Anglo-Boer War at the end of the nineteenth century was not to get the better of it.

The racial problem was born with the creation of the colony. There were too few Whites, and every day more food and cattle were needed for the ships. Van Riebeeck never stopped asking for slaves to carry out the heavy work. In 1658 a first batch of 398 were imported, bought in Angola in exchange for red and black beads. This was a great historical error. From the influx of slaves, later imported from the East, were to be born the Coloured people of the Cape, and the habit of the Whites, which they have not lost, of carrying out only the best-paid work, of importing foreign labourers and later of engaging the Bantu as servants, rather than of encouraging European immigration.

They are paying for this comfort by their dangerous demographical situation. There are today only 3,000,000 White South African citizens and 12,000,000 of other races.

Today the drama of South Africa lies in the fact that there is now an irresistible trek of the Bantu towards the ever-increasing industrial domain of the Whites: just as there was in former times a trek of the Boers towards the infinite horizons of the veld. By means of inverse *placaats*, which are the laws of apartheid, they wish to dam the flood. They want to build frontiers of hedges and ditches; but the tide is flowing and the White man is caught up in it.

CHAPTER 2

SOUTH AFRICA'S THREE MILLION WHITES

I

Who are the Whites of South Africa and what do they think?
I must reply to this question, and also to a parallel question which
will be asked further on: what are their attitudes to the establishment
of independent Bantustans?

From the point of view of their attitude to independent Bantu-
stans the Whites in South Africa can be classified into Afrikaners of
Dutch origin, and "English" of British origin, a rough and im-
perfect approximation since the three million Europeans include
Jews who are neither Dutch nor English, Frenchmen, Germans,
Italians, Portuguese, Greeks, etc.

I think I can affirm rather loosely:

1. That the Afrikaners favour the establishment of Bantu states,
and that the "English" are against. This is, of course, a generalization since a number of Afrikaners oppose the policy of the government;

2. That this issue is the main factor dividing the Afrikaners and
the "English"—although other important questions (the establishment of a republic, for example) have also found them divided,
and still do;

3. That the Nationalists are for apartheid and that the United
Party, the Progressives and the Liberals are against, but each of
them with nuances which makes this *for* and *against* sometimes a
political platform, sometimes an ideal, sometimes an alibi, and
rarely the basis of an active, comprehensive and logical policy.

II

However, all these Whites have many points of view and attitudes
in common about the Bantu problem: Smith and Smit are in agreement about the essentials.

What they have in common is, first of all, the impression—as

Anne-Marie Labarraque puts it so well*—of losing more each day:

"They suspect everybody of wishing to get rid of them, and they spend their lives in fear. They begin by fearing their own White brothers. The Afrikaners, usually farmers or civil servants, accuse the English and the Jews of monopolizing key-posts in industry. The English, on the other hand, feel frustrated by the electoral laws established by the Afrikaners. The Jews are worried by the Nazi tendencies of certain Nationalist organizations.

"The White population, in the first and last place, fears the Blacks. They are afraid that they will rob them or commit acts of aggression against them. House-owners never completely trust their non-White servants, and they are continually wasting time hiding their cupboard keys and then looking for them again! Cottages are often disguised fortresses, with thick doors armed with heavy bolts, and burglar-proof windows. The head of the family possesses at least one fire-arm. For, more than a burglary or an isolated attack, the White man fears a massive open revolt. The *tête à tête* with people of a different colour worries the White man more and more."

Fear, the worst of advisers, makes the Whites take up attitudes which a foreigner can only see as contradictory. The Leader of the Opposition does not want separate representation of the Coloured people in Parliament, but he agrees that there should be separate representation for the Bantu; he does not want Bastustans, but he wants social and residential apartheid. The Anglican Church condemns official apartheid, but applies it in its schools. Most English-language journalists fight on all fronts against apartheid, but would never dream of sending their children to a mixed school, and segregation is applied in the columns of their newspapers right down to the "society news" items. One would probably not find ten thousand Whites in the whole of South Africa who would accept sacrificing the right of the Whites to exist as a racial and national community. A journalist on the *Vaderland*, one of the moderate Nationalist newspapers in the Republic, told me one day about his childhood on his father's farm in the Transvaal, about how close he felt to the Bantu, how without any feeling of condescension, prejudice or hatred.

"When I am with them in the Reserves, or in a location," he said, "I sit down with them, on their bench, in their smoky hut, and I drink tea or eat a meal with them. Believe me—except for conditions

*"L'Afrique du Sud, pays des contrastes et de la peur" in *Réforme* 14.5.60·

28

of hygiene—I feel as at home as with Whites. Separate post offices, benches marked *Whites Only* and *Non-Whites Only* do not shock me, unless the facilities that we offer the Bantu are greatly inferior to our own. In the political field, I know that a majority of Bantu cannot live for ever without rights."

But after a long silence, the journalist said: "That's what I think with my head. But my heart feels differently . . ."

This is the feeling of most South Africans. Smith and Smit really want to give the Black man his freedom, whatever the consequences. They want to have a pure conscience. But their whiteness must not be threatened. Smith and Smit are in agreement about this.

In a book about the South Africans* there is a parable which clearly summarizes the average feeling of the White man in the problem and the problems it contains:

"The White man has awakened the native, and, like a dream, the old savage life is ended. He has been called. He has arisen. He is on the road—travelling in the shadow of the white man, carrying his chattels.

"The white man looks around at this being he has himself aroused, who is following him; who is serving him; who is dependent on him; for whom, on the journey, he must provide. And he thinks how useful it is that someone else's back shall be bowed under his burden, while he is free to exult in the air and sun of Africa.

"The native follows patiently. Now it is time to take food. The white man throws the native a scrap. They go on again. The native is useful to the white man but also he makes demands on the white man's resources. The master begins to wonder, a little resentfully, if he would not, on the whole, have been happier without his servant.

"The journey is an arduous one. The white man opens up again his bundle of food, and thinks that, really, he cannot afford to give any more away, that he needs it all himself. He begins to be resentfully conscious of this creature who makes demands on him. If only he could shake him off, he mutters to himself. He begins to feel that he is being dogged. He begins to suspect that the native isn't keeping a decent distance. He begins to distrust him, to fear him. The native, he knows, is not getting enough to eat. What if he were suddenly to take it into his head to spring upon him, and rob him of his means of sub-

*Sarah Gertrude Millin: *The South Africans*, Constable & Co., London, 1937.

sistence, and run away ahead of him, and leave him there to starve?

"How can he get rid of the native? How can he get rid of him?

"He begins to make suggestions to the native that he should retrace his steps, return home to his beginnings.

" 'Look here,' he says, 'this journey of ours has been a mistake. You and I can't do it together.'

" 'It is hard for both of us,' admits the native.

" 'You'd better leave me,' says the white man. 'You'd better go back home.'

" 'Go back?' says the native. 'Home? . . . But the road has fallen in behind us. And my home is broken up. How can I go home now?'

" 'You are taking the bread out of my mouth,' protests the white man.

" 'But I am carrying your load.'

" 'I could have carried it myself. It would have been better.'

" 'Then why did you call me?'

"They face one another, unable to move forward, unable to move back.

"And 'I wish to God I never had called you,' mutters the white man."

III

The *National Party*,* which for the purposes of our study we are identifying with militant Afrikanerdom, thinks, however, that they must separate. The road that has fallen in must be rebuilt, and the ruined homes replaced.

The National Party has a very simple doctrine: for each race it must be possible to develop, materially and spiritually and in its own territory, to the full its innate gifts and capacities, and for this the territorial and political separation of the Bantu is necessary.

Everything predisposes the Afrikaners to this drastic attitude. Bantu nationalism, which they foster, is the complement of their own Afrikaner nationalism.

*At the dissolution of Parliament in 1961 the state of parties was as follows: National Party—98; United Party—42; Progressive Party—11; National Union Party—1; Coloured Representatives—4. Total: 156.

The Afrikaners are largely members of the working classes of the White population. They live in the less smart suburbs of the industrial towns. Although this simplification may not be quite true now, the days when it was so are recent enough for the Afrikaners not to have forgotten them. The Afrikaner is thus in direct daily contact with the Bantu. Very often he does the same work as the Bantu, but he enjoys the privilege of higher wages because his skin is white. The Afrikaner worker resents the threat to his privileged position represented by the Bantu worker. Segregation is for him a guarantee, and sometimes the only *reality* which distinguishes him from the Bantu.

From a historical point of view, the Afrikaners became a nation long before South African "nationality" existed. They learnt very early on to shoot first and to worry afterwards about the shadow in the bush; to despise the civilized comforts of the "flesh pots". Their enemies were brutal and cruel; Potgieter, one of their first leaders, was flayed alive by the Makapans, and his skin exhibited to the curious. The life in the wilds made them strong and hard. It selected them.

Foreign observers too often neglect this dominant factor of the South African scene: the will-power of the Afrikaner people who form the majority of the White population, and who have inherited from their still recent pioneering past characteristics that are seeking adequate outlets. These people feel they are coming into their own. They struggled for a long time to set up their republics in the Transvaal and in the Orange Free State. When they lost them, in 1902, they struggled for the equality of their language and culture, and obtained it in the Act of Union in 1910. England had won the Boer War, but the defeated emerged victorious. While their English-speaking countrymen were building up the economic prosperity of the country, they slowly consolidated their political position. Today these people are a nation in their own right, and they have completed their victory by creating the Republic of South Africa in 1961.

Not to take into account the dynamism and the faculty of "counter-logic" possessed by these people, would be a grave mistake. To condemn their vision by saying that the wrong Bantu policy will cause the gold mines large losses, is completely irrational. On the contrary, one must count on this potential dynamism in order to achieve a just solution to the problems of South Africa.

It is true that the Afrikaner people have developed the typical characteristics of a "young" nationalism. In this respect, they are no more mature than certain Black nations in Africa. People cannot be encircled, at the extreme point of Africa, and exposed to the "wind of change" sweeping away frontiers and régimes, without suffering from claustrophobia and some impatience. In addition, the Afrikaners have no central sanctuary of their national existence which could survive the loss of their outposts. They know that they will live or die on the soil of Africa, with their history, their culture and their language.

One cannot, of course, deny that this feeling has sometimes led them in regrettable directions. The fact that a number of Boers wanted Germany to win in the First World War, can be explained by the help they had received a decade earlier from Germany in their war against the British Empire. Their opposition to the active participation of South Africa against the Third Reich, in the Second World War, reveals, to say the least, that they did not understand the meaning of the war. On other levels, which have nothing to do with international affairs, one saw an extremist cultural organization of Afrikanerdom during the war years call itself the *Ossewabrandwag*, the "guards of the ox-wagons", a name which clearly reveals their desire for ethnic isolation; and even to-day one sees movements like the *Voortrekkers* next to the Boy Scouts, the *Noodhulpliga* next to the St. John's Ambulance Brigade, and the *Rapportryers* next to Rotary. One sees the *Boerenasie* building ivory towers for itself in the name of its *volkseie*, its national identity, and the *andersdenk-endes*—those who think otherwise—are less well thought of than the most liberal English. Of course, these extreme cases never teach one much about the average mentality. But one cannot help shuddering at the story of the young *ware Afrikaner*, this true patriot of Brits in the Transvaal, who received the gold medal of the Anti-Asiatic League because he refused food in the hospital where he was being treated when he learnt that there were Indians in the kitchens!

Most Afrikaners would be prepared to condemn the stupidity of the *ware Afrikaner* of Brits, with his gold medal, and the McCarthyism of the Anti-Asiatic League. The Afrikaners are beginning to understand that power entails responsibility, that they are not alone in the ship they are steering, and that others, together with them, will either reach the blessed shores or go under, depending

32

upon the direction they take . . . This book hopes to describe the course that has been taken, to point out some of the rocks and to map out the right course for this dangerous journey.

IV

The others are all those who do not believe that militant Afrikanerdom can establish parallel states for the Bantu. These "others" are not only the "English" but also many Afrikaners who believe in a policy that differs from that of Dr. Verwoerd.

When the Opposition condemns the discriminatory laws of apartheid, it takes a stand on moral considerations. One can and one must subscribe to any firm condemnation of racial discrimination, and I shall examine in detail these discriminatory laws in a later chapter. The non-Nationalists also condemn the positive content of apartheid (the separate development of the Bantu states) together with the discriminatory laws, and in spite of their well-developed arguments, I very often had the feeling that they were condemning more the authors of the policy than its content.

When this condemnation is not purely emotional, it is based on economics. We then hear much of the crime against sound economic development which aims at exiling the Bantu to the Bantustans, instead of fully employing all the available forces of the population. We hear of the error of ideologies which see the Bantu only as intruders, and not as immigrants who do not need to immigrate. Critics bemoan the short-sightedness of the Afrikaners who do not see that joining the economic interests of the Whites and Blacks, in a richer South Africa, would create a more powerful nation than their present conflicts and mutual distrust.

The *United Party* is the official Opposition. Its policy can be summed up in four words: "White supremacy with justice". Contrary to the Nationalists, this party does not believe in a rigid system, in great theories. "We do not claim," Sir De Villiers Graaff told me, "to solve the problems which will confront the country a hundred years from now."

The party wants the Bantu to be considered a member of the South African community and to be allowed to develop within it, not separated from the Whites, but in such a way that White and Black share the fruits of Western civilization. Economic integration is not

33

only a fact but a dynamic necessity, which must be regulated, watched over and controlled. The normal corollary of this growing economic integration is political rights which must be granted to the Bantu but "after a long period of training in the ways of democracy and, particularly, in its responsibilities."

In practical politics, the United Party wants to maintain social and residential segregation and to establish parliamentary representation for the Bantu, but with separate electoral rolls and the franchise granted only to educated Bantu, according to norms which have not yet been defined. It condemns the establishment of Bantustans. To prevent the political and cultural swamping of the Whites, it advocates a massive immigration policy, which would allow for a total White population of fifteen million by the year 2000. With regard to every stand it takes, the party insists that their proposed measures "must not endanger the leadership of the White man, who remains, for the foreseeable future, the guardian of Western influence in South Africa." The great majority of English-speaking South Africans belong to this party.

The *Progressive Party* goes far beyond the official Opposition. It accuses the Nationalists of wanting to partition the country, and the United Party of wanting to perpetuate the hegemony of the Whites. The ideology of the party could be defined as "a common front of civilization against backwardness". The party wants to abolish all discriminatory laws. It thinks that the play of natural economic factors will bring the situation to normal: that the Bantu will cease to pour into the towns when normal wages are paid in the country and when the reserves have been developed.

The Progressives want the franchise to be granted to all, on a common electoral roll, and subject to the same qualifications. The party accepts the possibility of a Bantu majority in Parliament and of a Bantu Prime Minister. To prevent the domination of the White minority by a Bantu majority, the party advocates a form of racial federalism, which would consist in entrenching a certain number of fundamental rights in a rigid constitution, beyond the reach of a racial majority. This constitution would preserve the national interests of minorities by not allowing a majority vote to amend the constitution, the laws on the use of the official languages, the closing of schools, eligibility, etc.

Consequently, as long as the Whites remain the majority of civilized people in the country, they will rule. When the Bantu group has more civilized members, it will gain control. People will rule because of their degree of civilization, and not because of the colour of their skins.

The *Liberal Party*, at the other end of the scale, has a doctrine of absolute equality between all races. It envisages universal suffrage on the common roll to all adult South Africans with a Bill of Rights entrenched in a rigid consititution, and based on the Universal Declaration of Human Rights, which will protect the rights of all individuals. The party does not think in terms of racial groups and envisages the establishment of a non-racial society.

What chances have these divergent policies of succeeding?

In my opinion there is something basically immoral in the United Party's policy. They wish to perpetuate the rule of the White community, at least in the foreseeable future, but they refuse to allow the Bantu community the possibility of freedom. This policy is also based on the dream that the White population could be increased five-fold in less than forty years!

The doctrine of the Progressives is probably even more of a dream. The notion of a rigid constitution guaranteeing minority rights, is blindness. The history of all the minorities persecuted in spite of legal barriers is proof of this. A democratic régime can only survive as long as it is not overthrown, and if it is the constitution of the former régime is no longer any help to those enslaved. No senate, and no right of veto can do anything against physical force. Professor D. V. Cowen, who drew up an "alternative to apartheid"* in which the thesis of a rigid constitution is defended with all the skill of a constitutional historian, is obliged to admit in the end: "Constitutions can make the way of the transgressor difficult; they can delay a determined majority; they can do much to tame power and prevent its abuse; but they can never, of themselves, provide complete security and create a healthy society."

It seems to me that the only opposition doctrine which is consistent is that of the Liberals, who accept the implications of their generous doctrines, without claiming to hold back the forces they are seeking to liberate. The policy advocated by the Liberals is as honest in accepting the political or biological consequences of a total and

*"Constitution-making for a democracy"—Supplement to *Optima*, Mar. 1960.

individual emancipation of the Bantu, as the doctrine of the Nationalists who desire their total and *collective* emancipation. Liberals, as
well as Nationalists, are reconciled with the idea of a Black Prime
Minister. The Liberals accept the eventuality of a Black Prime
Minister in Pretoria, the Nationalists prefer this Prime Minister in a
capital of his own.

V

The antagonism between the Afrikaners and the English is super-
imposed on these conflicts of doctrine.

Passengers in the same boat as the Afrikaners, the English nonetheless put on, during this dangerous journey, a detachment which
exasperates their fellow-citizens of Dutch origin. In *Inside Africa**
John Gunther observes that the "Boers" write "Europeans only" on
reserved benches. The English would doubtless prefer: "Natives,
please keep away." This is both true and significant. The roots of the
Afrikaner people plunge deep into pre-industrial Europe, the brutal
Europe of feudalism and dynasties. The English arrived in South
Africa after the industrial revolution, which had transformed their
country and international ethics.

"The English," Anton Rupert said to me, "are masters in the art
of evolution without revolution. We can learn from them . . ."

This is what the Afrikaner people have not ceased to do during the
common history of the two communities, but they have always
revolted against the discipline of this master who taught them some
of the indispensable facts of life, but who, at the same time, took
away from them many illusions and many liberties.

Did not the Englishman import English, the language spoken by
the whole world, a language which made the Afrikaner pale with
jealousy because his own language was understood by nobody
abroad? Did not the Englishman, with his missionaries, open the
Kingdom of Heaven to the Hottentots, spoiling their usefulness on
earth?

Did he not compel the Boers of the nineteenth century—with
force because it was necessary—to accept the twentieth century?

Did he not, by imprisoning the fiercest Nationalists during the

*Hamish Hamilton, London 1955.

36

Second World War and by taking away their guns and by forcing them to participate in a war they did not like, save the honour of the whole country and that of the Afrikaners by making them participate, in spite of themselves, in the victory of the free world over the Nazis?

The English did all that . . .

And isn't even the gradual emancipation of the Bantu, the policy of the Nationalist government of building Bantu states, in keeping with strict British colonial tradition, according to a process which is the opposite of integration?

"By and large," writes Raymond Cartier, "the English in South Africa would like the laws applied to the Bantu to be more flexible and more human. They would like the racial policy to be modified so as to attract to the side of the Whites the one-and-a-half million Coloured people and the half a million Asiatics, instead of welding them to the Blacks by applying the same treatment to them. The English plead for careful handling, but the idea that White supremacy could be destroyed, that the equality of the races could be applied, that the Houses of Parliament in Cape Town could be engulfed by a majority of Black men is as inconceivable to them as to the most obstinate Boers.

"In the eyes of the latter, the English are guilty of cunning and hypocrisy. They are also guilty of intellectual frivolity and lack of foresight. They treat the racial policy of the National Party as a weapon for the Opposition, instead of expressing the essential solidarity of three million Europeans faced with the storms of Black nationalism. As deeply racialist as their compatriots of Dutch or French origin, they are playing around with the problem, whereas the Boers see themselves as openly and courageously seeking solutions. *The English are losing the future in order to improve the present moment.* They crown their incoherence and their defection by supplying arguments, and sometimes even names, voices and pens, in order to blacken in the eyes of the world the principles and the aims of the Afrikaners . . ."

In actual fact, I believe that the English are the moderating "Senate" of Afrikanerdom.

Their "progressive" ideas and their "liberalism", as we defined them above, have no chance of becoming a practical reality, even within their own ranks. But these progressive ideas moderate the

Afrikaner demand for that spiritual and political autonomy which is out of place today, and which was expressed long ago in violent doggerel:

Als ooit 'n wêreldkatastroof
ons liewe aard in twee mag kloof,
o God, geef dan, dat Engeland
*hom niet bevind aan onze kant.**

*If a cosmic catastrophe were to befall us
and our beloved world to split in two,
o God, let England
not be on our side . . .

WHY SOUTH AFRICA IS DISLIKED

I

We must now stop and think.

The Whites of South Africa are unpopular. A journalist who told me about his South African adventures shortly before I set out on my own journey of investigation, hoped that they would all die, and he felt the same kind of hatred towards them that people had felt towards the Nazis.

Why?

Why do we feel so strongly about South Africa?

Five years ago, when "Operation Evacuation Sophiatown" began in Johannesburg, the world echoed with violent protests. The Archbishop of York solemnly proclaimed "that this evacuation of sixty thousand Africans could be compared with the mass deportations carried out by the Nazis and in the Communist countries". An irreparable blow would be struck at individual liberty, and the human dignity of a Black population would be irrevocably trampled upon. Hundreds of journalists who had come from the four corners of the earth with their cameras and television equipment, focused their lenses on the removal lorries and the police cordons and waited for the explosion. Public meetings had been banned in Johannesburg for fear of a spark igniting the powderkeg. In actual fact, nothing happened. And when the superintendent of Meadowlands, the new "camp for the deportees", was asked whether he had had any difficulties with those under his control, he replied: "Yes, I had numerous difficulties—and I still have them: how to get rid of the people who are clamouring to come and stay here".

In spite of the facts, a film was shown on television and in cinemas throughout the world, and this film claimed that it gave an objective picture of South Africa. One of the sequences about Sophiatown showed "the systematic destruction by bull-dozers of African houses whose owners had spent years paying for them". Nobody mentioned the fact that this move was in the interests of public health. And yet, the film producer could have shown the scenes of public rejoicing organized at the time of the expulsions, the comfortable houses which took the place of the old slums, and the queues waiting at the municipal offices to be moved of their own free will. The film critic of the *Rand Daily Mail* (a newspaper opposed to Dr. Verwoerd's government) called this reel "one of the greatest hoaxes in film history."

One must have visited the slums of South Africa to understand that Sophiatown in Johannesburg and Cato Manor in Durban are gangrenous sores. A single group is interested in perpetuating these moral ulcers: the gangs of tsotsis who, with their razor-blades and their coshes, extort "protection money" from the honest families they terrorize; the brothel-keepers and bootleggers who have no chance of survival in a "location", with its straight streets, its numbered houses and its large green spaces—in short, in a well-policed built-up area. For all the other inhabitants of the slums who camp without water, without light, without garbage disposal, without heating, without shelter under the rusty corrugated iron and biscuit tins, under tents of sacking with wooden supports; for all the Whites who know them, it is unthinkable that anyone can prefer the horror of these cesspools to substantial houses which have a roof, heating and proper sewerage, and which gives the individual the benefit of clear, much desired social advancement. And I am deeply convinced that whoever wrote a line against the forced destruction of the slums had either never seen slums or was animated by base motives. The Rev. Blaxall, who built up a wealth of documentary evidence against South Africa, was forced to admit that "Whoever compares this rehousing of the Bantu to the deportation of the Jews does not know what he is talking about, and gives the South African Government an opportunity to point out that public opinion abroad does not know the truth . . ."

In one of his best books, *Le Droit Raciste*, Jacques Maritain has shown the genesis of anti-Semitism in the collective consciousness through the power of propaganda.

"Direct the attention of people along a certain path", he writes, "and they will immediately see incidental data which serve as a pretext for spontaneous systematization, however absurd it may be. If you were to repeat with all the methods of intensive propaganda that all the inhabitants of Fifth Avenue are crooks, the other inhabitants of New York would end by noticing that such-and-such a citizen against whom they had a grudge was, in fact, living on Fifth Avenue. And then another one, and then another one . . . The unpleasant people we have to suffer in other parts of the town, escape this searchlight which is thus fixed on us. And after a few months you would have created an 'anti-Fifth Avenue-ism' that is just as reasonable and as well founded as anti-Semitism".

One cannot help thinking of the power of abusive generalization, when one looks at South Africa. For motives which I will try to make clear, our field of vision is very narrow when we look at South Africa—and we do not see the other countries on the same continent, and all the other countries on all the other continents where Black, White and Yellow are deprived of the fruits of civilization for all kinds of motives which are not nearly as valid as the simple fact that they are not yet mature.

When the Bantu Education Act was passed, the curriculum, even before its contents were known, was denounced as being retrogressive and inferior to the curriculum of the Whites. When a school for sons of chiefs was set up at Tsolo, the South African Opposition vehemently denounced this perpetuation of tribalism; and when I visited it I observed that a great many of the pupils were commoners who were brought there owing to their scholastic success. Nobody tried to get any profit from this important shade of difference. The British Press never stops printing stories that South Africa is on the eve of a catastrophe, and public opinion in Great Britain seems to be convinced of it. And yet British investors, known for their prudence, have sunk £600,000,000 in this burning volcano since the fall of Smuts in 1948. And each time that anybody speaks about an imminent uprising, it takes place in Kenya, Nyasaland, the Belgian Congo and Rhodesia or simply in Brixton or Nottingham. And when the Mau Mau kill the Whites in Kenya, they even go so far as to blame the Whites. When it is a question of South Africa, they call it a racial riot (that is to say an uprising of the Blacks against the Whites) when the police swoop on a shebeen and White and Black policemen have to deal with a mob. Up to now there have practically been no riots of Blacks against Whites, nor has a single Black been lynched by Whites in South Africa.

Whatever may be the hard South African reality, there is an unjust prejudice against this country. This prejudice is cultivated chiefly by those who have no right to throw the first stone.

India is vehemently asking the United Nations to intervene in South Africa. This is in terms of Article 55 of the Charter which recommends the implementation of basic human liberties without distinction of race, sex, language and religion. However, the Indian delegate to the General Assembly of the United Nations in November 1956 declared with regard to the conflict between his country and Pakistan "that he would never subscribe to any statement or any proposition which had been submitted to the Assembly that did not take into account the sovereignty of a member state." The Hon. Sardar Patel, Deputy Prime Minister of India, himself declared at Bombay that he would not tolerate "any intervention in our internal affairs, even if it means the end of India, the end of Pakistan, the end of the world." And did not the Soviet Union itself, which is always so ready to denounce the violations of the rights of man by the government of Dr. Verwoerd, at the third session of the General Assembly maintain that "the internal laws of the Soviet Union do not concern the United Nations" when she was herself accused of "violating the fundamental rights of man, the traditional customs of diplomacy, and other principles of the Charter"?

If one comes down from the level of relations between state and state to that of individual judgments, one finds the same prejudice against the South African people.

As soon as the grandchildren of the Boers come up for discussion, all the dark sides of the country are given the limelight, and as soon as there is a fault, it is immediately given prominence. It is almost impossible for an article to be published in New York about the development of the Reserves or the creation of a Bantu university at Turfloop: but it is almost certain that the smallest police raid in a Durban suburb will have front-page honours in London. Yet we could remind critics that the situation of the Bantu in South Africa is, above all, the heritage of a century of British administration; that passes, segregation, and the herding together of Bantu in the mines of English capital are the heritage of the preceding régime; that in 1960 the eleven million Bantu had an income of £400,000,000, which is not much, but certainly a good deal more than the £48,000,000 they had in 1910, that is to say £33 per head instead of £6, or three times as much, taking into account devaluation.

Before 1948 a good deal more blood flowed in South Africa than since the Nationalists came to power, but in those days the blame was inevitably laid on the Bantu and the régime of General Smuts received every indulgence. Criticism of the present political and social system in South Africa and complete silence about the position before 1948 are the rules in the Press and in literature throughout the world. The most idiotic nonsense has been written about the recruiting agencies which supply labour to industry, the mines and trade. They are often said to be agencies by which the state recruits slave labour from the Bantu population. Has anybody written that they replace the odious system of recruiting agents who were paid commission on each worker they procured for their bosses and who, in order to pocket their capitation "fee", recruited any man, no matter how unsuitable, simply so that they could add him to their lists? These men were often torn away from their native villages by bribery, exorbitant promises or even by threats.

In many ways South Africa is being unjustly attacked. This is immoral in itself. In addition it allows South Africa to escape the explanations one is justified in asking.

I will come back to these explanations and I will then tell the leaders of the Afrikaner people what I think of their abuses and their errors, as I am saying here what I think of the abuses and errors of their opponents.

And, while we are about it: when correct perspectives are deformed under the weight of propaganda, we must sometimes ask ourselves why, if South Africa is such a hell for Black people, hundreds of thousands enter as illegal immigrants; and a good number of them do not hesitate to brave the crocodiles of the Limpopo and the wild animals in the Kruger National Park on the borders of Mozambique.

III

Yes, for what reason?

The simplest one which I have just pointed out is, of course, the fact that South Africa does not merit only reproach.

We must make our criticism correspond to reality, and not torture and twist the truth to the point of justifying any reproach, no matter what. Otherwise we will find ourselves morally disarmed when there really are (and there are!) dark sides and tragedies to be corrected. But does the world know enough about the way sensational newsmongers dishonestly provoke events so that they can then "objectively" record them?

The techniques of the American news cameramen who photographed lions in a zoo in Mozambique because they had not been able to find any at the right time on the South African side of the frontier are not dangerous. But their English colleagues who used the same method in a department store in Salisbury last autumn so as to be able to film an "explosion of racial hatred" by inventing it, should, to my mind, be severely punished.

Three times they photographed three Blacks who, very correctly dressed and with perfect manners, entered the cloakroom for Whites. As nothing happened, they came back accompanied by an African woman who posed as a customer at the hat counter. They got a photograph at the very moment when the salesman was politely inviting her to go and try a hat on in the room reserved for Coloured people. He was lifting his arm to take back the hat that the African woman had put on her head.

Of course it is absurd that in Salisbury, as in Johannesburg, the cloakrooms may only be used by people with the right skin colour, and that the hats of the Whites should be thought to be contaminated by some mysterious disease once they have touched the heads of Africans. But what must we think of the methods used by these people who try to fabricate an incident with no other motive than to picture, or provoke, something which must be studied much more deeply before its true significance can be seen, or before an attempt can be made to change it? Do people know that these rehearsals can degenerate into bloody disorder?

The White man sees in the non-White peoples, who were yesterday completely subject and worthy only of police action, only very remote, very improbable enemies situated somewhere on the other side of the Third World War when the victorious White block will be confronted in its turn by a then mature non-White block of nations. The White man confronted with the non-White peoples feels only an immense complex of collective guilt for the imaginary and real injustices that he has inflicted on them. His noble humanitarianism which has brought them education and medicine, the very foundations of their emancipation, is being degraded. His liberalism is being demoralized. He is becoming incapable of correctly evaluating what is real in the efforts of South Africa to solve her problem.

And he quite naturally turns South Africa into the scapegoat because he must transfer his guilt onto a far-off object. Besides, South Africa has laid herself open to criticism. She labels herself segregationist and she has put herself under the banner of apartheid; others are more astute and cover up with fine words a reality which is much worse. There is, in the clumsiness of the Boer who is honest enough to define things clearly when a lie would have protected him from many reproaches, a source of the deep prejudices which are felt against South Africa.

Moreover, "separation" has for so long and in so many places been synonymous with *inferiority* that it is very difficult to see in it, even at the end of the road, parallelism and equality. One is not yet ready to see in this "separate development" a Bantu "Zionism" with all the weight and the resources of a government willing to achieve it. Do the United States, which believe so mistakenly that the states of their South are *not* their colonies, imagine that they would not also have set up a constructive policy of apartheid if they had had five hundred million Negroes in their territory instead of fifteen million, and fifty million Indians instead of 350,000?

Do they really believe it, these Americans who are made of the same spiritual flesh as South Africa? They, whose farmers in love with wide open spaces sang, like the Boers, *give me land, lots of land . . . don't fence me in*, whose popular tradition of meals under the vaulted sky, which are called barbecues or braaivleise, recalls their very close pioneer ancestors; whose subconscious memories are haunted by the same images: the family gathering around the ancient black Bible; the trek towards the hinterland for new lands to conquer, the wagons formed into a circular *laager* to resist the hostile attacks of Indians or Blacks, with the same valiant women in their long cotton skirts loading the rifles of the same colonists with their large felt hats . . . Who, in circumstances similar to those of South Africa, has behaved differently—and who *would* have behaved differently?

If the Press, the government and public opinion in Great Britain are in the vanguard of those who denounce Dr. Verwoerd's government it is because the British feel more strongly than anyone else the guilt-complex towards the ex-colonial peoples, because they treated them with great severity, and their aggression complex is most acute. Great Britain is not motivated by humanitarianism. Was she human in Cyprus, was she human in Palestine?

Great Britain is so adamant in her denunciation of Dr. Verwoerd's government because she will not accept having lost in 1948 the last battle of the Boer War. In the same way she has never been reconciled to the independence of Eire. When the United Party was in power, discrimination and apartheid, which then had other names, was a just and good policy. At heart, the only thing that the decidedly imperialistic British people cannot easily pardon the Afrikaners, is that they have a political majority in their own country, and are leading it, and are calling their streets Voortrekkerstraat, Van Riebeeckstraat, Krugerstraat. And are not the Afrikaner people the only people since 1066 who have succeeded in dominating a people or a country of British origin, and is this not indeed an intolerable psychological position for a country which normally dominates or absorbs—or, at the very least, refuses to intervene?

Here lies the germ of the unwavering hostility between British ideals and Afrikaner nationalism. If the Afrikaners wanted to make complete Afrikaners of the Bantu, they would not be allowed to do so either. And what can the voice of the Afrikaner people, stammering in a language which is not in tune with the great movements of contemporary civilization, do against the vast means of expression and influence of an Opposition press, linked to the complex network of an English-language press which weaves—for better or for worse—over the whole globe?

I remember in what scornful way an Englishman of the Cape spoke to me of biltong, "this filthy delicacy of the Boers," and of the horrible Voortrekker Monument which "resembles the stone dreams of Hitler, only bigger and uglier".

And yet, biltong is delicious; and I agree with many of my Boer friends who prefer simple beef biltong, which is fatter, to buck biltong which, of course, keeps better during long rides over the veld. And I am also ready to forgive the Voortrekker Monument in Pretoria many faults because, at heart, I understand this stone language of a young nation, with its bas-reliefs in two tones of granite, white for the wagon-hoods, and brick-colour for the wood, the style appropriate to a pioneering nation; because of this museum where are assembled a few relics of the heroic times with the powder-horns, the Bibles, the wooden wagons of their ancestors, direct symbols which say much more than the most majestic ruins . . .

And then: can one say that the great memorial of Cecil Rhodes in Cape Town, with its colossal and cold granite, the rival to the Voortrekker Monument, is more beautiful and more subtle? Or must one simply accept that dreams in stone are allowed only to celebrate the glory of a great Englishman and to symbolize the Empire from Cairo to the Cape?

CHAPTER 4

ELEVEN MILLION BANTU

I

Who are the Bantu of South Africa?

Out of a total population of 15,850,000 in 1960, there were 10,810,000 Bantu, 1,500,000 Coloureds and 480,000 Asiatics. These Bantu do not form a homogeneous group—neither with regard to their language, nor with regard to their social distribution. Black Africa—and Black South Africa—is composed of nations that differ as much from one another as the Norwegians differ from the Italians, speaking languages as different as English and Hungarian, which are, however, both European languages. In South Africa there are four principal ethnic groups: the *Nguni* (about five million Bantu, or 60 per cent), consisting of the Xhosa, Zulu, Swazi and Ndebele peoples; the *Sotho* (about three million, or 35 per cent) consisting of the Southern Sotho, the Northern Sotho and the Tswana; the *Changaan* (about 250,000, or three per cent); the *Venda* (about 150,000, or two per cent). When the members of these great linguistic groups wish to communicate with one another, they are obliged, as everywhere in Africa, to make use of the languages imported by the Whites: in South Africa, Afrikaans and English, and in their contact with Blacks outside the frontiers of South Africa, English only.

This Bantu population is increasing more rapidly than the Whites.

The Whites increased from 2,462,000 in 1951 to 3,068,000 in 1960, that is to say by 16 per cent. During the same period, the Bantu increased from 8,561,000 to 10,810,000 or 26 per cent. Only the Coloured people increased more rapidly (35 per cent), from which one can infer that, in this part of Africa, they will be the "race" of to-morrow. The statisticians predict that in the year 2000 there will be a demographical situation even more favourable to the dark races: 21.5 million Blacks, as against 4.5 million Whites, 4 million Coloureds and 1.4 million Asiatics. The Whites will then constitute only 14.7 per cent of the population, as against 21 per cent in 1950.

The Blacks of South Africa are not only more fertile than the Whites. They benefit from a much higher rate of immigration. South of the Sahara, South Africa has remained an Eldorado, where Blacks receive the highest salaries in Africa. The neighbouring territories, and also very far-off countries, such as St. Helena, Mauritius, Madagascar, the Belgian Congo, Kenya, etc., get rid of part of their excess population in South Africa, in the form of migratory labourers who often take root there. Nearly 800,000 of them reside in the Republic, and 50,000 settle there every year, as against 4,000 Whites.

What do these Bantu do?

A more realistic classification than the linguistic classification, one which takes into consideration economic and political realities, distinguishes three groups among the population: the Blacks who make a living in the Bantu territories (where "nations" can be distinguished) by farming and raising cattle; Blacks living on the farms of the Whites; and the urban proletariat, the labour force of White industry (where the "nations" are mixed). These three categories each form roughly about a third of the Bantu population. But their social structure, their way of life, their economic activities, their degree of civilization and their aspirations are very different. It is not possible to apply the same policy to all of them because they have different problems. A common remedy can be found only by going beyond these differences, by reducing to a single cause the political misery of the more developed Bantu in the towns, the economic misery of the backward Bantu in the Reserves and the social misery of the Bantu living under a system of paternalistic "Uncle Tom-ism" on the White farms.

II

Professor Serton tells the story of an ethnologist who visited the Bantu Reserves a few years ago, and who, stopping his car in the veld, asked his Black guide whether he should lock it.

"No," replied the man. "It's not worth the trouble. There are no Whites here."

While this anecdote, though probably true, must not be taken at face value, it does give an indication of the primitive state of the Reserves. Thefts take place there, of course, but life is certainly simpler and closer to nature. Indeed, it is so close that it is one of excessive poverty, as borne out by statistics: 50 per cent of a family's income is spent on food (mealies, flour, chick-peas), 30 per cent on the coarsest kind of clothing, and the remainder on saucepans, pots, soap, salt, wire, nails, tools, etc. It is an economy of misery for the greater part of the rural populations, who only have an average income of £30 to £60 a year for a whole family!

This situation is due to a backward agricultural economy.

The very system of collective land ownership (the land belongs to the tribe) prevents a "natural selection" of farmers. In the individualistic economy of the White sector, an enterprising farmer increases his lands if he succeeds better than his neighbour. In the tribal system, where the land and the pasture-lands are distributed equally amongst all the people, no one has an individual interest in the use of modern methods of stock-farming and cultivation, and the level is that of the lowest common denominator.

The old belief in witchcraft thwarts the normal play of economic competition. The farmer who produces better crops, who has solid furniture and fatter cows is soon suspected of having had recourse to magic. Until very recently, the individual was careful to avoid any deviation which singled him out owing to his economic success, and which might cost him his life. The result has been a terrible lack of economic incentive, a levelling at the bottom. Although, in the collective psychology of the Bantu peasant, magic is no longer the principal cause of success, he has not yet—and rare are the exceptions—recognized that economic success is directly due to deep ploughing and the selection of seeds. In fact, "deep ploughing makes the oxen too thin"! We shall see further on that the cattle complex is to a large extent responsible for the misery of the Reserves. The Bantu hardly ever eats meat. Instead of using his money to buy more consumer goods, or investing it, he uses a great deal of it to increase his herd. The productivity of the herd is practically nil because no importance is attached to the quality of the cattle; they hardly give any milk; they die of hunger and thirst during droughts; but, nonetheless, they remain the only external sign of wealth, and, during initiation ceremonies, the adolescents, initiated into the duties of adult life, are exhorted to buy cattle rather than to spend their money "in the European way" that is to say, on houses, clothes and food.

In addition, the land is cultivated in open rebellion against the laws of nature. The one-crop cultivation of maize exhausts the soil: the Reserves—which, as we shall see further on, possess vast untapped resources—cannot support their total population, and almost all the able-bodied men leave for the towns and the agricultural regions of the Whites, where they are offered decent wages and food every day.

This movement sets up a vicious circle. Poverty and insufficient resources force the young people to work outside the Reserves. In turn, this exodus perpetuates the misery of the Reserves, because the young children, the women and the old men who remain there cannot go in for productive agriculture.

In the Reserves and in the White areas, the migratory labourers create complex economic and social problems.

Families, sundered for months and years, inevitably end by separating. Illegitimate children are, so to speak, the rule amongst the Bantu. The quality of the migratory labour force is mediocre. Because he is temporary, the worker frequently changes his job after his "visits" to the Reserves, and the result is economic waste and low productivity. It is estimated that a migratory labourer only works effectively during half his active life. I saw the case-histories of 148 Bantu families who were studied in order to obtain the typical economic position of the Bantu in the Reserves. Let us take that of X.B., born in 1892, who "retired" in 1945 and who has since lived in his village in the Reserves. X.B. began to work in 1908, and his biography reveals the classic and typical fluctuations of Bantu labour: 16 jobs with 16 different employers, 13 rest periods at home. The average length of employment was eight months, and the average length of the rest periods, six months. In all, a "normal" working life—a tragically wasted life.

This is the almost unvarying biography of a third of the Bantu people.

It is true that the coin has a better side. For most of the illiterate peasants who find work on the mines and in industry, expatriation is their first contact with civilized life, and the lessons learnt in Johannesburg are felt right up to Tanganyika. They learn the discipline of work and hygiene. They become familiar with machines and tools. Newspapers are read to them through loud-speakers. Films teach them the unknown horizons of the world. Evening classes, for many of them, are the first and the only school they will ever attend. They bring back from the mines the rudiments of useful trades: carpentry, simple mechanical jobs, gardening. It cannot be denied that the migratory labourer brings back home, not only money, but some cultural equipment. In the process of drawing from the Reserves their surplus labour resources, the mining companies have created transport systems, have built roads and bridges where there were none before, have drained marshes in order to transport their labour and have built air-strips for the 100,000 Bantu whom they fly to the towns every year.

III

The four-and-a-half million Bantu in the Reserves create a collective problem, which demands a national solution. The three million Bantu who live outside the Reserves, scattered on the farms of the Whites, create individual problems.

In a way, their lives are easier.

From a social and psychological point of view, the protection of a White farmer who looks after all the needs of his Black peasants offers the Bantu agricultural worker and his family the comfort of security and freedom from care. This is a paternalistic system which makes each farm a world of its own, according to the mentality of the masters, and it cannot be easily schematized. One finds White farmers who treat "their" Bantu like their own children, who get up at night to care for the ill, who celebrate together family and religious festivals, while other White farmers are convicted for having whipped to death farm-labourers guilty of petty theft. Between these two extremes lies the whole range of human patterns of behaviour. As a rule, the family of the farm-labourer can be sure of a roof over their heads, running water, fuel, medical attention, a school for the children, a church near by.

From an economic point of view, this situation is, in most cases, more favourable than in the Reserves.

In exchange for their work, the Black family can cultivate their own plot of land and raise a herd, and the farmer himself often ploughs their fields with his own tractor, and lends them manure and seed. Milk, vegetables and fruit are supplied free, as well as a certain quantity of corn or maize, which forms the bulk of the wage.

In addition, the farmer usually pays wages to his labourers. They vary between 10s. and £1 10s. a month. Statistics show that the average annual income of a Bantu family in the Transvaal comes to £176, an income higher than that of a peasant family in the Reserves. Of this, £55 represents wages paid to the Bantu farmer in cash and kind; £24 the wages and rations of the women employed as domestic servants on the farm; £38 the wages and rations of the other members of the family, employed as casual labourers; £23 comes from the sale of crops; £12 from the sale of cattle; £12 is the value of the agricultural products cultivated and consumed by the family; £12 the value of the lodgings, water, fuel, transport, etc., supplied by the employer. Of course, wages are higher in the towns. But, according to the same statistics, a Bantu official earning £15 a month in Johannesburg, spends £7 10s. on food, £2 7s. 3d. on lodging, and £2 17s. on transport. He has only £2 5s. 9d. for his remaining needs, in other words, he has to tighten his belt—literally and figuratively—to almost all the joys of life . . . Thus, the Black agricultural worker is, apparently, better off.

It is from a political and legal point of view that the situation of the farm worker is much worse. He is not a tenant farmer, a "share cropper" who pays rent in kind. He is an occupier with no title-deeds, a squatter, literally attached to the land—whatever the conditions granted to him by the White farmer—owing to the fact that residential rights are only granted to him as long as he is employed, and he can only remain in a village for 72 hours to seek new employment. Since the towns are practically closed to him by the system of urban influx control, it is not an exaggeration to say that the farm labourers, as a class, are particularly disinherited with regard to civic rights, and their happiness on earth is directly related to the very low standard of living they are used to. But how long will this habit last? This class of occupiers without freehold rights will only be emancipated from its servile condition when it is free to offer its labour in a free market. This also implies that its productivity will have to be improved by means of agricultural training, which is to-day almost non-existent.

However, in spite of its low rate of productivity, the Bantu labour force is much in demand from White farmers. This is clearly shown by the employment of common-law prisoners in the country. The prison system, functioning in a way equivalent to the parole system, puts them at the disposal of farmers in large numbers. The farmer has no right to deprive them of their freedom or to use force to prevent their escape, but this principle is frequently a dead letter. In addition, the police force is a supplier of agricultural labour. The police systematically offer delinquents who are guilty of minor offences (breaking of curfew and pass regulations) the choice between working on a farm and appearing in court. This system also gives rise to abuses because the Bantu offender often does not know that the punishment inflicted—a fine of one pound or seven days in prison—would be much lighter than 90 days' work on a farm. In addition, he does not realize that these days on a farm will be effective working-days, not including Sundays, public holidays, sick leave or rainy days . . .

The economic exploitation of the backwardness and the misery of the Bantu by farmers who are in many cases rich enough to fly to Johannesburg in their own aeroplanes, is something scandalous.

IV

It is said in South Africa that the only problem is that of the Bantu in the towns: that the problem of the Reserves can be solved through the creation of Bantu states or through money spent to improve the country areas; that the problem of the Black agricultural workers is not urgent; that all that counts is the political impotence of the four million workers, civil servants and members of the Bantu middle class in the big towns and cities. These are the people who suffer most from the discriminatory laws, who often live in slums and who get massacred at Sharpevilles. It is natural that those who make political demands are not the "savages of the bush", but those who have tasted the delightful fruits of civilization, and who know the Paradise closed to them, because they live next to it and do all the heavy labour for it.

The Blacks in the towns have, to a large extent, broken their tribal ties. Even if they maintain family and spiritual allegiance, they have adopted the way of life of the city-dweller and desire integration within the White community. They have been western-ized. The Gospel has been preached to them, and the doors of the factories have been opened to them. In the economic life of the country, they have been given the most important place, that of

54

producers. It is in vain that they are denied access to the social and political life of the country: they do not understand, and will not in the end accept, the fact that a certain number of doors are opened to them and others are shut in their faces. Nevertheless, although the urban Bantu have been westernized, both they and the Bantu of the Reserves have preserved their identity. I remember a peaceful Sunday in Johannesburg. The hall of my hotel was empty. I came down the staircase and, there, in the marble hall, was the lift-boy, resplendent in his scarlet uniform, dancing alone with the same gestures, the same supple movements as the naked dancers in the bush. The truth is often revealed by little furtive touches.

Fifty years ago there were 100,000 Bantu in Johannesburg. To-day there are 725,000, without counting the 350,000 migratory workers in the mine hostels. This means that Johannesburg has a second and a third generation of Bantu who have not known life in the country, generations of children who do not know that milk comes from a cow, generations of women who have evolved and who do not accept the tribal custom of the "levirat" which, at the death of their husbands, makes them automatically the wives of their brothers-in-law and hands on the household property to the male side of the dead man's family. Each South African town has its population (often the majority) of urbanized Bantu. And yet, people still see the Blacks as temporary residents, and one heard this contradiction candidly stated by the Minister of Bantu Administration and Development in Parliament in 1959: "The Bantu often remain in urban areas for two or three generations; but it has never been the policy of this Government that they must remain there permanently . . . Therefore, we say that they are there temporarily, and sooner or later they will go back to their own areas."* In 1922, the Stallard Commission, appointed by the Smuts government, declared that the towns were the creation and the special possession of the Whites and that "the Native should only be allowed to enter urban areas . . . when he is willing to enter and minister to the needs of the White man, and should depart therefrom when he ceases so to minister." Most people still continue to adhere to this paradoxical concept of temporary residence for three generations. The law applies this principle rigorously since the only Bantu who have the *right* to live in an urban area are 1. a Bantu who has resided there without

*House of Assembly Debates, May 27, 1959.

55

interruption since birth; 2. a Bantu who has worked there for *the same employer* for ten years; 3. a Bantu who has resided there legally for fifteen years, and who, in addition, works there and has never received a sentence exceeding a £50 fine. Only the wives, the unmarried daughters and the minor sons of Bantu in these categories also have a right to stay in the urban areas. In other words, all the other Blacks in South Africa, in order to acquire residential rights, must work ten years for the same employer, or for fifteen continuous years in the same town. But a Bantu who has lost his job and is looking for another one, cannot legally reside in a town for more than 72 hours . . .

This situation is clearly amoral. The Bantu in the towns are regarded as easily interchangable tools. Yet, since the first generation, they may be so "urbanized" that their discharge to the Reserves is a real cruelty. There is no comparison between them and the migratory labourers who come from outside the frontiers of the Republic, or with the Italian workers who come and work in the South of France. These labourers have just what the Bantu of South Africa have not got: another nationality, by virtue of which they have certain rights. Man is an entity in himself. Prostitution buys a service, but marriage implies the noble obligation of accepting one's partner for what he or she is, with all the joys and obligations which this entails. The Bantu of the urban areas are to a certain extent in a state of legal "prostitution". They are allowed to sell their services, but excluded from the community. In South Africa, the place and the share that individuals and groups have in the economic life is not in proportion to the services they render, but to their race.

This situation is also an anachronistic one.

It is true that the Bantu were formerly inhabitants of the country, who sold their labour, temporarily, to the Whites in the towns. To-day, industrialization has created a Black proletariat who form the majority in most of the towns of the Republic, and who, because they are increasing much faster than the Whites, are becoming an overwhelming majority. The mistake of the Whites is to imagine that this movement of the Blacks into the towns owing to industrialization is incidental, impermanent and unnatural. The illusion of the Whites consists in imagining that they can use political devices to perpetuate a social order which is being daily destroyed by economic expansion. The history of contemporary South Africa is a double migratory movement: that of the Whites, with their trade; their factories, their investments, their administration; and that of the Bantu towards this new world created by the Whites.

"One cannot stop the movement of the Bantu except by stopping the industries of the Whites," I was told by Mr. H. A. Fagan, former Chief Justice of South Africa. Mr. Fagan is one of the men who feel that this dilemma is a desperate one.

One evening I visited him in his home in Bishopscourt, Cape Town, overlooking the most beautiful town in the world, where he was then living in retirement. We were gazing at the lights twinkling below us in the valley when he said: "Can you imagine that a Black man born in this town has to ask for a pass to return to it if he has gone to stay in a neighbouring municipality? He must have a permit if he wants to work here or bring his wife here. I can't sleep when I think about it... Don't you think," he said sadly, "that they must be given the *right* to live normally, not just the right to ask the administration for permission to live normally?"

The Bantu in the towns are claiming this right.

"We are townspeople," the Rev. Thema of Pretoria said to me. "The people of the towns, whether they are White or Black, think like townspeople. The farmers, White or Black, are farmers, and the mistake the Whites make is to place the Bantu automatically in a country setting. The Bantu who have their homes in the town think of work in the town, of wages, of freedom... here. I haven't met a single Bantu from Pretoria who is interested in Bantustans.* We

*The composition, programmes and activities of the main Bantu opposition movements, the African National Congress and Pan-African Congress, have deliberately not been analyzed in this book. They are very well known in South Africa. The A.N.C., led by Chief Albert Luthuli, under its black, green and yellow banner (black for the people, green for the country and yellow for gold) has a political platform of moderate and gradual integration. The P.A.C., led by Mr. Robert Sobukwe, goes far beyond integration in a multi-racial South African nation: it stands for Black anti-White nationalism under the slogan, "Africa for the Africans", meaning more or less "Africa for the people who were there before the Europeans".

It is obvious that solutions to the Bantu problem (or the White problem) can also be found by implementing these policies. Maybe they will be ... To me, partition seems a more reasonable process. In the long run, a Federation between a White Republic and a Bantu Republic, both sovereign, could lead to integration between equals for which I see more hope than for the present trend of integration of Black individuals into a very reluctant White body politic.

live in an industrial area. Our people want homes, security and good wages. Our problems here are the threat to our economic security, the restrictions on our freedom of movement, the fact that we have no voice in public affairs.

"Yes, we were backward. We have had the chance to get to know civilization. Our ideal is now civilization. It is not a *problem*.

"And yet, we are denied the right to go to the end of a road we were told to take.

"We are called temporary visitors—but you can't change an apple into a melon by calling it a melon.

"We are told that rights are denied us here because they have given and will give many rights to the Bantu in the Reserves. But that is like taking away a man's coat in order to give it to his brother.

"Why does the government not consult me as the official representative of the Bantu in Pretoria? The Whites, by obstinately leaving us out of public affairs, are condemning themselves to becoming more and more ignorant about what is happening on this side of the racial frontier. This is unhealthy, because if nobody is allowed to be a spokesman for my people, then agitators will take hold of the megaphone. By destroying the bridges between us and them, the Whites will one day find themselves without any means of action and co-operation with the Blacks: like the man who lost his glasses and who is so short-sighted that he can only look for them once he has found them . . ."

The misery of the urban proletariat is not only political and social: it is also (in the first place) economic, to such an extent that one sometimes wonders whether the struggle between the races in South Africa is not merely, for the great mass of the Bantu, a class struggle. The Rev. Arthur W. Blaxall goes so far as to affirm that the absorption of Natives in industry has resulted in the Whites becoming a "White aristocracy" (white by accident) and the Natives "the Black proletariat" (black by accident) of a new mixed nation in South Africa.*

This is true but deserves a few observations: the South African Bantu is better paid, better housed, better fed and better clothed than the Black man in any other country in Africa. In fact, the "racialist hell" attracts Blacks from beyond the frontiers, who

*South Africa's policy of apartheid—unacceptable, Heidelberg, Transvaal, 1956.

come thousands of miles in order to enter the country, sometimes illegally, and who pay up to £20 for a forged pass. It is true that South Africa spends 16s. a head each year on Bantu education, and £1 7s. on sanitary services, that is to say a total of £2 3s., whereas Great Britain, who criticizes her, spends 10s. in Bechuanaland, three shillings in Nyasaland, five shillings in Uganda and nine shillings in Kenya. It is also true that thousands of Bantu earn £60 and more a month, and that certain skilled workers get more than £80 a month. If the desirable minimum wage, established by the International Labour Organization, is taken to be 100, South Africa pays 55 to its Blacks, French Equatorial Africa 40, the Congo 38, Ghana 31, Kenya 26, and Tanganyika 22. These figures speak for themselves. But the prosperity they indicate in the case of South Africa is entirely relative. It certainly represents astonishing progress if one thinks of the poverty of a century ago, but it is estimated that 60 per cent of the Bantu wage-earners earn less than £10 a month and that 35 per cent earn from £10 to £15, while only five per cent earn more than £15. And yet, the most prudent economists regard about £25 as the minimum wage for a man not to be hungry, cold, and ashamed of his poverty, his nakedness and the destitution of his family. Here again, figures speak for themselves.

The causes of this situation are first of all historical.

The Bantu, like people in Europe during the industrial era, were attracted to the towns by the magnet of an exciting life and wages which, to backward peasants, seemed fantastic. They did not realize that in the country they paid nothing, or almost nothing, for lodging, transport, food and fuel. The fantastic flow of Bantu into the towns, under governments which did practically nothing to stem the tide, which, under a policy of free enterprise, fixed the wages of the Bantu workers at its lowest possible level, led to the shanty-towns, to over-population, to the high incidence of crime in the dormitory-towns, to the "squatter camps" which sprang up like mushrooms during the industrial expansion caused by the Second World War.

This over-abundance of labour led, in turn, to chronic wastage of it. It has been calculated that out of 1,400,000 "man-years" available at a given moment, only 480,000 are used. Consequently 920,000 are lost. Moreover, the average length of time spent in one place of employment by a Bantu is 17 months—in other words, he changes his job nearly every 18 months.

An industrialist, Harry Goldberg, told me: "In the past it has been general custom to regard all Bantu workers as readily inter-changeable units, having no particular individual aptitudes, and suited to engagement and employment in gangs or undifferentiated groups. This mental attitude of employers can be traced back to the days when large numbers of peasants, unaccustomed to industrial work, flocked into the towns as migrant workers to provide labour for new industries. These workers were employed to carry materials and merchandise, to wield picks and shovels, to sweep and clean, and generally to perform simple tasks requiring physical strength and stamina, but, under the conditions then existing, needing no judgment, manual skill or intelligent understanding of the work performed.

"Although conditions have now changed radically, most employers have nevertheless not yet learned to look upon Bantu work-seekers as individuals with a wide range of different aptitudes and natural talents.

"In Johannesburg, for example, there are about 120,000 new engagements every year, as against a total male Bantu labour force of about 230,000—indicating a labour turn-over of more than 50 per cent per annum.

"The financial losses suffered by employers as a result of this excessive labour turn-over can only be guessed at, but, taking into account the direct and indirect costs of engaging the worker, equip-ping him with protective clothes, training him, losing production during the training period and thereafter during the time that his work proves to be unsatisfactory, and the cost of discharging him, the amounts involved must be considerable and to a large extent are an avoidable waste of money.

"If a worker has two or three such unhappy experiences in suc-cession, his disappointment, frustration and financial losses are bound to build up in him an attitude to work, to his employers and to our society in general, which can only be harmful to everyone concerned."

"A few years ago," Dr. F. J. Meyer, of the great Iscor steelworks, told me, "I visited one of our rolling-mills. Machines were being installed. A low concrete wall, about four feet high, led towards a concrete-mixer in operation 150 feet away. Along the 150 feet of this wall were spaced out 50 Bantu who were passing a bucket of mortar from hand to hand. An empty bucket was coming back along the line in the opposite direction.

"I couldn't believe my eyes!

"Only two workers were needed to do the same work, that is to say to carry the full bucket half-way, exchange it for the empty bucket and come back to the mixer. I pointed this out to the foreman. He said: 'You are right, sir, but these Natives were here in any case, so I used them.'

"The Bantu are badly paid", concluded Dr. Meyer. "But it is very expensive labour when it is used in this way . . . It is ruinous labour."

This poverty, which is costing South Africa so much to keep at the same low level, is one of the worst problems in this rich country.

V

A German film-producer, Kris Marker, called one of his documentary films *The Third Side of the Coin*, a sibylline title which could well apply to one of the most disconcerting phenomena of the life of the urban Bantu: the dormitory-towns built along the edges of the White towns, "locations", separated from the White towns by a buffer zone which usually consists of the factories where Black and White meet during working-hours. The coin has a happy and a sinister side; the locations form the "third side". They combine both the pleasant and the sinister. When compared to the shanty-towns which they are slowly replacing, they are splendid achievements in urbanism and social regeneration with wide, tree-lined streets, proper sewerage, electricity, schools and cinemas. They are "camps" if one looks at their rectilinear arrangement, and if one considers the way they are controlled by the authorities. This control is very real, even if there are no observation posts and barbed-wire. Due to their isolation, access to them can be forbidden by stopping the trains, while their resistance can be reduced by such measures as cutting off the electricity and water, which are always controlled by White superintendents at a safe distance.

Of course, dreadful nonsense has been written about the destruction of the shanty-towns. Products of the industrial revolution, they had precedents in Victorian England. Their replacement by solid houses at a cost of tens of millions of pounds, an act of the present government, will remain one of its titles to glory. I visited one of these shanty-towns of rusty corrugated iron, rotten planks and torn sacking—Cato Manor, in the suburbs of Durban. The chief of police at Cato Manor had shown me his personal horror museum, where I saw stacked up piles of rusty weapons, clandestine stills confiscated by his men, truncheons, and all kinds of sinister instruments found on the local toughs, the "tsotsis". A few days earlier, at the Baragwanath Hospital in Johannesburg, I had spent a painful morning visiting the victims of the previous week-end's incidents: men with their sex-organs mutilated in brawls, women raped, covered in petrol and burnt by their violators; young men skilfully knifed in the vertebral column with bicycle spokes sharpened like daggers. All these people had been picked up by ambulances patrolling the locations. These patrols are routine, for the authorities know what to expect over week-ends when the shebeens sell their illegally distilled alcohol to the wretched and irritable mass of badly housed, underpaid, ill-fed people in the shanty-towns. Remembering these horrible sights, I was thus happy to see my shining Buick escorted by a Saracen with a loaded machine-gun. A White man does not venture into this cess-pool of mud, rags, smells and crime. The number of Blacks who kill each other there each week is not known: and they are victims of the shanty towns.

I will not easily forget Schauderville, Kfar Ford, New Brighton and Kvasakele, locations on the outskirts of Port Elizabeth. Eleven years ago, Kfar Ford was a shanty-town built out of the packing cases in which the components of American cars arrive for assembly at the factories. In 1960, I saw real towns, with greenery, bright shops, tarred roads, hedges, shutters painted green, schools as good as those of the Whites, a swimming-pool and an open-air theatre. These locations do not have the air of concentration camps. The mortar and the bricks used to build them are the same as those in Johannesburg, but the spirit underlying their erection was not the same. Separation was, of course, desired, but not discrimination or inferiority. In Port Elizabeth, bricks are held together by the cement of human dignity and concern for one's brother.

One man, Adolf Schauder, wanted these gay towns and he built them. Schauder, a former solidier who fought on the side of the English during the Anglo-Boer War and who found a new home in

South Africa, guided me through the town which bears his name. The Blacks who pass him greet him with respect and take off their hats to him. On his seventieth birthday they named him *son geba*, "the merciful one".

"What we did," said Schauder, "was simple. We did not force anybody to move. When the people who obstinately clung to their shacks saw the new houses, they themselves burnt their slums and came to beg us for houses. That's all."

I left Port Elizabeth with a feeling of astonishment and gratitude.

Schauder's houses cost less than prisons and hospitals. Could not a brotherhood, an order of devoted "knights" with a thousand Schauders, moved by an ideal, save the country in a new crusade without a cross?

Anyhow, even with lesser people than Schauder on the job, it is ridiculous to criticize the government of South Africa for its policy of rehousing the Blacks. The sooner the festering sore of Cato Manor, which has a hundred different names in a hundred parts of South Africa, is cleared, the sooner the gangs who act as "protectors" to the human swarms of Sophiatown are done away with, the sooner the illegal drinking-dens are wiped out, the better. At the National Building Research Institute in Pretoria, I witnessed tests carried out to lay down standard health and building conditions for the Bantu towns. I saw a hail cannon simulate hail in order to determine the resistance of materials; an experimental stove gave off carbon dioxide in order to determine the best method of ventilating the houses; insulation was tested by means of an artifitial sky These are samples of a definite contribution made by the White man to the happiness and progress of the Bantu in Africa.

VI

In spite of their different functions, the Bantu (in the Reserves, in the country and in the towns) have in common their own particular culture. A great French statesman, Edouard Herriot, said that culture is what remains when one has lost everything. Even those Bantu who are the most solidly rooted in the towns, and who lost their country roots three or four generations ago, have kept the cultural treasures of their race—and the contrary would have meant the impoverishment of human civilization, which is made up of diverse contributions, and cannot be enriched by a general uniform levelling of culture. The Bantu are different from the Whites. They are not Europeans with a black skin. It is to be hoped that the Bantu will continue to bring their specific contribution to the common progress of civilization. Bantu culture confronts us with two apparently contradictory aspects: a strong drive towards conservatism, or negritude, and a faculty of adaptation to and adoption of "whiteness", which manifests itself in many curious ways.

In the first term of the contradiction are to be found all the manifestations of Black "racialism". Apartheid is not only the White man's reflex to and reflection on his position. It is also one of the Black man's reflexes. No more than the White man does the Bantu seek social contact with the Coloureds and the Asiatics. When his emotions run high and he becomes violent, he attacks the schools, churches, hospitals and irrigation canals built by the Whites for his own good, because deep down inside him, he sees them as symbols of an intrusion into his way of life.

In the other term of the contradiction, there is the Bantu's immense ability and desire for adaptation. When flying from Paris to Johannesburg, with stops in Nigeria and in the Congo, you meet at Kano wonderful specimens of Black men in English uniforms. They stand stiffly at attention, with sticks under their arms: the spitting image of the models they are trying to imitate. In Brazzaville, the traveller is welcomed by easy-going and somewhat untidy figures. They are good-natured gendarmes who wear the familiar *kepi* of the French constabulary. Once again, the models have been well imitated—apparantely without the slightest effort—and the result, in both cases, seems perfect. In all the other fields of acculturation, one can observe the same malleability. Islam and Christianity are equally successful. It all depends which missionaries get there first. The Black man thinks all the virtues of whiteness are to be acquired through the external signs of the White man: a hat and a brief-case, which is often empty or which contains a snack for lunch. Chiefs grow moustaches or wear glasses, which are to them the symbols of the intellectual. Illiterates buy newspapers. Popular magazines—such as *Bona*, which is both the *Match* and the *Elle* of Black South Africa—publish whole pages devoted to face-creams, "miracles of modern science," which allow you (yes, you too) to have a lighter skin, and shampoos which straighten crinkly hair . . .

64

One of the New Year wishes is "May Heaven grant you a light-coloured skin."

These two extreme reactions, despising whiteness, and imitating whiteness, are inevitable. Cultures are not static phenomena, and only cultures which have completed the full cycle of their evolution, can be described as dead cultures. Cultures which are still burning realities in the soul of a people affect one another in a living way, bearing the pollen of progress from one nation to another. It is normal that the world should be subjected simultaneously to the apparently contradictory influences of americanization and the spread of the Soviet ideology, to decolonization, and colonial rear-guard skirmishes, to the levelling civilization of plastics, and the corresponding, growing demand for hand-made remains of the past. Our universe is an expanding one, and contact is always made in both directions. The contact between Blacks and Whites reflect the contact between Africa and Europe, the meeting of two civilizations. It is this contact—consisting of a thousand and one little soldered joints—which is building the edifice of a modified Bantu civilization. It is here and now that one must seek its reality: it would be useless to seek it elsewhere, in the galleries from which the rich ore has already been extracted, or in the vein which the pick of the miner has not yet touched. Culture is a visible aspect of time.

In its present state, this Bantu culture offers complicated mixtures to be prudently investigated, rather than finished and labelled products displayed in a show window. The result of contact between different cultures is never the sum total of the cultures which have combined, or the difference between conflicting cultures. The two cultures come out modified: they have lost their malleable envelope; the loin-cloth has been exchanged for the top-hat (sometimes the sun-helmet for native head-gear which gives greater protection), but the deep identity of the people has remained intact, and it stamps new acquisitions with its particular mark.

Thus, when *Drum*, a magazine for the Bantu élite, organizes a literary competition, a certain number of manuscripts of the short-stories sent in by its readers illustrate themes of violence, cruelty and destruction—a crystallization of the "live dangerously" psychology that the Bantu has known from centuries of living in the jungle, and a reaction to the new difficulties he faces in the jungle of the big towns. This addiction to violence also accounts for the high rate of crime in the towns: violence is sometimes even taught to adolescents, notably amongst the Pedi, where corporal punishment is the rule for children who show pacifist tendencies.

The old belief in witchcraft, which is still prevalent amongst the primitive Bantu, this doctrine of *the end without the means*, makes itself felt in the lives of even the civilized. The Mau-Mau chiefs called themselves "field-marshal", "bishop", "Winston Churchill", and they believed that these names endowed them with power. When the Belgian Congo became independent, a good many Blacks thought they would acquire the qualities of the Whites by appropriating the insignia of independence. These vestiges of a belief in the magic power of symbols, even when these symbols are examinations and diplomas (which give one status without the need of further effort), are an essential component of the culture of the Bantu: a belief which has, besides, its parallel in the conviction shared by many Whites that the colour of their skin is the magic short-cut which does away with the need for effort and merit . . .

Are these beliefs the sign of an inferior culture?

At the heart of the matter is the fact that there is no such thing as a hierarchy of cultures and races. Barbarians are sometimes the ancestors of the most civilized people; and the Nazis, in Germany and other places, have shown to what depths of barbarism highly civilized nations can revert. The Bantu culture is in no way inferior to Western culture. It is a different culture. The Bantu is not a backward Englishman or Afrikaner. He is a Zulu, a Xhosa, a Sotho. To tell a Zulu that he has nothing to lose and everything to gain by bartering his culture for the culture of the Whites, is nothing but racial arrogance. The culture of a people is made up of all their efforts to adapt themselves to a milieu, and these efforts are exerted in different, sometimes conflicting directions, and with different degrees of intensity which depend on the problems to be solved. The large flat nose of the Bantu is not "uglier" than the straight nose of the European: nature gave him a flat nose the better to breathe with in the humid tropical conditions under which his ancestors lived. His dark skin is not a stigma, but a means of protecting himself against the equatorial sun. His lack of initiative is the result of centuries of malnutrition and endemic diseases, and disappears, slowly but surely, with a normal diet and sanitation. Man looks at life through coloured glasses—the colour of his particular culture.

He has a point of view, a *Weltanschauung*. If you show an ox with horns four feet long to a Bantu and to a Hamite, the Bantu will find them long and the Hamite will think they are short. Their sense of values is influenced by their culture, not their judgment. They are both capable of expressing length in feet, and of using the ruler and the slide-rule for more difficult measurements . . .

The different Bantu peoples, like every other race, are culturally orientated. The Nguni will not eat yaourt at the home of somebody who is not related to them. In this tribe, those who commit incest are killed without trial. The Basuto favour marriages between the children of brothers and sisters. When a Bantu servant, in the bewildering city of Johannesburg, does not get up at the sound of an alarm-clock, it is useless to accuse him of being lazy: his culture has conditioned him to rising when the sun warms his skin and to going to bed at nightfall. They have other criteria and other artistic traditions. They draw conceptually and not visually, like children. They draw what they *know* to exist, not what they see. The test of the man and the elephant produces the reply that the elephant is

The test of the man and the elephant

nearer the man, and that the elk cannot see the hunter owing to the hill between them, because they have no tradition of convention in art . . . But who would dare to assert that unconventional art is "inferior" to our tradition of convention and symbolism?

All this is culture. A culture is neither inferior nor superior. The languages of the Bantu are based on sounds of a variety and

67

richness of which we know nothing. Anyhow, there are no universal criteria for tastes and colours. When the White man wishes to impose the totality of his culture, he is indulging in collective ego-centrism, or ethno-centrism. The principle of the right to political self-determination of a people has been recognized everywhere, as long as the rights of the other man are respected. The Whites, instead of ethno-centrically imposing their own, should consider it their duty to help the Bantu to adjust their culture to the needs of progress. Is it the right of the Whites to determine what Bantu customs the Bantu should abolish and what European customs they should adopt? Is it for the White man to determine the criteria of acceptance or rejection?

"The Whites", Hugh Tracey (an expert on Bantu music) told me, "brought a type of provincial Christianity to Africa. They had the mentality of an elderly spinster. They taught the Zulus to get married in white veils and gloves, as if they were in a London suburb. In this respect the missionaries were lacking in real religious feeling, and, at heart, they believed just as much as witch-doctors in external signs, and their faith was so difficult to communicate (because it was church-going more than real religion) that they were satisfied with communicating mere appearances. This resulted in a Zulu running into a debt of £200 in order to get married in a white veil, with gloves and so forth, so as to acquire by the power of the White man's magic the qualities of the White man from Chelsea or Pimlico who gets married in such an outfit. And so they brought to the Black man many shades of White culture. The ideal of the Belgian native was to become a *nouveau riche*. The French brought their humanist conception—sometimes a little too noble. The Portuguese contributed the approach of the simple, practical peasant: plant, or you won't have anything to eat. The English, by dint of much teaching, were persuaded that they could produce African gentlemen everywhere they went."

Hugh Tracey has an exceedingly thorough knowledge of the African mind. The walls of his house are adorned with primitive musical instruments. He studies the soul of the Bantu through their traditional songs, the simple refrains from which one learns their real thoughts about work, children, women, and all the miseries and mysteries of life.

"The cultural evolution of the Bantu", he said, "has reached the

A cinema and restaurant in Meadowlands, the new Bantu township outside Johannesburg. Some critics compared the removal of the Bantu to Meadowlands with the mass-deportation carried out by the Nazis and the Communists

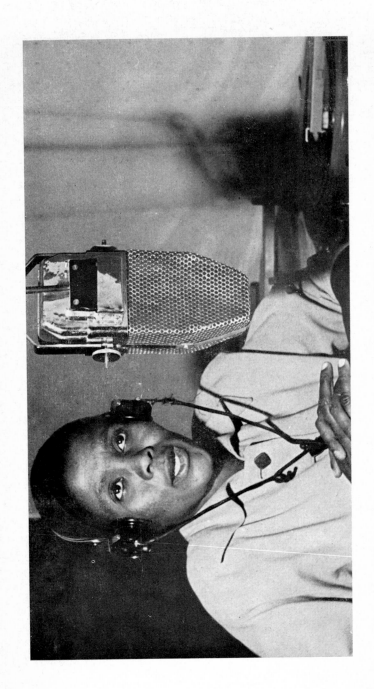

Mrs, Silvia Moloi, a part-time announcer for Radio Bantu, a division of Radio South Africa. Mrs. Moloi is in charge of children's and women's programmes

stage of a peasant society suddenly caught up in the industrial revolution of the big towns, where bus journeys are expensive, where one drinks, where four children out of five are illegitimate. In order to understand this state of affairs, one must look at things from the point of view of African culture. Then one will find the formula for a suitable cultural interchange . . ."

Cultures have a soft outer shell, where exchanges take place easily, while on the inside there is the hard kernel, composed of a universal supply of fundamental decency, which is indestructible, which cannot be applied elsewhere, but which is so valid that the foreigner recognizes it as a timeless and noble substance. Each people has its own kernel. These kernels are like mother-cells, the chromosomes of nations. Each people names them. We speak of French humanism, the American way of life, Afrikanerdom. There are traits in each of them which cannot be communicated, but which are universally respected in each one. The culture of the Xhosa people for instance has its hidden Xhosa kernel: *isiko*, the custom based on the psychological needs of the individual; *isiko* is the most valid approximation to a specific and major culture of the Bantu.

Noni Jabavu, one of the best writers in Black Africa, the example of an evolved African whose culture is firmly established, fully mature and adult, has given some subtle examples of it.

Isiko demands that a family who has lost one of its members should "retire to the forests" in ritual seclusion. The custom has deep social significance: the continuous flow of community life must not be interrupted by the stresses and strains caused by the distress of those afflicted.* *Isiko* is the feeling of belonging to a nation, which has given its name to the great Zambezi river, called after the *uku-zambeza*, the stripping of the ancestors who during their journey south entered these waters naked, driving their herds before them and whose weakest members were lost, the prey of the swirling waters or hungry crocodiles; but the survivors emerged from the waters baptized to a new life as a stronger, more virile nation. *Isiko* is the scorn felt for cringing slaves, the belief that a man is a man, that he can look any man in the face, for no man is worth more or less than another man. The political culture of *isiko* is completely summarized in the unwritten law "that a chief is but the spokesman of his people and a bad spokesman will be done away with."

Drawn in Colour, John Murray, London, 1960.

Noni Jabavu writes: "Indeed one does not deny that we tribes lacking pomp and circumstance are simple people; nevertheless, the more thoughtful of us nowadays generally feel that this lack of 'ancient tradition', fossilized claptrap we call it, is an advantage because it makes cleaner slates of our minds as it were; leaves us more ready to take to new techniques and new attitudes which come, at any rate in Southern Africa, with the arrival of industrialization, Western standards of living and philosophical heritage. We have accepted all that; what does it matter that 'Poor Whites', negrophobes and other undesirable types also arrive at the same time? Seldom that anything comes without flaws."

Is not this political philosophy the essence of a culture? This aristocratic contempt for "poor-whitism", arriving together with the good things in the same wagons, putting on trial, judging and imposing sentence upon the whole of White colonialism in three words—is it not very high up in the hierarchy of ways of accepting life?

VII

Apart from their culture, the Bantu are united by the laws which oppress them.

The point of contact between Blacks and Whites, the dividing line between the colours, is a well-defended Maginot Line. Its blockhouses are called the Job Reservation Act, the Immorality Act, the Group Areas Act, Influx Control etc., etc. They are all effective means of refusing to allow the Blacks to enter the vital sphere of the Whites.

Evelyn Waugh* recounts the amusing effects of strictly-applied segregation that he encountered during a journey by sea from Cape Town to London. Everything was perfect on the South African ship except that people were squashed together like sardines. "We were four in a cabin, and there was simply not enough room for all of us to sit on deck or in the saloon. I forget how many baths and lavatories there were, but I remember there was usually a queue. One black man travelled with us. In deference to South African susceptibilities he had a four-berth cabin to himself. More than this he had a lavatory, a bathroom and an armchair all placarded: *For the use of non-European passengers only*. He was a man of

*A tourist in Africa, Chapman & Hall, 1960.

70

studious disposition and he had a very comfortable voyage. I greatly envied his three weeks solitude . . ."

Unfortunately, there is very little to envy in the situations the Blacks find themselves in. They are rarely amusing, always humiliating, sometimes tragic.

I knew a Bantu commercial traveller who represented a big firm of cleaning products. Like his White colleagues, he had a car and sold the same soap. He worked harder, because it is more difficult to persuade the Bantu to buy. His White colleagues worked on a 10 per cent commission basis. He got five per cent.

In April 1960, the *Sunday Times* published figures to show what education costs Black school children. Their Matriculation fee is £1 10s. more than that for the Whites!

The Black man cannot make the most simple gestures in life: enter a café when he is thirsty, take his family to a restaurant or to the cinema of his choice, or take the first bus coming. The cafés and the restaurants, the buses, the benches and the beaches are separate. After 10 or 20 years of a happy life with a woman he may be accused of "criminal sexual relations" and be separated from the mother of his children. He has not the right, unless he was born there, to live in a town with his family, and he can lose this right (the South African law stipulates this!) if he leaves the town *for one night*. It is also law that his son, when he turns 16, can be sent back to the Reserve where he was born if the White superintendent of the location where he lives so decides.

If you encourage a Black man to stop work, and he does so, you both run the risk of the lash, five years' imprisonment and banishment.

In many towns, when the sirens go off in the evening to indicate curfew-hour, which is at nine o'clock, ten o'clock or eleven o'clock, according to the town, the Bantu must be at home in their locations and ghettos. All of them. The rough illiterate peasants, who have just emerged from the bush; the doctors, the lawyers and the poets, all those with black skins who were born on the wrong side of the colour-bar. The law makes no distinction. It is colour-blind, and even, one could say, blinded by colour. It is idiotic.

Influx control aims at preventing the White towns (where the Whites are already in the minority) from being swamped by Blacks

71

from the Reserves. Influx must not be confused with immigration. It seems quite normal that the Republic of South Africa, if it wants to, should forbid Blacks from abroad coming to seek on its territory what they can't find at home. Everywhere in the world, immigration is controlled. In the light of possible further partitioning of South Africa, it is even normal that the interests of the Whites should be the first consideration in the future White region.

But it is not a question of immigration. The "immigrants" are South African citizens. At this point of our analysis we are not trying to discover whether these measures are justified or not. We wish to determine the effects of discriminatory laws on the Bantu population. This leads us to state that "influx control" forces the Bantu to ask for work and residence permits; even if he merely wishes to move from one suburb of a town to another he must obtain a separate permit in order to be able to live with his wife; he only holds these privileges by right, as we have seen, if he was born in the town, or after 10 to 15 years of continuous employment, and loses them as soon as he stops working; and so, in the end, a great number of Bantu have no established residential, work or family rights.

In order to prove, at any and every moment, that he has the right to be where he is, to sleep where he sleeps, to work where he works, the Black man is given an identity card, the "reference book", the "bewysboek", the pass. Many foolish things have been written about the "pass". It is a banal document, which is at the same time a birth-certificate, a receipt for taxes, a work permit and an exemption certificate (from curfew regulations, the law prohibiting Bantu from buying alcoholic drinks, etc.) In our time of controls and permits, it is perhaps the closest thing to a Kafka-like vision of a "life-card" which regulates everything, right down to the right to breathe and to reproduce. Perhaps it appears detestable mainly because it materializes the manifold restrictions and controls which surround the Black man: the monthly stamp of his employer, the residence and visitor's permits, etc. We, who have our pockets full of other permits and documents, prefer not to dwell upon it . . . Because there is worse in store . . .

Job reservation is the basis of economic discrimination against the Bantu, the Coloureds and the Asiatics. This complex law is aimed at maintaining White preponderance in skilled jobs and confining the non-Whites, whatever their aptitude, to unskilled jobs, and thus to low wages.

Ministerial decisions periodically define the categories of reserved employment. These regulations are extremely complex. Determination No. 4, gazetted in November 1958, reserves for Whites the posts of ambulance drivers and attendants, firemen and traffic policemen above the rank of constable in the service of the Cape Town City Council. It added that at least 82 per cent of the constable's posts in the traffic police should be reserved for Whites, that no further Coloured constables should be appointed, and that any vacancies or additional posts created should be wholly reserved for Whites. After protests and discussions, 20 Coloured ambulance drivers were allowed to transport non-emergency cases of non-White patients. Their services may not be used in cases of emergency, nor in cases where non-White patients are immobile and where first-aid stretchers are required.

Determination No. 5, in force from 4 January 1960, reserved for Whites the work of operating passenger lifts in the municipal areas of Bloemfontein, Johannesburg and Pretoria, in estate agencies, building societies, insurance, banking, finance and investment undertakings, the commercial distributive trade, hospitals and nursing homes, educational undertakings, the printing, newspaper and mining industries, municipal and electric supply undertakings, employers' organizations and trade unions. It made two exceptions: non-White employees might operate passenger lifts used to convey non-White persons or goods, or goods and personnel employed by the firm owning the lift.

Determination No. 6 (effective March 18, 1960) provides for the building industry in the Transvaal and Free State. In urban areas, many of the less skilled activities, such as operating sand-papering machines, bagging down walls, digging foundations, mixing concrete, outdoor paving in broken slate, etc. are excluded from the definition of "work" and may be carried out by Coloured men. All other skilled occupations are reserved for Whites.

Determination No. 7 deals with the section of the iron, steel engineering and metallurgical industry that is concerned with the manufacture for domestic use of metal cupboards, shelves or sinks, hollow-ware, refrigerators, washing machines, electric stoves, geysers, electric kettles or pots. It reserves for Whites 27 listed categories of work (except in the Western Cape where 23 instead of 27 types of work must be performed by Whites only.)

These are examples.

The regulations are so detailed that they define the slightest brush-stroke or movement with a trowel that a Black man may legally make. Private householders in White parts of urban areas may now employ Bantu to construct stone walls to enclose their premises. Owners of businesses and persons responsible for the management of institutions (except in the Western Cape) may use Bantu to renovate or maintain their buildings only if the Bantu concerned are in their regular employment, and are not especially engaged to do the work concerned. Furthermore, not more than one such Bantu may be employed in each business or institution or branch thereof (except for lime-washing walls, for which more than one Bantu may be employed). Besides renovating and maintaining the buildings, an African in the regular employment of an institution or business may apply protective anti-corrosive or bituminous coatings to walls, pipes and machinery!

One could fill pages with the lists which cover all sectors of the economy. These laws, by confining the Bantu to the bottom of the ladder, not only rob them of all incentive and any prospect of promotion, but also, by artificially and automatically protecting the White worker, they thwart healthy competition, encourage incompetence and discourage productivity.

They are also partly responsible for the very small numbers of the White population. Australia, Canada and New Zealand, are countries of immigration, because the White man, even without big financial means, can make a living there. In South Africa the millions of Bantu do the menial work, so that the White job-seeker and potential immigrant is restricted to the trades and professions, to positions requiring higher training, to the role of the capitalist. Usually, the average immigrant is not a capitalist, nor a highly trained scientist. In this way large numbers of immigrants are automatically prevented from reaching South Africa. Their fresh blood is reinforcing Australia, Canada, New Zealand instead.

The Industrial Conciliation Amendment Act (*1959*) completes these regulations by preventing the Bantu from organizing to sell their labour under better conditions.

Bantu trade-unions are not forbidden, but they are not recognized as competent in negotiations with the authorities or the employers. The trade-union interests of the Bantu workers are supposed to be represented by "industrial councils" composed of representatives of the employers, the White trade-unions and prominent outsiders judged to be competent with regard to the working conditions of the Bantu. The Bantu do not have the right to strike. It is a criminal offence. The mere fact of belonging to a Bantu trade-union makes the worker suspect and often costs him his job. The Bantu are also excluded from legislation dealing with the training of apprentices, and unemployment pay is only paid to Bantu whose wages exceed £273 a year, which means that the vast majority do not receive anything!

The brute labour force of the Black man is accepted. But that part of him which can be elevated and which is capable of professional refinement, his brains and his sensitivity, is rejected.

The muscle is used, the man himself as a human being is rejected.

The Group Areas Act is the law which most clearly strikes the foreign visitor. One does not see at first glance whether a man crossing the street is suffering from malnutrition or whether he is eaten up by frustration. One does immediately notice that South Africa is divided up into residential ghettos.

"Do you know," a fierce opponent of the present régime said to me, "how Dr. Verwoerd envisages the ideal city of the future? It will be round, cut into sectors which radiate from the centre, like a cake cut into slices, with a different race living in each slice. And so, you see, each race will be able to get to the centre without ever crossing the territory of another race . . ."

The real facts are neither so simple, nor so much of a caricature.

The law is not only aimed at creating racially "pure" residential areas for each community, but also at controlling property rights.

When an urban zone has been declared a White, Bantu, Indian, or Coloured "Group Area", the disqualified residents must leave it. They must be given at least a year's notice. They can remain the owners of their property for the rest of their lives, but their heirs must sell within a year of inheriting the property.

The individuals and the communities who have been uprooted do not only suffer from a moral point of view. In many cases, they are financially ruined. The Indian traders, whose customers are traditionally to be found amongst the Bantu, lose them. Proprietors must sell their houses below their real value, and buy land at high prices. In most cases, the zoning uproots non-White communities to the benefit of the Whites who extend their domains, and they are removed from the urban centres to peripheral zones which are always further and further away. Naturally, the traders do not receive compensation for the loss of their investments.

"This law does not merely want to cut up our towns like a cake," concluded the relentless opponent of the government. "It is designed to make the life of the Indians so hard and so bitter, that they will leave the country . . ."

Social discrimination comes under the heading of a series of *laws on immorality and separate "amenities"*. I will show what is meant by "immorality" by quoting a few examples, and indicating the consequences of "immoral" behaviour.

Shortly before the Second World War, a young White man in the Cape became friendly with a young Coloured girl. After the war the young couple decided to live together.

In January, 1959, the man was charged under the Immorality Act of 1950, which had made inter-racial sexual relations a criminal offence. The prosecution was wise enough to abandon the case, after it had been established that the couple had been living together for many years. The White man had only one way of legalizing his situation: to register himself as Coloured on the population register. This meant losing his job, destroying the bridges between himself and the White community. He did so.

In 1954, a German sailor who called at the Cape had a love affair with a Coloured girl. Back in Germany, he learnt that she was expecting a baby. He joined her, and, not being allowed to marry her, he lived with her. He was also charged in 1959, when his companion was expecting a second child. He declared to the judges that he would leave the country he had made his own. He was given a suspended sentence. A Berlin newspaper offered to pay for the return journey of the whole family.

These examples of immorality are tragic; some are burlesque.

In 1960, a South African court had to judge a strange case of outrage to public decency. A waitress in a restaurant accused a Black man of having hurt her intimate feelings because he had photographed her between two Black men. The accused based his defence on a coincidence. He was busy taking a photograph of two Black men in front of an open door when the White woman suddenly stood in the doorway just as the camera clicked. That very same day I knowingly photographed a White woman worker in the printing-works of the *Journal of Bantu Education*. She was next to a Black margin cutter. I don't know whether I was guilty of a most reprehensible immoral act.

Cases of this kind are frequent. Many are much more dramatic. Couples, married for years, have been arrested, separated and accused of illicit relationships. And yet there was no real problem to solve. South Africa was in no way threatened by an epidemic of "immorality". Statistics show that there were only 92 mixed marriages in 1943, 99 in 1944, 92 in 1945, and 97 in 1946. Was this a matter for legislation, or for accusations of *Rassenschande* against couples who had grown old together, and who had had grown-up children for many years?

In any case, the law has not prevented anything. On the contrary: bad laws always have bad results. It has perhaps added the additional attraction of stolen fruit to the tang of the exotic. Relations between races—which the Whites are supposed to abhor—continue. From 1951 to 1958, 19,014 people were brought before the magistrates. Obviously, there must have been many times more, not caught *in flagranto delicto*. In this conflict between the Minister of the Interior and God, what chance has man? And when this "immorality" is situated on such a high level of affection, in spite of racial barriers, that a husband does not hesitate to brave ostracism by his own people, and economic ruin, in order to join his companion belonging to the "wrong" race, it is really ridiculous to bring the law to bear on it.

In all the other fields of inter-racial contact, separation is easier to establish and to control, and infringements are more easily dealt with.

The blankets on South African trains are green, with a big mark on those used by the Blacks, so that they should never be used by the Whites, even after having been carefully disinfected.

The beaches are separate, and the separation goes right down into the water. However, three miles out to sea, it becomes legal to swim side by side. The Minister of Bantu Administration has the right to prevent Bantu, as individuals or groups, from attending a religious service or a meeting outside the "locations" reserved for them. A

Black man cannot enter a building belonging to a White man unless he is performing his work, or unless he has permission of the owner or lawful occupier, and no White man can go into the "locations" of the Bantu without permission. All public places are kept strictly separate, although there are still a number of restaurants where people of different races eat and even dance together. Even the law-courts have two witness-boxes so that a White man does not have to set foot on the same floor where a Black man has just testified. The aim of the legislation (whatever its positive intentions, which we shall examine) is to make inter-racial co-operation impossible by means of an iron curtain. This legislation is particularly serious, because it means that Blacks and Coloureds are offered public services and "facilities" at a lower level. Until 1953, the principle of *separate* services was associated with the obligation to provide equal services, and in a famous judgment, the Appeal Court acquitted a Bantu who had used the White waiting-room in Cape Town railway station, on the grounds that the facilities available to him were far inferior to those provided for Whites. But the Reservation of Separate Amenities Act (1953) introduced the principle of giving each sector of the population facilities in accordance with "circumstances"—that is to say, separation in *inequality*.

Arbitrary methods of enforcing these laws make them worse.

Too much power is vested in the police and the administration. The case is reported of a farmer who had almost beaten a Black man to death: he was sentenced to a fine of £10. A Black man who incited Blacks to burn their "passes", had to pay a fine of £500.

A Black servant attempted to poison her master, a "platteland" farmer. He had savagely beaten her while she was pregnant and the day after she had given birth. The only proof of the attempt to poison him was the confession of the servant. But the same confession also contained an accusation against the master. The judge did not even ask the police to investigate this accusation.

For a long time until 1961, policemen had no numbers sewn on their collars or uniform. This gave them the terrible and threatening superiority of those who remain anonymous. Until a short while ago the police went so far as to arrest Blacks *on the front-door steps of their own homes*, because, at that moment, they did not have their "passes" on them. Seventy per cent of the wounds inflicted on the Bantu at Sharpeville show, without any possible doubt, that they were shot in the back. One of the leaders of the present Bantu political opposition became a fierce enemy of the Whites on the day when a policeman asked him for his pass ("Kaffir, show me your pass . . .") and, having found it in order, threw it at his face. This man was a university lecturer, who was worth a hundred times more than the ruffian in uniform. The policeman's aggressive and stupid attitude of racial superiority was an insult not only to the Black man, but to his own White people.

The Government has discretionary powers. *The Suppression of Communism Act* allows it to exile and imprison Communists, but it also considers Communist any doctrine which aims at promoting a change in the political, industrial, social and economic conditions by means of disorders or illegal acts. The executive may "deem" anyone a "Communist" whom it thinks has advocated anything calculated to achieve these "aims of Communism" . . .

A Black man cannot obtain the aid of the law if he has been evicted, even though wrongfully, from his house. He can only claim compensation, once he has been unjustly expelled.

"The handling of a non-European by a police officer, in the enforcement of pass or tax laws, the demeanour of a servant," writes Harry Goldberg, "these are the things which are studied by foreign observers. It is effects, not underlying intentions, which are recorded in the newspaper reporter's notebook or the press photographer's camera."

And the foreign observer sees more. He sees what the others no longer see, a tragic mentality at work: the separate blood banks, and the husband who forbids his wife, in danger of dying, to receive "Black" blood! In a Durban bus he hears a fat White woman giving vent to her indignation:

"Yes, you can hardly believe it, but at home, we have a Black minister and he and his slut of a wife sit out on the verandah, in the easy chairs and chesterfields of the former White Pastor! And they even use the bathroom, with hot water in it!"

I remember a typical scene in a Johannesburg building.

I was in the Black lift. Another White man got in. It was an automatic lift which stopped at every floor where people wanted to get in. At the first stop, the White man swore at the Black lift-attendant. "Man, can't you see, I'm going down. Why are you stopping my lift?"

The man did not reply, and the White man complained at every stop. His excitement grew until he literally barked at this "bloody lot of Kaffirs."

Finally, I said to him: "Man, this is an automatic lift, and this man can't do anything about it. Besides, you are in the wrong lift . . ."

When he had gone, the Blacks said to me: "They are always shouting at us, and we can't answer back."

But one day there could be a reply—a terrible reply—to this useless arrogance which one might describe in the famous words of Fouché as "worse than a crime, a mistake."

It is estimated that 50 per cent of all the men in the Police Force are permanently employed in applying the discriminatory laws.

This is too many.

This means that they are bad laws.

There is a law which forbids Blacks to buy brandy (at the time of going to press, September 1961, the new liquor act was not yet in force). Yet, everywhere in South Africa, I was told that they buy it from the Coloureds, from the Indians, and even from the Whites themselves.

The object of the law (to prevent the Bantu from starving their families owing to drink) has not been achieved. The contrary is achieved: for the Blacks who have a certain social standing and fortune are those who have evolved and who benefit from exemptions. The poorer classes are those who pay high prices for black-market liquor. A bad law always has bad effects.

Must everything be regulated? Has the state, which has the power, the moral right to go further than the average wishes of the population?

Three hundred years ago, a governor tried to forbid the sale of spirits to the Red Indians. He also forbade the consumption of white bread, less healthy than black. Three hundred years ago, he did not succeed. The gap between right and the law is like the gap between conjugal fidelity and the harem system. Who would think of praising adultery? But did the people who technically eliminated adultery through the law of the *purdah* and the harem have the right to do so? Must one pay such heavy prices?

It has been said: if one accepts the Black man because his muscles are needed, then one must accept him with his brain, and, to put it crudely, with his genitals as well. If South Africa is not willing, then it should try to do without the Black man for a little while.

But if one only accepts part of the Black man, by sending back his children and his old people and his political ideas to the Reserves, one is slowly forced to surround oneself with a wall of defences, and one ends up by living in the situation of a besieged garrison, in a *laager* with rules and regulations which in the end curtail your own freedom. This happened to Sparta, which died because it enslaved the Heliots. Fifty years ago, Olive Schreiner wrote these prophetic words:

"It is ordered by the laws of human life that a Nemesis should follow the subjection and use, purely for purposes of their own, of any race by another which lives among them. Spain fell before it in America; Rome felt it; it has dogged the feet of all conquering races. In the end the subjected people write their features on the face of the conquerors . . . The continual association with creatures who are not free will ultimately take from us our strength and our own freedom, and men will see in our faces the reflection of that on which we are always treading and looking down. If we raise the dark man we shall rise with him; if we kick him under our feet, he will hold us fast by them."

And then, the White race will go down . . .

PART THREE

ANATOMY OF A SOLUTION

"The law is everywhere anticipated by
the spontaneous impetus of action—
action which, amongst many particular
disorders, yet contains the new order,
and which in advance realizes the law
soon to be made."

MICHELET

CHAPTER 1

THE ROOTS OF APARTHEID

I

Egoism and generosity, cruelty and benevolence, a whole range of apparently unresolvable contradictions are problematically interwoven in the theory of apartheid as soon as one starts discussing it. The fact of apartheid confronts you in the streets, in your hotel, in the difficult and embarrassing contacts between race and race. But life is made up of so many difficulties and restrictions, one lives with so many constraints, one suffers from so many controls, one is the victim of so many social ostracisms, if one travels, if one has lived in war-time Europe, if one is a Jew, or rich or poor; and so in the long run the segregation of the Blacks and the Whites in South Africa appears as one of the numerous burdens which make up the human condition. It is terrible to observe it, to have to admit it: but it soon becomes a habit, all the more so as the individual attitudes of the Blacks and the Whites largely correct by good nature and good humour what is deeply cruel in the enforced separation of the law. The practical result of this human application of inhuman principles is not always unbearable.

But when I passed from facts to theories, when I discussed apartheid with my South African friends, I entered into a world of their own, a world which was outside my habits and ways of thought. I really entered into the *laager* of the besieged, and I got the impression that at the very moment when enemy fires were crackling round their camp, I was asking why they were standing guard at their look-out posts. A certain Professor Cilliers had written a letter to the *Cape Times* on the subject, and a sentence in this letter became an obsession with me, sometimes to the extent of paralyzing my curiosity and drying up my questions. "But, sir," the professor had written, "does it need a carefully argued and documented study to convince you that if you lie down before a steamroller you will be flattened out?" Perhaps it was really necessary to have ancestors with large, grey felt hats, perched on ox-wagons, and a grandmother scalped by Sioux or disembowelled by the Zulus, to understand how this complicated problem is rooted in history, a problem that I had come to study superficially—I who had never lived in their camp? They explained to me the reasons for their struggles, for their laws, for their feelings. I understood the rational reasons, and yet . . .

I remember a night in the Cape Province. Eva had climbed up with me through the vineyards onto the mountain overlooking the wide valley of Paarl and Stellenbosch.

I had spent the day talking to learned men. The town was now sparkling with a thousand lights. In the wind which was chilling our bones, Eva talked to me with deep seriousness of the country in which she was born. She did not know any other. She had spent her early adolescence on the platteland of the Transvaal on her father's farm, where Whites and Bantu lived together in patriarchal simplicity, and for a long time she had not known that there was a problem. Eva had been greatly shocked by this problem in Johannesburg. In the Paarl night, she spoke to me words which have never ceased to astonish me—words which have been an important lesson to me, such a lesson as I have seldom received.

"Paul," she said to me, "the spider gets its poison out of the same flower from which the bee gets its honey . . . Paul, this is our single and utmost problem. Put it in your book."

II

It is almost impossible to define the word apartheid. Literally, it means the fact of being on one part, aside. This implies the statement of a difference, plus the putting on one side. The putting on one side, in its turn, can be static: apartheid, then, is segregation, and the word must then have a derogatory implication. It can be dynamic, and it then creates, for the entities which have been separated, new possibilities which are sometimes worse and sometimes better than before separation. Apartheid is all this. Sometimes apartheid is seen as a generous programme for the complete uplift of the Bantu, having as its aim the granting of the maximum of civilization and rights; at other times apartheid is condemned as the exploitation and persecution of non-Whites. Between these two extremes lies a whole series of degrees of acceptance and criticism. What apartheid really is, I will try to express with nuances, with figures and with facts throughout these pages. For the majority of South Africans, apartheid is a philosophical and political system trying to assure a parallel development of the Whites and the Blacks, each with their own characteristics, with a view to an ultimate separation which will be as complete as possible in all points of contact; economic, political, social, cultural, biological and territorial.

At the starting-point of apartheid there is an instinct. It is the instinct of the White man which is a driving thing, with all the blindness of instinct, to preserve his country, his culture, his people, inviolate from a mixing which would mean quick swamping by the Bantu. This instinct is selfish. The White man has a privileged position in South Africa today. The real Europeans from Europe know this better than the South African, who does not possess a keen awareness of his privileges. He has been used to them for too long. He thus simply defends what he thinks is his right.

"When two men are seated on a horse," said a farmer from Pietersburg to me, "one of them must sit behind the other. It is normal for the one who is guiding the horse to sit in front."

The Whites and the Bantu of South Africa are in the uncomfortable position of horsemen on the same mount. The White man who is holding the reins, and who has the spurs, does not want to get off; but he is beginning to understand that it would be wise to give the Bantu another horse—a black one, perhaps—and that the Bantu could then ride at his own sweet will.

The White man is afraid.

His leaders talk facts and figures, and he understands them. The most optimistic provisions, based on an increase at the present rate, and a big White immigration, foresee some six million Whites in the year 2000 as against sixteen-and-a-half million Bantu.

The "pessimistic" estimates, which foresee a decrease in the death rate of the Bantu and only a slight increase in the rate of White immigration, give the figures of four-and-a-half million Whites and twenty-one-and-a-half million Bantu. The Tomlinson Commission has adopted the second point of view. The greatest sociologists, economists and statisticians of the country have signed a verdict which says in capital letters: *It is the second estimate which appears as the most acceptable for the future*. Within a little while there will be four-and-a-half times as many Blacks as Whites. A policy of integration of the Blacks would give them a majority in elections.

The fear of the White man is fanned by the tumultuous awakening of the African giant at his frontiers. He sees in the Bantu of South Africa the vanguard of the 200,000,000 Blacks of the continent. There are governments who have taken up the slogan "Africa for the Africans." Plans for an African union are on the agenda. The vast majority of South Africans think that a multi-racial state would be a Black state in which the White man would no longer have any kind of right or security. The example of the Belgian Congo haunts them. A multi-racial state would be perfect, but almost as realizable as the cohabitation of lion and lamb.

In addition these Europeans with legitimate rights feel at home in this country which they have built with their own hands. To what country can the man return who has built his own home in Africa, and who knows no other? The fear of the White man is not just panic, born of despair, but a rational fear based on years of contact with a more prolific community. Fear is one of the unalterable realities of human nature. It provokes instinctive reactions in individuals, as in groups. But the fear of the White man in South Africa is not the absurd fear of the mentally ill. It is the type of fear which serves a useful function in the life of individual human beings. It is the instinctive desire of a people to preserve themselves.

The White thus wishes to maintain his political position: through apartheid he excludes the Black man from his own world.

He also wishes to preserve his economic status.

To a certain extent the "laager" that is built round the White domain has as its chief aim to prevent the influx of Blacks from lowering the standard of living. The Blacks and the Coloureds will for a long time to come sell their muscles and their brains cheaper than the Whites. A *laissez faire* economy would put salaries on the lowest common level.

One of my Afrikaner friends, proud of the rapid increase of the power of his people in the industrial urban areas which had long been the field of the English-speaking people, explained to me: "In 1955, at the time when there was a scarcity of coal in Britain, the English miners demonstrated more vehemently than ever against the importation of Italian miners. The Italians were threatening their standard of living. Trade unionism aims to ensure better salaries and better living conditions. Do you think that the English miners 'hated' their bosses or the Italian miners? Neither do we hate the Bantu. But we cannot allow ourselves to let them compete against us in the labour market.

"And it is a field which interests Afrikaners even more than our English fellow-citizens.

"Most of us come from the platteland, from the Orange Free State and the rural Transvaal. We only 'conquered' the great industrial towns in the twentieth century. Until then we were living completely isolated in the countryside. The twentieth century with its money economy forced us to seek work in industry. We climbed the rungs of the ladders very quickly. But for the same reasons—because industry was needing hands—the Bantu also streamed into the towns. In 1929 there were 587,000 Bantu in the towns, in 1944 a million. There are three million at present.

"Do you know that our great national strikes in 1907, 1913, 1914 and 1922 had as their only aim the struggle against the economic integration of the Bantu? The Commission of Inquiry charged with establishing the causes of the strike of 1922 concluded that 'the trade unions had wanted to oppose the substitution of cheap Black labour for White labour.'"

The White wishes to preserve his economic standing: apartheid excludes the Black from free competition in the economy.

III

These selfish reasons for apartheid are not the only ones at stake. A generous impulse adds the milk of human kindness to the venom of fear and envy.

One of the ideas which most frequently crops up in the work of thinking South Africans who write about their problem, is contained in the word justice, in the word equity, in the word ethics. South Africans want to "do justice" to the Bantu. They proclaim that a policy of oppression of the Bantu is not only unworkable in the long run, but is immoral. They think that the Bantu must enjoy the same chances of developing themselves, and have the same freedoms as the Whites. Mr. J. G. Strijdom, the Prime Minister who immediately preceded Dr. Verwoerd, said: "The Bantu is a human being. We cannot remain indefinitely sitting on his head. Apartheid means that in his own territory he will be lawyer, doctor or mason—that according to his capacity he will be able to reach any level. Oppression means allowing a Bantu to live amongst White people, but at the same time refusing him the right to exercize the trade or the job that he is capable of doing: that is evil and unjust."

I have not met a single South African who wishes to oppress the Bantu. All those I have met wish to put their shoulder to the wheel to help the Bantu to keep his national identity, to rise on the economic ladder, to gain political rights—in their own areas, in a separate territory.

This is not a recent attitude. It is commonly believed that this "generous" Utopia is a smokescreen put up by the Nationalist Government to hide the cruel reality of discrimination, but in reality this attitude has very deep roots in the South African "political philosophy".

General J. C. Smuts, a great statesman, author of the preamble to the United Nations Charter, cherished this generous Utopia forty-five years ago. A speech that he made in London on May 22, 1917, at the Savoy Hotel was typical of his heart-felt convictions:

"A policy is developing in South Africa today which may have profound effects on the future of the continent . . . we have got into the habit of giving to the Natives their own separate institutions, which are parallel to ours . . . through this parallelism we shall solve a problem which otherwise would have been insoluble . . . each day we are more and more convinced that it is useless to try to govern White and Black under the same system . . . their political institutions should be different, but always on the basis of self-government . . .

"In our system of the ownership of land, in the form of our administration, our policy consists of separating the races . . . and so in the final analysis you will have in South Africa vast regions cultivated by Blacks and governed by Blacks . . . and in the remainder of the country you will have Whites governing themselves . . ."

On January 20, 1913, General J. B. M. Hertzog, a former Prime Minister, second in prestige to Smuts in the history of South Africa, defined his policy as follows: "Do not let us take the whole of the Union for ourselves. Let us divide it. Let us give one share to the Bantu, and let them develop there according to their own nature."

Theodore Roosevelt, on the very day of the proclamation of Union, May 31, 1910, spoke in London about "British policy in Africa". He declared that British administration in Uganda "had been particularly well advised in trying to develop the Natives according to their own way of life, instead of trying to make Englishmen out of them."

If the principle was right in Uganda, is it less right in South Africa? Is the chain reaction of political emancipation in Africa anything less than the political application of apartheid?

The generous impulse which encourages the South African (and especially, the Afrikaner) to desire a distinctive national development for the Bantu is a curious transference of nationalism. Where most of the Bantu intellectuals (who would be called *evolués* in the former French colonies) think of their political future in terms of rights to be conquered within the setting of White society, the Afrikaner intellectuals think of the political future of the Bantu in terms of the national autonomy of the Bantu. In this respect they are better integrated into the "African context" than the Bantu themselves, and they cannot understand why other people fail to recognize the unselfishness and the idealism of their attitude . . . They often told me: "It is absolutely impossible for the Bantu to find in a mixed society the adequate expression of his personality, the realization of values which are most dear to him. They have their language, Zulu or Xhosa, for example. Could they be added to Afrikaans and English as official languages? They have their traditions of marriage. Are they ready to reject them? Nothing is more disagreeable for a Black man than to see a White man hanging round his wives. It is just as disagreeable for him as the inverse situation is to the White man. In a multi-racial society, would marriage or mixed cohabitation, even if legally permitted, please the Black man?"

Most South Africans see no inconvenience in dual nationalism or multi-nationalism. South Africa already has two capitals, Pretoria, seat of the Government, and Cape Town, seat of Parliament. It has two languages. It had, until 1958, two flags, its own and that of Great Britain. Why should it not have two nationalities, one for Whites and one for Blacks, symbols of two different economic, cultural and political destinies?

In this respect, the Afrikaner is, of course, infinitely more "Bantu nationalist" than the English-speaker. The word *nation* and the whole complex of feeling and ideas that the word arouses, has different connotations for the Afrikaner and for the Englishman. For the Afrikaner, the nation is an exclusive concept, for the English, it is an inclusive one. For the Afrikaner, a conference is national when nationalists, in a political or cultural sense of the word, get together; for the English when all the languages, the cultures and the people to be found within the frontiers of the same state come together, even though by chance.

For the Afrikaner, *nasie* or *volk* is an ethnic, cultural and historical reality. For the Englishman, the word nation embraces a mechanical entity, independent of a common culture, subject to a political or state authority. In the United Kingdom the nation consists of the Scottish, the Irish and the English.

In South Africa the imperial concept which for centuries has been part of the English mentality, includes the Afrikaners, the English, all the Europeans, all the Bantu and all the Asiatics; it is an ideal which is completely foreign to the Afrikaners. It is for this reason that the Afrikaner works more willingly than the Englishman for the realization of Bantu nationalism. It is for this reason, also, that he fears it more than the English, because, through his own experience, he knows its potential force. He knows that nationalism is a fundamental, primitive force which is dangerous to the extent to which its aspirations are opposed. If he wants to canalize it, and to give it shape parallel to his own national development, this is because he knows that steam always seeks to escape, that dynamite grows in explosive power through constraint, but that steam and dynamite used in the correct way are powerful factors in our civilization. He wants to give Bantu nationalism its cultural and political escape channels.

Within the framework of this generous inspiration, which is, as we have seen, natural to him, the White man makes perhaps one mistake. He wants to help this Bantu nationalism to flourish peacefully and in terms of a balanced and gradually introduced progress, by giving the Bantu houses, hospitals and schools, but very few town halls or parliaments and, for the moment, no flag.

Nationalism, however, is first and foremost the aspiration to political freedom: political freedom is for a people what self-respect is for the individual. The taste for political freedom asserts itself regardless of the price to be paid in the struggle, the dangers to be faced, and the poverty to be endured. With a subjected people the struggle of nationalist parties is an emotional and sentimental impulse towards freedom, which takes short cuts regardless of rational arguments, material and economic interests. The man with self-respect, chooses freedom even when it means hunger, rags and homelessness, otherwise he has the mentality of a slave. People who have been given a taste for freedom want to govern, and to govern themselves badly if necessary, rather than to be governed. Completely irrational and certainly regrettable, such is the genius of true *nations*.

This doctrine, except for the difference in dosage just indicated, is similar to the political conceptions of most of the heads of state of the new Black republics of Africa. Their *negritude* is emphasized with pride. The arts, the culture, and the customs of the Blacks are revived with loving care and the Whites are often accused of having stifled them. Is there really any difference between the struggle for the emancipation of the Blacks by all the Nkrumahs, the Sekou Tourés and the Bandas, and the concept of the emancipation believed in by the apostles of vertical and radical apartheid?

IV

The doctrine of apartheid is also based on a mystique of segregation that is essentially religious. The South Africans, and in particular the Afrikaners, are a people deeply steeped in "this strange spirituality of their incomprehensible, cold, cruel Calvinism which supplies Biblical justification for the least Biblical acts".* This description is a little harsh: such a state of affairs no longer exists. The *predikants* of the Dutch Reformed Churches of South Africa no longer preach that the Black are "sons of Ham", destined from all eternity to serve as "hewers of wood and drawers of water". But the consequences of this primitive conception still influence the Whites of the *platteland*. The practice of segregation in all the Dutch Reformed Churches implicitly condones segregation in all other spheres of life. The South African Protestants are still deeply attached to the doctrine of predestination imported by their ancestors in the seventeenth century, and its practical conclusion in the idea of a chosen people

*Garry Allighan, *Curtain Up on South Africa*. (Purnell and Sons, Cape Town, 1960.)

93

elected by God for a special destiny has in their eyes been shown in the history of South Africa.

Totius, a great South African poet who was a professor at the University of Potchefstroom, stated in his *Racial Policy of the Afrikaners in the Scriptures** that God did not want unity, but favoured diversity. God is a differentiator. That is why created beings are not born mixed, but each according to his species, and God created each species from the beginning. God ordered us, he added, to prosper and to multiply and to fill the earth. That means to move: that means to give birth to nations.

"When our fathers," said Totius, "left the low country near the Cape to seek the high plateaus of the interior, we began to become a nation. Our Great Trek completed this process. God ordered us: Fill the earth. God approved the birth of nations." Each nation is called by God and its sacred duty is to maintain itself as a nation. Nations and kingdoms, but not empires, are created according to the will of God. Dr. A. Kuyper, the Dutch theologian, adds in his *Common Grace* that the Boers of the Cape would have *resisted the will of God* if they had not trekked in 1834 to separate themselves from the other inhabitants of the country!

To this conception of the divine right of nationhood is added another theme: that of the sin that stems from the non-separation of peoples.

When one reads through the scientific publications of S.A.B.R.A. one is struck by the number of studies, a sort of theological popularization, devoted to this subject. They often invoke the injunction of Paul to the Corinthians: "Be ye not unequally yoked together with unbelievers: for what fellowship has righteousness with unrighteousness, and what communion has light with darkness?" (*II Cor. 6 : 17*), and all the former commandments to Israel not to mix with the pagans. For historically the dividing line between believers and non-believers coincided for a long time with the dividing line between civilized and non-civilized, White and Black; in such a way that the Biblical command aimed at the non-believers ended by meaning the non-White. This historical fact certainly persisted until our time in the religious heritage of the South Africans.

The symbol of the Tower of Babel is also very frequently invoked to uphold the "natural order" of separation desired by God. A

*Congress of the People, 1944.

very complete commentary on this key idea appeared in 1955*
and has been copiously commented on by Press and reviews.

The building of the Tower of Babel must have been undertaken
in a spirit of rebellion against God. In violation of the explicit
commandment of God: "Be fruitful and multiply and replenish
the earth and subdue it"; (*Gen. 1 : 28*), the rebels built a city and a
town where humanity "would hold together" instead of remaining
scattered. It was thus an attempt at unification as against the divine
command for diversity.

God replied with a punishment intended as a warning example.
He divided the language spoken by Man into various dialects, and
he split the Chosen People into various peoples. In this way God
created the true model for the type of relationships which ought to
govern peoples.

The coming of Christ has certainly not, in practical theology,
modified the teachings of the Old Testament on this point. The unity
rediscovered in Him (a unity "where there is neither Greek nor Jew,
circumcision nor uncircumcision, barbarian, Scythian, bond nor
free" (*Colossians 3 : 11*), transcends the diversity but does not
abolish it or make it undesirable. Is it not said of this unity that
"there is neither male nor female" (*Galatians 3 : 28*), which cannot
mean in the providential order of things the confusion of the sexes
on a plane of human relationships? What this rediscovered unity
means is a plenitude of unity in a world to come.

Even then, adds an Afrikaner commentator, the diversity will not
have lost all meaning because in the multitude assembled "before
the Lamb", as John says in his Apocalypse, the origins are still
recognized: they are "of all nations and kindreds and people and
tongues" (*Revelations 7 : 11*). Consequently the racial, ethnic,
cultural and linguistic diversity corresponded to the divine plan:
one must respect it. It is a serious sin to undo this multiplicity, to
seek a unity contrary to the divine plan in a new Babel.

In 1944 the Synod of the Dutch Reformed Church of the Transvaal came to this conclusion: "The Word of God teaches racial
apartheid and the guardianship of Natives by the Whites." A still
more "logical" theologian, Professor Strauss, declared in 1950 at
the Calvinist Conference in Bloemfontein that the "Christian White

*The Scriptural Basis for Race Relations in Civil Life or the Community of
Nations* by Professor A. B. du Preez.

is invested with official authority over the native. The native must obey our orders. He must ever bear with our punishment in the name of the Lord because it delivers him from the slavery of sin."

Few South Africans subscribe to these extreme conclusions of a faith which has gone astray. But the extremes clearly show the direction taken by the thoughts of the average Afrikaner, although there is little doubt that they never reach the logical conclusion of those thoughts . . .

When the foreigner becomes interested in this phenomenon, he realizes the significance of a factor which seems very curious to people from Europe, something out of this world: a still vigorous and living religious feeling permeates everyday life, individual convictions and the policy of the nation. I was amazed to read the words "Christ or Chaos" carefully traced on the body of a Buick. On Sundays the bars are closed and alcohol is only served in hotels if one has a meal. There are not even any sports. In the Orange Free State fishing is forbidden on the Lord's day! In 1957 the British and Foreign Bible Society distributed 347,010 Bibles in 84 languages in South Africa. In 1956 the only countries where more Bibles were sold than in South Africa were the U.S.A., Germany and Great Britain.

In spite of the legal *régime*, and in spite of the harm done to individuals (and we have seen cases of this), nobody in South Africa has ever lynched a Black man, and this is due to the action of a living religion. The Bible was the only book the pioneers carried with them during their trek inland. As they moved inland, the Bible remained their only link with civilization. It kept alive the spiritual values of Europe. For generations the reading of the Bible took the place of schooling. The Voortrekkers were so permeated with its teachings that they gave the name "Nile" to the first river they encountered, because it flowed towards the North . . .

The Europe that the first colonists left was still, to a certain extent, the Europe of great religious movements and conflicts. A deep religious feeling was transplanted to Africa and was maintained there owing to distance when it had already disappeared in Europe. The Huguenots reinforced it. This is why certain religious problems which have been slowly eliminated from the spiritual life of Europe are still living for the Christians of South Africa. The Church was a real link for the Boers. It was the physical centre of their lives at a time when there was no other point of social contact for the farmers who were scattered through the infinite spaces . . . Christ or chaos . . . In a factory on the Rand, I was present at a service improvised by the workers amongst themselves during the lunch-hour in the canteen. This habit is widespread. In 1941 the National Party stated in its policy that it was completely opposed to "any non-Christian practice in national life" . . .

South Africa is full of moral principles, even at a time when South Africans seem to twist the meaning of the most generous commandments of religious ethics.*

---

*Until 1951 the Nationalist Party in the Transvaal had a clearly anti-Semitic policy and, until then, excluded Jews from membership. A good many Nationalist leaders were militant anti-Semites and did not hide their feelings of sympathy towards the Nazi rulers, before and during the Second World War. A pamphlet of the *Federasie van Afrikaanse Kultuurverenigings* went so far as to ask "whether the culture of the *volk* is not affected by a Judeo-imperialistic policy applied against Afrikanerdom with regard to the exploitation of our natural resources."

CHAPTER 2

BANTU EDUCATION

I

The most important feature of the Bantu's trek towards their future, full of the happiest auguries or darkest threats according to the angle from which one views the matter, is that of education. The Tomlinson Commission clearly saw "that it is of fundamental importance that education should not be a loose cog in the mechanism of Bantu society. On the contrary, it must be the large driving wheel which starts the machinery of development and keeps it going."

The child, it has been rightly said, is father to the man. Consequently, as early as 1953, legislation was introduced whose principles appear to us as healthy, whatever the defects: the education of the Bantu by the Bantu for the Bantu. It was aimed at both the individual and the community. It was meant to secure a Bantu education for the Bantu child in the same way as a child in France receives a French education and a child in America an American education, based on national culture and given in the mother-tongue. The community was to benefit from a "Bantucentric" education to counteract the strong centripetal tendencies which were progressively assimilating it into the culturally-different White surroundings.

This principle logically follows the policy of renationalization of the Bantu. Until then a dilemma had hung over the cultural destiny of the Bantu: the Black man had had only two alternatives: rejecting his negritude by attempting to adopt Western civilization, or remaining Black and uncivilized. He was now offered another choice: to remain Bantu with his language promoted to the dignity of an instrument for acquiring knowledge, of attaining civilization, and in so doing to enrich his own community in the spiritual, social and economic fields. In short he was offered the opportunity to leap ahead—an attitude which is rewarding and shows courage and vision.

The premises were certainly sound.

The normal thing for a child is to be educated in the surroundings in which he has to live as an adult. Most children, in any country, leave school only to go back where they came from. All educationalists agree on this point: the principles of teaching are universal, but the methods and the content of education must be related to the environment and the traditions. The school, too—it would be stupid to deny it—forms citizens, men nourished on the history that was lived by their forefathers and that they in their turn will continue to make, shaped by their knowledge and their acquired attitudes.

Attitudes are based on the impact of spiritual masters and heroes held out to them as models. Whether one likes it or not, the school conditions and shapes the personality. Bantu education seeks to prepare the Bantu child for service to his community; it seeks to inculcate in him that all doors are open to him within this community—which implies that many doors are shut to him in White society. It wants to inculcate in him that education and civilization acquired by the individual must not culminate in the ideal of being absorbed into the social life of the Whites, but must be used to uplift Black society. The emphasis is certainly put on the community and not on the individual. Dr. Verwoerd coldly but clearly defined this aim in Parliament on June 7, 1954: "It means supplying the Bantu with an education which is not centred on the interest of the individual, but which has as its aim the progress of collectivity." He does not aim at westernizing individuals but at uplifting nations. Whether this is a crime against the individual or a necessary disciplining of the individual as a means towards better progress for the nation depends again upon the angle from which the problem is considered. Clermont Tonnerre, speaking in the French National Assembly in 1789, faced a similar problem, that of the Jews who had to be assimilated into the French collectivity; he used precisely the opposite formula: *109800*

"All for individuals, nothing for the community," he said.

If the principle of and the necessity for a renationalization of the Bantu are admitted, could the indispensable means to this end be questioned?

The system in force before the "education of the Bantu by the Bantu for the Bantu" was not geared to this renationalization. There were schools for the Bantu, but were they Bantu schools?

As in Europe the churches in South Africa were the early pioneers

99

of education. One of the principal aims of the missionaries was teaching the Blacks to read: to read the Bible and by reading the Bible to throw off heathenism. Before 1954 the education of Bantu children was to a large extent still under the control of the missionary societies. Religious teaching had an important place in the curriculum. Co-ordination between school and family was rudimentary. Most of the missionary societies had their headquarters abroad, sometimes thousands of miles away, and the teaching often failed to root itself in local realities and to aim at local needs. Bantu children were made to learn by heart the interminable lists of kings and Emperors who had succeeded each other as the heads of European states, but they were not taught the importance of soil and water conservation for the economy of the Bantu countries. The school did not encourage a stern desire to serve the community.

In 1953 the British Secretary of State for Colonies had ordered an inquiry in West Africa into the system of education. The conclusions of this inquiry are valid for conditions prevailing in South Africa: "Too much importance has been given to the type of education which is customary in English primary schools and too little importance to the African environment, to the spiritual and physical facts which have significance for the African children because they correspond to their daily experience." In other words, there had been too much book-learning, a conditioning of the young Bantu for a social and political situation in an Utopian city which did not correspond to the city of his daily life, and for positions which did not exist for him in private and public enterprises. The school did not fit in with the other fields of the Government's social and political policy which was working in a "Bantucentric" direction. There were two opposing movements, centripetal and centrifugal. Very often their conflicting trends amounted to nil.

The schools were producing a Black *élite* for unemployment; this *élite* was not brought up in the ideal of promoting its own community; the schools were merely showing the Bantu an illusory way to the doors which lead to the green pastures of the Whites. But for all that the Bantu could not crop the succulent grass: culture and science did not give access; the keys to the kingdom were not in the hands of the teachers . . .

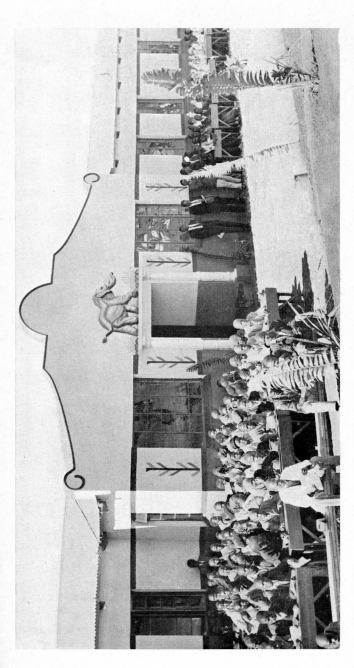

The Mphaphuli Secondary School at Sibasa, Northern Transvaal. The building was erected by a Bantu contractor using only Bantu labour. The elephant on the gable is the emblem of the Venda people. This photograph was taken at the opening ceremony of the school

Modern school-buildings with all the necessary facilities are steadily replacing improvised classes held under trees

The principal of the School for Sons of Chiefs and Headmen at Tsolo, Transkei, explains a point to some of his students

A White Paper of S.A.B.R.A. entitled *The Education of the Bantu,
Oppression or Opportunity* opens with a photograph of three beaming
Black school children on their way to school with their books and
exercise-books under their arms. As caption there is this terse statement: "A few generations ago most of the Bantu children were
playing naked in the warm sun near their primitive homes. Today
the 'Tom Sawyer' stage has already been reached, with almost half
the Bantu children attending the growing number of schools. A
generation from now they will all be at school."

This is true. The "Tom Sawyer" stage has been reached.

It is not a very satisfactory stage. But we know from figures
circulated by Unesco that there are 700,000,000 adults in the world
who cannot write or read—150,000,000 of them in Africa. Twenty-
five years ago 91 per cent of the Bantu population of South Africa
was illiterate. Today this figure has fallen to 58 per cent. This is a
practical illustration of the "Tom Sawyer" stage. I witnessed it in the
"royal" village of Chief Mohlaba Shilubani, near Tzaneen, with its
school inside the church, a mine-recruiting calendar on the wall
and a few road-safety posters.

Earlier in the afternoon Chief Shilubani had received me in his
Town Hall, a brick house with fifteen benches and a portrait of his
father, the late Chief. I had asked him about the top priorities for his
village, and he replied unhesitatingly, without consulting any of the
councillors who were present: "Schools! We don't want our children
running round the fields."

Then he led me through his mudhut village, and showed me a heap
of bricks in a shed.

"They were made last year," he told me, "to build at least three
classrooms. We stopped at three because we had no more money.
We are going to ask the parents for some. Perhaps we'll get some
from the Government . . . and our children will be able to go to
school."

The first stage of the state-controlled system of education which
was introduced in 1953 aimed at the abolition of illiteracy, through a
new curriculum including practical classes, suitable to the Bantu
tradition.

In order to extend to a maximum number of children the educational potential represented by each teacher, each classroom and each bench, primary classes were shortened to three hours a day, so as to allow two shifts. The Government has been criticized for this measure: it was said that this was an easy way, sending big numbers of children to school, but providing them with little real schooling, and that the aim was not only to attain a high figure of school attendances—the highest in Africa—but especially to keep education for non-Whites at a low level. We will see further on what is the truth behind this dark plot. In fact, in the former non-nationalized educational system, 50 per cent of the Black children only had two years of schooling, 10 per cent reached standard I, three-and-a-half per cent Standard VI, a half per cent Junior Certificate and a very limited number Matriculation. In other words, the Black child spends little time at school and it is necessary to educate him before he has been dragged into the normal economic circuit from which no one will be able to extract him in order to form him. The extension of primary schooling corresponds to the needs of an underdeveloped country from which one must eliminate illiteracy on as wide a basis as possible, and in South Africa the number of Bantu children at school has in fact increased from 56,845 in 1917 to 464,024 in 1940, 746,324 in 1950, 858,079 in 1953, 1,238,583 in 1958, 1,428,000 in 1959, and 1,500,000 in 1961. The leap forward is obvious since nationalization in 1953.

In order to provide the maximum amount of education to pupils who will only spend two years at school, the primary cycle has been divided into a lower primary, which gives a grounding in elementary knowledge in all fields, and a higher primary which gives access to normal schooling. The usual subjects of study are writing, the official languages, the mother-tongue, arithmetic, hygiene and nature study and to these have been added classes in social studies, a subject consisting of geography and history taken together, geography being the study of the *world* in which man lives, history being the study of *man* in the world in which he lives. As for the four practical subjects in which people have seen proof of the "degradation" of Bantu education—manual work, Bantu craftsmanship, gardening and that extraordinary course in "tree planting and soil conservation"—these should be made compulsory throughout Africa and Asia. Are not trees and soil the basic problems in this new black-yellow world taking shape on these continents?

The second characteristic of the education of the Bantu for the Bantu is the use of the mother-tongue.

The principle is certainly valid in the primary and secondary schools.

Transformation of the fluctuating, oral tribal culture into a written culture, the elevation of little-known literatures to literatures taught and analysed in class; the changing of dialects which are not rich in vocabulary into teaching languages, must eventually enrich these cultures, these literatures, and these languages for the benefit of the people who possess them. One enriches soil by feeding it with manure and by restoring to it the residue of the crops that it has produced and that have been harvested . . . The Bantu languages are being endowed with the scientific terminology required by modern education in all fields; the writing of textbooks will allow Bantu writers who wish to renovate their language to enter the domain of disciplined and methodical creation. With regard to the Bantu community, encouraging the use of the mother-tongue certainly represents a positive measure.

At the formative stage of the national personality the promotion of intellectual autonomy is a positive element. One immediately thinks of the formative period of the State of Israel and the resurrection of Hebrew. Theodor Herzl, the inventor of the Jewish State, thought that his language was German and his culture European. The Hebrew University, by firmly adopting Hebrew as a medium of instruction, has very quickly raised it to the function and status of a cultural language, endowed with every possibility of expression, from the slang of the military camps to higher mathematics. The language and cultures of the Bantu can only be enriched through the influence of the civilizing values of the West.

With regard to the individual—although this has often been debated—the advantages of mother-tongue education seem equally obvious. Montaigne asked for minds "well-formed rather than too full"; this has not always been the ideal of teachers in countries of recent scientific civilization.

A common phenomenon in former colonial countries is a confusion of *concept* and *terminology* in the minds of recent *élites* who studied and taught the European language, and continued to think in their own dialect. Their sometimes purely verbal knowledge, retransmitted in the form of definitions to the classes they had to

103

teach, often hid a deplorable absence of thought. This cultural verbalism revealed itself in their incapacity to coin definitions in their own language, that is to say, to restate in a different form what they had learnt. The mother tongue, an almost instinctive form of expression of innate emotion and knowledge, is certainly the tool best adapted for acquiring book learning, according to the infallible axiom of pedagogy which holds that knowledge is propagated from the known to the unknown in circles which nonetheless always retain the same centre, the same origin . . .

The third principle of the new deal in education emphasizes the last term of the formula: "by the Bantu".

The 1953 Act removed the Bantu schools from the control of the missionary societies under the four provincial administrations, upon which they had until then been dependent. Control was transferred to the central government, and locally to Bantu school boards, and, where they existed, to the Bantu Authorities.

Within seven years 7,093 schools have been placed under the control of 4,500 school boards consisting of 30,000 parents or other citizens interested in their progress, along with 27,767 teachers. These figures are important: they represent 4,500 meeting places where 30,000 Bantu persons can have a controlling interest in their own affairs and a training ground for their active participation in the management of their destiny. Through the education of the children the whole community is being educated, through the concrete problems of running a school, populations which have been spoon-fed for generations are taught that a book, a pencil, a school bench, a teacher, mean money and that they are not manna coming from the omnipotent and far-off government in the town but the fruits of an effort that the community which benefits from them must make. The system as a whole is thus certainly on this level a positive contribution to the development of the body civic of the Bantu and fits in very well with the guiding thought which theoretically underlies the whole edifice of apartheid: apprenticeship of national independence.

III

Segregation of Bantu education has nonetheless provoked the keenest controversy aroused by any measure of apartheid because its opponents rightly feared that it could become a fundamental tool for the "conditioning" of the Bantu. Was it going to be used to keep the Bantu for ever in a subordinate position in a mixed society? Were they going to try to turn out "good Blacks" by the millions, through an inferior education which was carefully calculated not to allow the Bantu to lift his head beyond a certain standard, and in which the spirit of servitude and patient submission would be taught? After seven years of this system the quarrel has died down because its most fervent enemies have not been able to discover the slightest thing in Bantu education which would amount to "conditioning" people for "slavery". But the dark plot had been ascribed to the Government in Pretoria with such an abundance of accusations and pessimistic predictions, even before the system came into existence, that we must clearly state here that these predictions were not realized and that South African educationalists agree about it.

The curricula are as full as those of the White schools, but the teaching methods simply take into account the local conditions of the Bantu school—and the elementary English textbook speaks of Nozipho, of Thoudi, instead of John, Mary and Jack, and of the nocturnal life of the village in terms of jackals which wreak havoc in the poultry yards.

What is inferior in Bantu education is that the Bantu children, although of the same age, are *normally* one or two classes below the White children. This is in no way due to administrative pressure, but stems from the fact that they come from a less cultured environment and that their economic role in their villages is that of herdboy; nor do their parents willingly free them from this obligation. Bantu education is aimed precisely at smoothing out this difficulty. What is inferior in Bantu education is that only four per cent of the children go beyond the primary stage, as against twenty-four per cent of the White children, and their examination results are not as good; but this shows only that one must lower rather than raise the academic standard of the Black schools so as to obtain better numerical results, and create a special "Black matriculation"—something which does not exist in South Africa. Finally, what is inferior in this education is that the State spends nearly £44 a year on every White pupil, £18 on a Coloured pupil but only £8 on a Bantu child. These figures faithfully reflect the general difference between the living standards of the three communities, and here one could indeed speak of inferiority. But things being what they are, one must never judge anything as an absolute. School buildings and teachers cost much more in Johannesburg than in the royal kraal of Chief Shilubani.

This does not mean that £8 will buy less culture than £44, nor that the culture taught at Tzaneen, in almost similar books with the same examinations in view, is inferior.

The problem of the quality of Bantu teaching seems to me to be situated somewhere else. It seems to me excellent that history, geography and ethics are being taught as a single subject, "social studies", and it would be a good idea to extend this principle to White schools. It is, after all, normal that the emphasis should be put on the Bantu environment rather than on the heritage of Western civilization and at a given moment one must stop talking about "our ancestors, the Normans"—to the descendants of Chaka and Dingaan. The true problem is the ultimate aim of the studies. Those who admit that teaching has a social aim, that its first function is to preserve and to propagate the culture of the group, are opposed, in Europe as well as in Africa, to those who affirm that man is an end in himself and that social institutions are but the means of fully realizing human personality. The problem of the naturality of education is particularly important in countries of recent indigenous culture. In South Africa they have clearly chosen to educate the Bantu *community*, rather than the *individual*.

But the independent states of the continent, building their new national physiognomy with huge strides and at tremendous pace have done the same thing. It is in this sense that the policy of autonomous Bantu education is without doubt the least reversible of all the policies which have been applied to the Bantu in South Africa, and the most positive step taken in the direction of Bantustans.

IV

It was at Turfloop, the young University College of the North for the Venda-Tsonga, the Sotho and the Ndebele, between Pietersburg and Haenertsburg, that I saw the most convincing illustration of the system, and also felt to what extent it works in the right direction.

Under a blue sky in the midst of red sandy countryside and rocky hills I stopped at a busy building site. Building sites have the physical effect on me of conveying certitudes. Working teams and scaffoldings do not need any intellectual explanation. Smokescreens are not built of bricks. At Turfloop, the smell of mortar, freshly quarried stone and the strong odour of white wood and the noise of the concrete mixers, made me think of Jerusalem, of the work camp of the Hebrew University; of Bangalore, India, of the work camp of the Bharat electronics plant. Here the world of tomorrow is being built, a world which is constantly pregnant with possibilities, a world potentially far ahead of today's world.

Had Professor Potgieter, the rector of this young university, this Afrikaner for whom apartheid is a generous mystique, been purposely chosen so young? Here was one of these people dedicated to an apostolate, a man who believes in his work.

"Ninety-five of my students are in their first year. The laboratory equipment for the second year has been ordered . . . We will grow, gradually, as our numbers grow . . . There are some who have no *ideals*. They want to earn money and go to a town where they can live according to 'White' standards. It is a curious thing, but they are the least intelligent: one would think that they are frightened of themselves, and they need the proximity of the Whites to feel themselves protected. For myself, I like the others better: those who have been sent by their own people with a scholarship from their tribe and from their regional authorities and who will return home to work amongst their own people. Our aim is not to produce 'evolués', people who will have an honourable but subordinate rank in the ante-chamber of a white advocate or in the dispensing room of a white chemist. In this university we want to form people who will stand on their own feet and who want to run a state of their own: people who want to serve, just as a Ghanaian student wants to serve Ghana."

Professor Potgieter's eyes were glowing as he pointed to a big poster on the wall above his desk, bearing the names of the Council of the Northern University and of the Advisory Council.

On the Council, which holds all legislative and executive power, there are the names of Richter, Le Strade, Van der Merwe, Young, Rautenbach and Brink. On the Advisory Council I read the names of Chiefs, clergymen, assistant inspectors of Bantu education; the names of Ramokpopa, Moroka, Kgware, Mphephu Rama-bulana.

"The Council is White," Potgieter told me. "The Advisory Council

107

is Black. But when you come back in a few years' time to meet the next Rector of Turfloop University, I hope you will find a Bantu Rector in my place. If in the long run this is not possible, it will be proof of our failure. One day the members of the Advisory Council will have to manage their own affairs in this university, and we shall have to go down to the bottom of the poster and become the advisers who will advise as long as the others want to consult us."

This is a healthy political idea. The decentralization of the Bantu universities can certainly contribute to reinforcing the national growth of the regions where they are situated. Universities are traditionally and naturally the breeding ground for nationalism and even the centre of patriotic agitation. I heartily agree with the idea that Fort Hare should become the political centre of the 'young Turks' of the Xhosa people in the Transkei, and Turfloop that of the Venda-Tsonga in the Transvaal, and the Zulu university of eNgoyi that of the Zulus. And one must welcome in the same way the creation of the Indian university on Salisbury Island in Durban Bay. All nations have national universities, with strongly pronounced national characteristics. The German, French and English universities all have their essentially German, French and English peculiarities, although all of them co-operate in the search for scientific truth.

The establishment of Black universities in the heart of the Black countries will stimulate their spiritualization, in the same way as Stellenbosch, Potchefstroom and Grahamstown stimulated the spiritualization of the White communities they served.

From an economic point of view these universities will stimulate the growth of university towns. In 1960 1,575 students were registered at the three Bantu universities. Two thousand scholars sat for the matriculation examination. Turfloop, built by Bantu workers, causes a constant flow of money to stimulate the Bantu economy. The bricks were made on the spot. The decorative motifs were chosen after competitions held in five Bantu technical schools. The students are housed on the spot and the teaching staff must be near by. This university population pays for services and products which stimulates local activity. Turfloop is the clear example of a seed sown in the right way.

But the system has limits to its efficacy, and there are perils attached to it.

First of all, years will pass before the education given at Turfloop reaches the level of the education the Bantu have been deprived of by not being allowed at the mixed universities. Whatever the long-term benefits that the Bantustans will obtain from them, time is running short, and long-term benefits may, eventually, never be paid . . . A real Bantu *élite*, in really big numbers, is needed today. Perhaps today is already too late. A system that makes one lose time at the very moment when all the processes in Africa are being accelerated—no matter what may be its theoretical merit—has a fundamental defect.

On the other hand the Government in Pretoria and the Governments which will tomorrow sit in Pietersburg and Umtata, and behind these governments the White and Bantu nations of Southern Africa, have certainly no interest in building up their *élites* in ethnic isolation. What is good and indispensable at the stage of primary education is perhaps no longer so in the higher classes of secondary education. On a higher level the influence of the popular background is acquired and contact with foreign cultures is indispensable. At an academic conference held in Tunis in 1959, Professor Cecil Hourani, an Arab educationalist, put it excellently:

"To become a modern Arab, a man must pass through the rolling mill of foreign cultures . . . to be completely himself he must for a time cease to be himself . . . to know himself he must see himself through the eyes of others. It is no use shutting oneself up in oneself . . . the University of Damas was a failure because it did not allow Arab culture to receive fruitful outside contacts. But a culture thus impregnated becomes creative in its own language and in its own domain."

The leaders of the Black and White nations who will tomorrow live in South Africa must not be formed in antagonistic camps. Whether one wants it or not, they will have to discuss their common problems of transport, water, hygiene and customs on all levels; their discussions will sometimes lead to quarrels about their political relations and like all peoples and all nations they will experience conflicts and may even make war on each other; they will sign peace treaties. But in what manner will they live near each other? What kind of wars will they wage on one another if they are separated during the formative years, at the very stage when conceptions of the world are formed which give to the worst enemies the basis of understanding? At university the ties and bonds of a common outlook are formed, which extend their influence beyond the lecture rooms right into the offices of cabinet ministers, editors, legislators and executives. The university provides a nation with the leaders for top administrative posts, finance, the business world, power. At universities the leaders of tomorrow acquire a common series of standard and intellectual values and the habit of seeing the other side of a question. One does not merely study civilization in books. One can study the theoretical rules of a game but the game is played on a sports field, and sooner or later one must go on the field.

Good neighbourliness is learnt in a living context. The leaders of the South Africa of tomorrow must have points of contact, the greatest possible number of points of contact. This is obvious and whatever works in the opposite direction is folly.

Consequently the existing system must be adapted to reality. It is in everybody's interest. If the *raison d'état*, the higher interests of the Whites and the Blacks, really inspire political thinking in Pretoria, the means must be adapted to the ends. If there is to be separation in dignity, if apartheid really is to be parallelism, a reciprocal feeling of dignity between Bantu and Whites must be built up—and they must be taught that co-existence which is proposed as the ultimate aim. If separate universities are desirable for the excellent reasons we have enumerated, the dangers which are also contained in them must be removed.

Once separation is an accomplished fact on the level of separate nations, a measure of contact must be restored on the level of the individuals belonging to the separated nations.

White students should be accommodated in the Black universities whenever their future position demands contact with their Bantu counterparts in their professional life. Exactly the same should be done with Blacks in the other direction. If the Bantu who are brought in today from the Reserves are one day to be received as true ambassadors and true foreigners—and I believe that those who claim this are speaking in good faith—one must give their fathers an adequate grounding, along with the means to attain that end. It would be both honest and intelligent. The University of El Azar provides an example of dangerous, aggressive fanaticism brought about by cultural isolation, placed in the very heart of the Arab world on the borders of Africa and Asia . . . It is certainly not in the interests of the Blacks of Africa—and certainly not in the interests of the Whites—to produce a number of El Azars rebelling against Western civilization.

V

These are the specific defects of Bantu universities. More serious shortcomings mar Bantu education in all stages from primary to higher. They do not in any way detract from the system of parallel development itself; they concern its application, which sometimes seems to me to be contrary to the aim.

It was a mistake to hand over the control of the education of the Bantu to the Department of Native Affairs, later subdivided into the Department of Bantu Administration and Development, and of Bantu Education. In South Africa everything which checks the advance of the Bantu, everything which artificially limits their aspirations, everything which implies vexation and control, comes from the Department. The Blacks have not yet understood that the same source is responsible for their progress. The staff of the Department consists mainly of hardened administrators. With some exceptions (and this book deals with some notable exceptions), they lack the milk of human kindness. Education and teaching are matters of mind and spirit and fare badly under constraint. Teaching and the control of illegal immigration are two different arts. The Department of Bantu Education decides with complete authority who shall study, what shall be studied, where people will study, and who will teach: at the present stage when the Black population has no representation in the central government its system of education is literally *totalitarian*.

The Minister of Bantu Education could inform a delegation of professors of theology that they would be allowed to open a theological college for the Bantu if the "secular subjects" such as psychology, philosophy and Greek were excluded. Even the teaching notes bought from correspondence schools by adult Blacks who get instruction through the post, will be subjected to the Minister's control.

The system of using indigenous languages as teaching languages must be adapted at university level, where problems are necessarily more difficult.

The use of Zulu for Zulus, of Xhosa for Xhosas, of Sotho for Sothos, must not increase the division between these nations. The old inter-tribal divisions led to wear and ruin. If the Government in Pretoria imagined (and I say imagined because I do not believe it holds this Machiavellian view) that it was necessary to divide the Bantu nations so as to rule over them all the better, it would certainly be making a mistake. At the point Africa has reached (and the conflicts in Kasai, Katanga and Kivu show this clearly) an inter-tribal war with the means of 1961 and its possible involvement in the cold war would benefit nobody, least of all a White nation.

What one must encourage is not division between the Bantu, but a Bantu inter-tribal nationalism, a multi-tribal nationalism which merges Xhosas, Vendas and Zulus in a common conception of the modern state, not its contrary. At university level, at least, a return to Afrikaans and English should be encouraged. The Bantu languages as intermediaries between the tribal mentality and Western civilization will have played their roles fully at the primary and secondary levels of education.

Finally, my last criticism goes to support the theory of apartheid. When opening any Bantu history or geography textbook one notices with satisfaction the signs of the new and constructive spirit that this education for the Bantu has brought.

"Look around in your own area," writes B. G. Grové and F. J. le Roux,* "and see who is the most successful agriculturist. Is he the man who spends little energy in his farming and takes small thought for such matters as the preparation of the soil, the selection of good seed and need to fertilize his crop? You will soon realize that the successful farmer requires education in his business of farming quite as much as the teacher needs sound training in his profession.

"In the Bantu areas the growing of maize is not yet as productive as it should be, for few Bantu farmers pay sufficient attention to the necessity of scientific production . . . Instead of returning the stalks of the mealie plants after reaping to the soil as compost, many Bantu people use it as fuel. This is one of the reasons for the decreasing fertility of so many lands in the Bantu areas . . .

"Through soil erosion deep dongas have been carved into the landscape. The lands have become infertile, many pastures have

*Social Studies for Bantu Primary Schools, via Afrika Publishers, Cape Town.

become barren, natural forests have disappeared and many streams have dried up." But these utilitarian observations do not reveal to what final end a better use of the nation's resources leads.

"The residence of the Chief of the Zulus is situated in Tongoland," observe the same authors. "Therefore this area can be referred to as the nuclear area of the Zulu nation." But what future is held out to this "nation"?

"In the Bantu areas today, Chiefs, headmen, demonstrators and other government officials are demonstrating good farming methods. They are also advising, assisting, and in some cases compelling farmers to co-operate in the rehabilitation schemes. In addition, government departments are making great efforts to regain the damage done in the past."

What is the aim of this rehabilitation? This building up of a new country and a new economy? Should not the Bantu child be told and taught that all this has a definite aim, and that this aim is the national independence of the Bantu nations of South Africa? Are people afraid to explain this programme honestly?

"Saving the Bantu areas and increasing their production has become a national problem. The future of the millions of Bantu who live in these areas has to be made secure. Not only must they be able to produce sufficient food for themselves, and make a comfortable living off the land, but they should also increase the production of the Union as a whole."

The Union as a whole? . . . Why do they talk about the Union instead of the positive idea of apartheid, the Union instead of partition, "these regions", instead of "these states"?

"The school curriculum," Dr. Van Zyl, an inspector of Bantu education, told me, "is economically and socially orientated. The Bantu child must acquire a sense of his own responsibility. The meaning and the understanding of the subjects taught only has value if the child has realized that he is a member of a particular community, that he is linked by ties of all kinds to this community, and that this community is to be found in his home, his school, his church, his village, and his tribe."

But why stop at the tribe?

This is the fundamental defect in the education of the Bantu for the Bantu by the Bantu: it lacks explicit references to the national independence of the Bantu and encourages a dangerous ambiguity.

THE AGRICULTURAL DEVELOPMENT OF
THE BANTU TERRITORIES

I

In 1958 the total area of land under cultivation in the whole of South Africa amounted to 16 million acres. Of this land 3.7 million acres, or 23 per cent, was in the Reserves.

During the same year, the Bantu harvested only 10 per cent of the total crop of the Union. These two percentages are eloquent. The land cultivated by the Bantu is little more than a third as productive than that cultivated by the Whites. Moreover, according to the experts, these figures are extraordinarily optimistic.

Improving Bantu agriculture by raising its productivity is one of the principal economic problems of the Bantustans.

When travelling through Bantu areas, one is struck by the nudity of the soil; the absence of trees, the scanty grass; plots scattered among the villages without apparent order; soil eroded by the rains and the maze of intersecting footpaths, each taking the shortest route from the huts to the roads or to the water supply; planted fields trampled without regard by man and beast; the flocks apparently straying where they want to, with no hedges or enclosures save the kraal into which ragged little children drive the very lean cows at nightfall—a picture of desolation interspersed very occasionally by the beginnings of improvement: hedges; geometrically shaped plots; cemented water-pumps and irrigation furrows.

There are numerous reasons for this situation.

First—the force of tradition.

The Bantu are not really agriculturists. They owe to their nomadic and pastoral origins a habit of brutal and anarchic exploitation of the soil. There was plenty of pasturage two or three centuries ago; whenever the grazing land had become exhausted, they moved their flocks, which had multiplied without control, towards apparently limitless horizons. No attention was paid either to overgrazing or to fertilization and seed selection. The Bantu certainly knew nothing of the rules of crop rotation. The agrarian law of the tribe was reduced to unlimited use of the tribal pasturage. There was neither individual nor collective responsibility for soil conservation or the maintenance of grass-land. Crops were raised on the same soil where grazing was allowed. The cattle wandered freely, feeding at will on crop or pasture. Trees were cut down for firewood or for building, but there was no reforestation. When this piratic system of exploitation had exhausted the land they resorted to the historic expedient of the African continent—war, which restored for a time the balance between the numbers of the population and the capacity of the land. This tradition, whereby the Bantu man is dedicated to the arts of war and the woman to tilling the fields has been perpetuated until the present regime, in which the White man's mines and factories provide the economic palliative which the Bantu no longer finds in periodic massacres. It allows the Bantu to satisfy to a certain extent his taste for a nomadic existence but it is responsible also for his poor agricultural output. Agriculture is no part-time job, no trade for the amateur, no hobby.

The negative impact of tradition is particularly strong in the realm of cattle-raising. Although the Bantu has not allowed his cattle-complex to reach the disastrous state of cow-worship practised in India, he still holds a worthy place on the ladder of bovine admirers. He measures his riches and his social standing by the number of his cattle. He will go hungry, rather than kill one ox, whose carcase he will eat only after having preserved it alive until the last possible moment. He allows his calves to drink from the cows because he wants fine calves as well as healthy children. He values the quantity of his cattle rather than their quality, and the external appearance, notably the horns, rather than the actual health of the animal. It follows from this that the ideas of the market value of the herd, the milk production of the cows, scientific selection and mating of animals, are quite foreign to him. It is a question of having the greatest possible number of animals no matter what the actual capacity of the pasturage at his disposal. The Bantu are so proud of their cattle that they manage to produce outsize, contorted horns by the infliction of all sorts of complex torments on the animals. The attachment of the Bantu to his animals is illustrated by the story of the herder who had taken his oxen to market and who anxiously watched the prices rising as the bidding took place. At the end of the sale the herder told the astonished auctioneer: "If they are worth all that money, I would rather keep them."

At Stellenbosch, modern agronomists have selected the Nguni breed of cattle as especially suitable to the taste of the Bantu. In this choice the aesthetic appeal has been considered as much as the biological, economic and ecological features. The Bantu likes the Nguni with its black coat spotted with white, and its erect and graciously thrown back horns. But the veterinarians have not been able to find out whether the colour of the animal is suited to its climate conditions, nor whether the peculiar shape of its horns would help its passage through the bush . . .

This regard of the Bantu for his cattle has an economic, social and religious background.

During the age of Bantu pastoralism and in the framework of the tribal collective economy, the wealth of an individual was not measured by his lands, which were neither bought nor sold. The man who cultivated 10 morgen was as "rich" as the man who worked 100. There was no industrial production. Cattle formed the only tangible merchandise and consequently the only visible sign of wealth.

In addition, in this polygamous society, cattle constituted a wife's guarantee of an adequate supply of milk for her children. On the African continent, where hunger was ever-present, this purely domestic consideration was of extreme importance, and gave rise to social customs which appear to be very far removed from their biological motivation. It has notably been responsible for the custom of *Lobola*—the dowry in the form of cattle which is received by the family of the bride—and which is observed even in the most civilized milieu.

The cattle-dowry has been made the focal point of marriage. There is fact as well as symbolism in the Bantu proverb: "The children are not begotten by the man but by the cattle given in payment for their mother."

Even to this day the possession of cattle also has a religious significance. The cattle being the Bantu's most precious possession, he has made the kraal a place where the ancestral spirits are venerated, and he considers his cattle to be the medium of contact with these all-powerful beings from the Beyond.

Social and religious traditions are not the sole cause of agricultural

116

backwardness. Psychological factors (which are to the individual what tradition is to the mass) have equally contributed to the Bantu's low agricultural level.

Eldred Green, an expert on Bantu mentality, reports the authentic story* of the agricultural demonstrator in the Transkei who had hoped to appeal to the imagination of the Bantu by concentrating his efforts upon the most important Bantu farmer in that district, of whom he wished to make an example of sound agricultural economy.

Having received the necessary authority, he spent an entire year on this one farm, using modern machinery, the best seed and manure and all the approved techniques. For the duration of his experiment, he was accompanied by the farmer, to whom each action and the purpose of each technique was explained in detail. The flock of sheep was reduced by selection and prize rams were bought. The same procedure was adopted for the cattle. The demonstrator sowed well, he cultivated assiduously and he reaped in abundance. At the end of the season the agriculturalist, well satisfied with his work, left promising to return in the spring. When he came back he had the surprise of his life. His modern methods had been jettisoned, the herds had degenerated, and the farmer's wives were scratching the ground with their primitive hoes. The farmer was again sowing maize as he had always done!

The expert was desperate.

"By all the powers of heaven, did I not show you the way to reap a good harvest?"

Eldred Green, whom I met in Cape Town in the editorial office of one of the country's most reputable newspapers, recounted the Bantu's reply to the agriculturalist:

"What do I want a good crop for? You got me such good crops last year that I shall not need good crops again for several years."

This lack of foresight, this custom of living from day to day, is deep-rooted. When the rains start, the Bantu farmer begins to prepare for ploughing. But by the time he is ready the rains have long ceased, the soil has become so hard that it is too late to work it, and the farmer resignedly starts waiting once more. His misfortune does not in the least encourage him to scan the skies for the return of the rain.

*Cape Argus, October 30, 1958.

117

Certainly, education is going against the current of inertia which tradition has inculcated. But this current is still very powerful.

The contempt in which "woman's work"—work on the farm—is held by the Bantu is a cause of much brain-racking on the part of the instructors in the agricultural colleges. How to accustom the young Bantu to the pick and shovel? How to accustom him, in general, to see agricultural school as the preparation for the life of a model farmer, when education (that magical "open sesame", whatever its subject may be) is considered to be the passport into the ranks of the white collar workers and when the young Bantu agronomist has but one desire as soon as he possesses his diploma—to leave for the town?

David Matshego, a Bantu student who is made of the stuff of the chiefs of tomorrow, has written these words which sum up the problem admirably:

"No race can prosper before it learns that there is as much dignity in tilling the fields as in writing a poem."

II

To give the Bantu a taste for modern agriculture is one of the positive ambitions of the policy of the Bantustans.

The adversaries of this policy take the point of view that no development worthy of the name is possible because these territories are too small. This statement is correct only in so far as there is actually not sufficient land to allow each Bantu male to live idly on the agricultural labour of his wife or wives, and from a herd multiplying on unlimited and—unfortunately—non-existent pasturage. The ideal conditions: a sparse population, limitless female labour, regular bloodshed by wars and the blessing of a high human and animal mortality rate will never return. The farming population of the Bantu regions must be reorganized along the lines of the economy of the White section, where 75 per cent of the population is concentrated in the towns, and the remainder fully occupied with cultivation. This 25 per cent gets the maximum production from their soil and their cattle, and can consequently live off the land. The economy of basic subsistence—and sometimes of penury—which results from primitive pastoralism and the monoculture of maize must be replaced by a scientific agriculture.

118

The Bantu are beginning to understand this need. "Land has not become more since the good God created it," Chief Pilane of the Bakatla told me, "but men, animals and the birds of the air have multiplied. The same area of land still has to feed all of them. We must take care of it. At Saulspoort a few years ago, a snake could be seen at 300 yards because the soil was bare—there was no grass. Control and organization of pastures was instituted. Today the grass grows thickly. Once we had to go several miles to find a pasture; today the cattle graze at our front doors."

III

Order and system is slowly being brought to Bantu agriculture.

It must not be imagined, however, that a blow is being struck at all tribal tradition. The co-operation of the mass of the people is indispensable, and deep-rooted customs have to be taken into account. The way in which the problem of the sub-division of plots is being solved, offers a good example of the technique and spirit of the reforms.

Traditionally, each of the wives of the head of a family possesses a plot of ground. On this plot maize, manioc and vegetables are raised, and the harvest of each plot is stored separately. When the granary of the first wife is exhausted, they turn to the stocks of the second, and so on. When all the supplies are drained they tighten their belts! The real nature of this system is a striking example of ruinous usage, since in the end the whole yield will be consumed by the same family although it will have been cultivated in portions. Its justification is that it guarantees "a share in everything" to each of the wives.

This system is being reformed, but in such a way that it is still acceptable to the villagers. There is no disruption of social traditions regarding the apportioning of land. The three or four family plots continue to belong, as before, to each wife, but each one is now specialized. All the maize is grown on the first, the animals graze on the second, and so on. The authorities have not been blind to tradition, but they have adapted it to modern needs. Such subtle solutions are not always possible.

Several laws organize the agricultural New Deal.

The Native Land Act of 1913 defines the regions occupied by the

119

Bantu, and reserves for them the exclusive right of owning and working 22.7 million acres. If the law had not excluded the White man from these lands the economy of the Reserves might, perhaps, have attained a higher level. But the Reserves would long since have been in the hands of the infinitely more enterprising White man. The Blacks would little by little have sold to them all their lands and "eaten" their national inheritance, and would have formed to-day a rural and urban proletariat. It would have been impossible to resettle them without dislodging the White purchasers, whose claims would have been in existence for decades or centuries.

In 1936 the Native Trust and Land Act instituted the South African Native Trust and vested in it the ownership of the Crown lands situated in the Bantu territories; more than 15.3 million acres situated in close proximity to Reserves, or enclosed by them, were to be released for acquisition and occupation by the Bantu and the Trust. The Trust is to return the lands to the Bantu Governments when they have been established. At a cost of nearly £12 million, this rehabilitation has been actually carried out on 10 million acres of land. In the year 1960 alone, £2.3 million was spent in this way. When the purchase of land has been concluded, the Bantu will possess an inalienable agricultural domain of about 42 million acres: 22.7 million set aside in 1913, 15.3 million defined in 1936 and 3.8 million bought by individual Bantu farmers.

What do these lands look like? The 64,348 square miles of the Reserves have a population of about four million, say 70 to the square mile (the total Bantu population of the Republic being 11 million). This area is about one third the size of France, or four times Denmark, or one half of Italy or twice Portugal . . . A large part of the area is situated in the warmest and most fertile part of the Republic and has the highest rainfall. Seventy-six per cent of these Bantustans receive more than 20 inches of rain a year. The remaining 24 per cent receive more than 15 inches. Of the whole of South Africa, 22.7 million acres have an arid climate and only 211,000 acres of the Bantu lands fall into this category. A rainy, temperate climate is considered to be the most propitious for farming. Of the 24 million acres in the whole of the Republic benefitting from this climate, 12 million are situated in the Reserves. The experts consider that, on an average, 100 acres of the Bantu lands have a similar agricultural *potential* as 147 acres of the White holdings, that these lands, utilized properly, could consequently be one-and-a-half times as productive as the White lands. Broadly speaking, the poorest North-West regions of the Reserves could be devoted to breeding on a large scale, the South-East to cultivation. In the Eastern Transvaal, Northern Natal and in Zululand breeding could be supplemented by cultivation. There irrigation is possible. The growing of fibres could be introduced and a more selective type of breeding could be practised. In the Northern and Eastern Transvaal, in the valleys of the Transkei and Ciskei, intensive breeding, cultivation of sub-tropical fruits, legumes, fodder, and the dairy industry could be developed. These are the best lands for cereals, afforestation and sugar cane . . .

IV

Here then, are the Bantustans. Despite their excellent agricultural *potential*, at the present they do not even provide subsistence for their inhabitants. What must be done to realize these riches?

During my wanderings in Africa, in Asia and in Europe I have met many strange specimens of humanity. I would class William Wessels amongst the most curious. He is of the race of those who want to collaborate with the Creator in order to beautify Creation. Maybe he is one of those, like Akiba, whom Turnus Rufus once asked which was the finer—the work of God or the work of Man—and received the astonishing answer: The work of Man! To prove his point Akiba brought Turnus Rufus some grains of corn and some cakes saying: "Here is a divine work and there is a human one, is not the latter the finer? . . ." He brought, too, some skeins of linen and a cloth of Beth Chean, saying: "Here is a divine creation and there is the work of Man, is not the latter the more beautiful?"

William Wessels puts his shoulder to the wheel. The Natives called him Moruti—meaning father, teacher—and he is a priest by calling, a pastor in the Dutch Reformed Church. I met him at Dikhali in the Northern Transvaal busy "preaching" with the calloused hands of a peasant—preaching, with pick in hand, the "gospel" of agricultural rehabilitation for six days of the week before returning on the seventh to his Church where he attended to the more spiritual and more abstract needs of his White "flock." Moruti takes an active part in the construction of a better world. He is

121

adding the touch of man to the bareness of Nature given by God. He is one of the thousands of White and Black instructors who are reforming Bantu agriculture.

"I have chosen this job," he told me, "because I think that to help the Bantu and the Whites to live better is an important thing. When I started, my Church decided to keep my services as a minister because they considered that this was missionary work. There is another minister like me in the Transvaal. I believe this has nothing to do with politics."

In his jeep Wessels jolted me through Dikhali—the semblance of a village—a little more ordered than the usual anarchic mushroom-like growth of huts. On a wall I deciphered the "Moketi Dikgale" the "Enter with Joy" of the Sothos of the North. The houses resembled real small farms with their earthern or brick walls decorated geometrically in blue on ochre or yellow ground.

Wessels said:

"We have built wells for the people of Dikhali. In exchange they have provided the labour for erecting fences. We have installed windmills over the wells. We have planted millet, maize and kaffir-corn. We have enclosed the summer pastures into which the cattle are not admitted in winter so that the land can rest. In winter the cattle are released into the harvested lands and they eat the stubble. Do you know why I have done this? So that the children of Dikhali can go to school. They are the cattle herders. When the animals are enclosed in pastures the children are free and can in their turn be shut up between four walls in order to be taught."

Reorganization of Bantu agriculture is not everywhere in the hands of enlightened missionaries. It is planned on a national scale and carried out, with variations, on several planes: crop rotation, fertilizing practices, grazing control, livestock improvement, and the introduction of industrial crops.

The improvement of the lands proceeds by stages.

It is never imposed upon a tribe. It is by persuasion, by the "preaching" of the new gospel of progress, that chiefs, headmen, farmers, are led to register their ground as improvement areas. The resistance of conservative elements is often strong. Once this has been overcome, the lands of the tribe are redistributed according to a standard pattern. A small piece is reserved for huts which are regrouped into a residential quarter; a water-point is established;

the kitchen-gardens are concentrated in one place and are enclosed by hedges; the pastures are delimited; rotation of crops is practised; the importance of the herds is defined; trees are planted and the struggle against soil erosion is set in motion by terracing and other means. This struggle against ignorance and waste is waged over a huge area of land—some 400,000 morgen a year. A total of 136,000 morgen were improved before 1948; 2,424,000 were re-instated until 1958; with 37,923 miles of strips of grassland against erosion, 12,661 miles of wire-netting enclosures, 1,200 retaining dams, 2,000 wells, 10,000 miles of roads, etc.

The immensity of the task to be accomplished demands that it is attacked in several stages, according to priorities.

When an area is registered as a betterment area, the first thing is to stabilize it—to stop the continual deterioration. The residential quarter is demarcated, the arable lands are selected, and the capacity of the pasturage is estimated in order to determine the potential size of the herd. It is a phase of consultation and it is limited to instructing the villagers where they must build, cultivate and allow grazing.

The actual reclamation begins in the second stage, with the construction of contour banks to retain the arable land, erection of fences, the building of dams. Next the surplus herds are reduced. Every year, the work of construction progresses at the rate of 500 miles of fences and enclosures, 200 dams and 300 miles of roads.

In the last phase, once the lands have been reclaimed, the rehabilitation of the people begins. During the preliminary stages of improvement, the men who seem capable of becoming good farmers are selected. They are given allotments from which they can derive a good living; they are taught the modern techniques of cultivation, especially the use of fertilizers. In the course of the last four years the production of maize in the Reserves has increased from 1,400,000 bags a year to five million. Three million bags a year still have to be imported to feed the population, since it forms their staple diet. But when the Reserves are self-supporting in maize they will have won one of the greatest victories in Africa—over hunger: yet neither the date nor the significance of the event will make headlines in the world press . . .

But the most important victory is on the battle-field of cattle-raising.

The Bantu are beginning to realize that the udder of the cow is more important than its horns, that the value of an animal does not lie in sentimental attachment, or in that obscure feeling of respect which descends on the farmer in the evening when he leans against the wall of the kraal and when the spirits of his ancestors seem to converge upon this most sacred precinct of the village. The value suddenly becomes the pounds, shillings, and pence (rands and cents, these days) which the butcher is ready to pay for his animal, and the butcher is a man who scorns the horns of the Nguni and the fine coat of the Bapedi. He look for good Frisians, Afrikanders or Swiss Browns!

An important change has been effected: each year 45,000 to 50,000 mediocre animals are slaughtered, 500 selected breeders are bought in the Reserves. The breeders are sold with a 50 per cent government subsidy and are reared in 22 model farms; vaccination of cattle is compulsory, stock fairs and markets are encouraged. The number of butcheries, which relieve the pasturages of their surplus animal population and which supply the human population with the proteins they have dispensed with for centuries, has risen to 460 in the Reserves.

The improvement in the bovine species can be translated into figures. In 1939, 7,000 head of cattle sold in the Reserves realized £33,000. In 1952, there were about 53,000 head valued at £763,000 and in 1958 about 51,700 valued at £963,000. Selection is guaranteed by progressive elimination of mediocre breeders, by improved methods of feeding and milking. The South African Native Trust possess a certain number of model herds composed of high quality stud animals, of the types best suited to local conditions and stationed at strategic points in the agricultural offensive, which are used for the improvement of surrounding herds.

The agrarian "revolution" is also concerned with the introduction of industrial crops. Some 126,000 acres have been designated as suitable for sugar cane plantations; of these, 20,000 acres belonging to 3,000 Bantu farmers, have already been planted in Natal and Zululand. The harvests have increased from 117,000 tons in 1955 to 204,000 tons in 1958. The reason that more cane has not been planted is that production in the Republic of South Africa is regulated by a system of quotas corresponding to the capacity of sugar factories.

Industrial fibres are beginning to make their appearance in the

Reserves. Sixty thousand acres are particularly suitable for sisal and New Zealand hemp. The cultivation methods are simple, and do not necessitate important investments, and the fibres are free from diseases. Up to the present, 5,000 acres have been planted in the Transkei, Ciskei, Natal and the Northern Transvaal.

The breeding of fish has been introduced on an experimental scale. This "culture" conflicts with tenacious alimentary prejudices of the Bantu: taboos prohibit the consumption of fish, which are associated with reptiles in numerous tribes. But the proteins obtained in artificial fish dams are much cheaper than those produced in the fields. Moreover, the artificial dams do not only combat soil erosion or impoverishment, but actually increase the quality of the humus by means of the organic material which accumulates there. This sector of agriculture could become a testing ground for the whole of Africa, when education has eliminated the strong prejudice which paralyzes it today.

Finally, afforestation offers the most important outlet for industrial labour in the Reserves. Some 687,000 acres have been chosen for forestry development and timber production. More than 25,000 acres are replanted every year. The area of Maputaland, which lies in Northern Zululand, with its 368,000 acres suitable for afforestation, represents the biggest single potential plantation in the Southern Hemisphere. Up to 1958, some 72,000 acres were afforested. This afforestation should not only provide the fuel which the Bantu have always squandered so recklessly—thus turning their lands into deserts—but also presents great industrial possibilities. There are already a good number of saw-mills, and at Umtata there is a furniture factory which belongs to the Trust. It has been named "Vulindlela"—the Xhosa term for "Open the way . . ."

Whether it opens the road to Bantu independence or not, the enterprise of agricultural rehabilitation brought to the Reserves is certainly the most irreversible and the least contestable of all the "racial" policies of the Government.

The struggle against erosion and over-grazing, the selection of seed and the importation of pedigree bulls are no political smoke-screens.

The work that has been done in these respects reminds me of the peasant whom I watched working one evening in a field near the frontier of a small Asian country surrounded by blood-thirsty enemies. He was digging the stones out of the ground. His house was a little distance away. Leaning on his pick he said to me in a calm voice, disregarding the near-by barbed wire fences and hostile pillboxes:

"It is unrewarding work but it's the task I prefer above all my other duties. As far as my house is concerned, they can take it from me, or maybe they'll burn it. One day it will fall into ruin in any case. But these stones which I am removing from the ground, and which have been there since the good God put them there, will never be replaced by anyone. This is something definite and it is for all humanity."

CHAPTER 4

THE INDUSTRIAL DEVELOPMENT OF THE BANTU TERRITORIES

I

Letaba is a Bantu district in the Northern Transvaal through which the tourist passes on his way to the Kruger National Park, via the mountainous and wooded "Little Switzerland" near Tzaneen. At Letaba the visitor is struck, as everywhere in Bantu territory, by the great number of women, children and old men, and the small number of male adults, sitting in front of their huts, in the enigmatic pasturelands where sparse vegetation is graced by emaciated cattle. Where are the men?

And yet the demography of the Bantu in Letaba is "normal": out of 42,000 families in the district, 36,000 able-bodied men are in Johannesburg or in the factories. They stay away for six to nine months to earn a living that the land, eroded, parched, treeless and over-exploited, refuses its inhabitants who are stagnating there.

"Men are increasing in number, and the land grows no bigger," a despondent Zulu prince told me in Durban. The 36,000 bread-winners who left Letaba form the local contingent of the army of Bantu migratory workers; and they leave behind them a contingent of temporary widows and orphans who for weeks, months (and years or even in vain) wait for the return of a father or a husband on short holidays.

It is easy to see what social, family and moral disorders are brought about by this situation.

Only industrialization can neutralize and then reverse the two factors which today cause the Bantu territories to be bled of their able-bodied men: the poverty of the soil, which forces starving people, who cannot get food, to go into exile; and the increasing demand for labour in the industrial regions of the Whites, which attracts these exiles to Johannesburg. An increase in the viability of the reserves and the creation of a demand for labour in Umtata, Pietersburg and Tsolo or in the heart of the Zulu country—these are the conditions of the real economic independence of the Bantustans. The official policy of the Government is to encourage the Bantu's economic development in their own territories, and to displace the centre of gravity of the Black community from the heart of Johannesburg to the heart of the reserves.

Of course, displacing a centre of gravity is a complicated operation. Calculations concerning people are subject to intangibles, to the variable human factor. And if one wishes to substitute for the powerful magnet of the big White towns a counter-magnet, it must exert a more powerful attraction than the first one, otherwise it would be useless.

II

The establishment of industries in the Bantu regions is a healthy phenomenon within the framework of the total economy of the Republic of South Africa. The opponents of the Bantustan policy often claim that the Nationalist Government would not hesitate to ruin the economy of the country in order to impose its pipe dreams, to subordinate the general well-being of the country to its ideologies, to sacrifice reality for Utopia. This is false on two levels: in the first place the Nationalist Government is not really sacrificing very much in order to transform this Utopia into reality; and in the second place it would be in the general interest of the country if they did. It is in the interest of South Africa to decentralize its industry for reasons which are very far removed from the scientifico-religious theories of Totius the poet, or of the Synod of the Transvaal clergy, to whose ideas I have referred.

Most South African economists agree on one of the implications of the apartheid policy: the Reserves must be developed, whether this development leads to Bantustans or not.

Almost all the industries of South Africa are today concentrated in four urban areas: the Cape Peninsula, Port Elizabeth, Durban-Pinetown, and the Witwatersrand and Pretoria. Eighty-two per cent of the total industrial production of the Republic comes from these four centres. Seventy-six per cent of the industrial labour force is concentrated on three per cent of the country's area. This concentration is particularly dense in the Transvaal and it increases every day. In 1916-17, 23 per cent of the total labour force of South Africa was working on the Rand. In 1956-57 this figure was

46 per cent, and in 1961 50 per cent. These figures show that industry is concentrated on the Rand—and Bantu labour as well. The White population increased by 296 per cent between 1910 and 1959 in the four towns, as against 682 per cent in the case of the Bantu. In 1928 there were 101 Bantu for every 100 Whites in these areas, as against 172 in 1953 and 200 in 1961! The Tomlinson Commission estimated that there would be 780 Blacks for every 100 Whites in Johannesburg in the year 2000 unless the tide of history was checked!

Even the most orthodox economists, and those least likely to be influenced by political considerations, would do anything they can to stem this tide.

This concentration is due to natural causes. In the Cape, Port Elizabeth and the other coastal regions the sea-ports were responsible, and on the Rand an almost unique conjunction of natural resources: the water of the Vaal River, coal, iron ore and gold, with an ideal climate to boot. Moreover, industry, once established at a particular point, tends to take root and expand there: big industries become even bigger. Raw materials are naturally less expensive in Johannesburg than in the veld: they are mined on the spot or else brought there at lower cost. Water, electricity and transport have been there for a long time. Accommodation and public services exist and can be extended. Skilled labour is available. Spare parts and repairs present no problem. There is immediate contact with customers, banks, and the authorities. All the secondary industries which maintain supplies are very close.

All these facilities encourage industrial concentration on the lines of the Ruhr. But sooner or later industrial concentration may become unhealthy for social, economic and political reasons (particularly in view of the racial problems of South Africa). This is happening in Johannesburg. The price of land is continually increasing. Workers' dwellings are consequently further and further away from the centre of the towns and from the factories. More and more miles of railways must be laid to link the residential areas with the factories. Transport is more expensive and the workers spend more time, without any profit to anybody, in coming and going. The costs of entertainment, of food distribution, of postal services, of maintaining order—in short, of every service, keeps rising. The Viljoen Commission, which in 1958 inquired into the growth of industrial complexes, clearly saw that the concentration of masses of badly lodged and underfed people whose social and family life have been broken up, who have to cover enormous distances to and from their place of work, and who are therefore an easy prey to immorality and political subversion, represented the price paid for the industrialization of this country. Great Britain had the same problem in the nineteenth century, at the time of the Industrial Revolution.

An explosive situation had then developed amongst the proletariat, even though the English formed a united national community. But in South Africa the demarcation line between the proletariat and the political masters coincides with the racial frontier.

III

In all the countries of the world, industrial complexes, when they begin to reach gigantic proportions, are dealt with by decentralizing industry in order to benefit regions with a surplus labour force. There are few countries in the world where this economic venture is further complicated by the resettlement of a "national minority", let alone a majority, as in the case of South Africa. The methods of encouraging decentralization may vary greatly; but the basic idea is the same, whether in Italy, France or England.

In South Africa, decentralization is in the general interests of the country, not only for the reasons I have just enumerated, but also for reasons of military security, because almost all her industries are centralized in one place. South Africa, which imports nearly £600 million worth of goods a year (31.5 per cent of her national income) is the country with the second highest import rate in the world, and she possesses an enormous margin of potential industrial expansion. She can therefore effect well-planned industrial decentralization, which would amount to decentralized industrial expansion rather than a transfer of industries. To these positive factors are added large untapped reserves of raw material, vast empty spaces, the cheapest coal in the world—at 10 shillings a ton, i.e. only one-third of the price paid in the United States and only one-sixth of the price in Britain—the most modern mining methods and an abundant and cheap labour force. But unless all these factors are co-ordinated in a master-plan of general development, the spontaneous interaction of these natural forces will undoubtedly increase the influx of Bantu into the White towns. Some people think that it is too late to check this movement, that the industry of the Whites depends so much on the labour force of the Bantu, and is so deeply rooted in the unproductive employment of a cheap and non-specialized labour force, that it is impossible to slow down, let alone stop, the easy flow of the Bantu towards the Rand. If this analysis is correct, then there is very little hope for the political future of the Whites if, as predicted there will be 780 Bantu for every 100 Whites in Johannesburg in 2000 A.D. But if this viewpoint is courageously rejected and if the restoration of Bantu nationalities is fanatically pursued, there is every reason to resist the influx of the Bantu, the separation of families with all the moral and social disorders which it brings in its wake, the chronic impoverishment of the Reserves, and the political and demographical swamping of the Whites.

The industrialization of the Bantustans and the decentralization of White industry are inseparable.

However, industrialists will not yield to decentralization unless compensation is given for all the attendant disadvantages and inconveniences. The advantages of Johannesburg are well known. On the other hand, the Bantustan areas mean that water, electricity and roads still have to be supplied. The principal markets in South Africa are far away; capital investment in the future Bantustans may be subjected to political risks; a less skilled labour force and consequently more White technicians, who will ask for higher wages because of the inconvenience they will suffer; and more expensive accommodation, entertainment and general costs of living; transport of goods and building materials will be more costly because of longer distances; much larger stocks of raw materials and spare parts will have to be held, with the attendant risk of obsolescence and difficult redemption of capital. These are a few of the innumerable factors which increase industrial costs, and compensation will have to be available for them in the form of lower wages for local workers, inexpensive industrial sites, the eventual availability of local raw materials, and fiscal advantages, that is to say, state intervention. This is the heart of the matter: factory owners will decentralize their industries only if it proves possible to produce more cheaply than their competitors.

Does the industrialization of the Bantustans offer any prospect to the industrialist? Once again, a policy has been formulated but its practical application lags behind. Indeed, one is faced with a fundamental difficulty. If one wants to, a Bantustan can be built out of almost nothing. The United Nations include states which are less democratic and less endowed with representative and administrative institutions than the Transkei in its present stage. Indeed, to call the territorial assembly in Umtata a Parliament is not dishonest because there are parliaments throughout the world holding magnificent powers on paper but exercizing in actual fact very few prerogatives. But what can be done on the political level often is impossible in the industrial field. You can choose tribal chiefs, grant them powers and see them carry out their tasks effectively, but you cannot simply create industry at the touch of a magic wand. Once the South Africans have been separated in the industrial field by an ideal demarcation line, there will remain White capitalists and entrepreneurs on one hand and, on the other, a Black mass with no technical knowledge or capital.

Under the application of separate development the Bantu in the Reserves would be incapable, under present conditions, of developing anything, because there is nothing to develop.

It was decided, therefore, to industrialize the White regions bordering the Reserves instead of attempting an immediate development of the "bush". In this way the necessary life-blood of wages, industrial habits and skills could slowly be pumped into the Reserves.

The Government advocates this policy mainly for political reasons.

It holds that the Bantu territories must be reserved for the Bantu and that the initiative and the capital of the Whites should be excluded because the aim is not only to develop a *region* but a *community*.

If it was merely a question of developing a region this could be achieved at a lower cost by freely allowing White investment. But where the aim is the promotion of a nation, self-development is the only possible formula. There is no question of spoon-feeding the Bantu; he must be taught to feed himself. The Government doctrine is to see a class of Bantu capitalists develop gradually from a slowly maturing spirit of initiative awakened and cultivated by example and apprenticeship, not to superimpose White enterprise in the Reserves.

The "morality" of this attitude is often stressed in South Africa. "If the development of the possibilities of the Bantu areas by the Bantu himself proceeds slowly," declared Dr. Verwoerd, "the position would still be that he would retain his opportunities in his own areas. There the same consideration applies as with land: if there had been no protection of the territory in the Reserves for the Bantu, every single Bantu would have lost his land already. In the same way, then, it is the duty of the community to take steps to safeguard the possibility of economic development of the Bantu areas for the Bantu himself."

There is reason in this attitude.

If the Whites are allowed to introduce their capital and their factories freely into the Reserves these industrialists must be granted property rights over their industrial sites and guarantees of stability. Instead of diminishing the number of "White spots" which are scattered throughout the future Bantustans, they would be increased.

The Whites would have to have managers, foremen, houses for their families, shops, churches and schools for their children. It would be the exact opposite of a creative retreat of the Whites from Black affairs. The meagre autonomy which the Bantu enjoy in their own territories would disappear.

The creation of border industries has none of these drawbacks. The Minister of Bantu Administration and Development, Mr. De Wet Nel, has proclaimed this policy "without ambiguity and solemnly" on several occasions. "As far as industrial development is concerned," he told the Chamber of Industries on November 5, 1959, "I wish to state once again unequivocally and most emphatically that the Government regards the development of industries owned by Europeans and requiring a labour force of which the majority will consist of Bantu, in suitable European areas near Bantu territory as of the utmost importance for the sound socio-economic development of the country as a whole and of Bantu areas in particular, and that the Government is determined to take the necessary steps to create the conditions for attracting industries to such areas." A committee has been set up which consists of all the interested Departments—Bantu Administration, Transport, Commerce and Industry—as well as the Industrial Development Corporation to study the potentialities of the Border areas. In March,

1959, this committee designated 57 White towns in South Africa situated at strategic points, for decentralization, and indicated for each the conditions of climate, resources, communications and population which would enable it to be linked with adjacent Bantu zones from which it could obtain its labour force.

"The problem," Dr. Diederichs, the South African Minister of Economic Affairs, told me, "is to create Bantu capital and a demand for products in the Reserves. As long as there is no Bantu capital, there will be no Bantu industry; as long as there is no purchasing power in the Reserves for more goods and services, we won't ge primary and secondary industries to produce the goods or tertiaryt activities to sell the services.

"At present the Bantu who work in the White areas spend almost all their money in those areas. The problem is how to bring this money back into the Reserves and thus create buying power and capital.

"The border industries will easily fulfil these conditions. Instead of migratory workers who visit their families twice a year, you will have workers who go home every evening or at worst every week-end. We will have solved the greatest social problem of the Bantu in the Republic: the separation of families. The mass of wages brought into the Reserves will stimulate the growth of a number of economic activities. We have planned Bantu towns in the Reserves, real industrial towns which will encourage the development of the building industry: brickworks, furniture factories, timberworks, steel foundries; and all the urban trades: bakeries, cleaners, traders, transport. It will be a chain reaction. It is estimated that 100,000 Bantu working in the factories on the peripheries of the Reserves, would make employment possible for two-and-a-half million people in the industries, trades and services which they would create, including agriculture, which would be stimulated to produce for an industrial population."

The fundamental defect of this scheme, however, is that it has hardly been started. Very few industries have been decentralized, and we will see later on that where it did occur, decentralization was not always successful.

With a naivety that the Minister of Economic Affairs must have taken for cynicism, I asked him for a copy of the law on the industrialization of the reserves. He replied that there was no such law, that in each particular case the conditions desired by any particular industrialist to establish an industry, were discussed with the Railways, who agreed to special tariffs, and with all the departments concerned. I had imagined that there would be a dynamic law which freely granted the best facilities to whoever wanted to establish industries in these border areas. I discovered that, in order to translate the dream into reality, South Africa was counting chiefly on the spontaneous movement of industry wishing to benefit from the cheap labour of the Reserves and that deserving cases could then be helped by a slight tariff concession!

"We expect something quite different from the Government," an industrialist said to me. "A government must govern. We want it to create a psychological shock. If it created regions of industrial development with water, roads and electricity, and it offered us these fully equipped industrial sites on conditions which we could accept without hesitation; if it helped us to accommodate our White technicians while in 'exile'; if it provided for automatic and generous depreciation concessions; if it subsidized the expenses of moving; if it provided guarantees against devaluation of our equipment; if it even built factories and offered them on lease; if it created technical colleges in the Reserves to assure us of skilled Black labour—then we would go.

"Solving the problem of the Bantu is a national problem. And until the Government does things like this, it will not even have begun to solve the problem."

And even then one cannot be sure that it will be the ideal solution. Moving White industry to the borders of the future Bantustans does not mean that the Bantustans are being industrialized.

In spite of the additional buying power created in the Reserves, many problems will remain unsolved. There will be as little opportunity for the Bantu in the border areas as in the White territories: within the framework of the present laws, they will not be able to rise above a certain degree of professional skill. The masses will feel the salutary effect of Bantu capitalization only after a long time. In order to diminish the volume of Bantu migration, migratory industries will be created, but only *near* the Reserves or the Bantu states. If these states become independent, there will be a frontier between them and "their" industries—which consequently will not be theirs. This leaves the industrialized nature of the Republic un-

135

changed, at least in the immediate future, and emphasizes the proletarian and dormant character of the Bantustans. If the border industries are to have any salutary effect, they must draw such a large number of Bantu and pay out such an amount of wages that the economy of the Reserves will really be revolutionized.

In order to counteract the attractions of Johannesburg, the border industries must attract the Bantu in their hundreds of thousands, but before that can happen, the border areas must attract industrialists with the force and magnetism that Johannesburg, the Cape, Port Elizabeth and Durban now possess. And if decentralization proves to be unfavourable to the industrialist as compared with centralization the difference will have to be made up by the State.

V

How will the policy of decentralization and the industrialization of the Bantustans be carried out?

In 1956 a rayon factory was established at Umkomaas in Natal, and it obtained its labour force from the near-by Bantu areas. Other undertakings were also established near some of the Reserves, including a banana dehydration plant at Port Shepstone, a pineapple canning factory in Empangeni, a chemical products factory in Umbogintwini and a steel-foundry at Isipingo.

The greatest measure of decentralization has, however, taken place in the textile industry. Several clothing manufacturers from the Rand, Durban and the Cape moved their factories to the borders of the Reserves. They produced sports-shirts, pull-overs, trousers and under-clothing. Since they paid much lower wages (thirty and sometimes fifty per cent of the wages paid in Johannesburg), they could offer their goods at very competitive prices, and as a result a certain number of factories in the White regions of South Africa had to close or at least suspend production of certain articles.

Then there developed, in the business world, in the trade unions, and amongst the Whites generally, a feeling of impatience, even of hostility, which revealed the wide gap between the idea of Bantustans and their practical realization. The Wage Board instituted an investigation into the recession in the textile industry attributed to the "emigrant" industries and demanded that the wages paid by these unfair competitors should be raised. The Minister of Labour pointed out, with due objectivity, that the recession on the Rand was caused by the general state of affairs in that industry; that it could not be blamed on the Reserves, which had only fifteen of the Union's 600 clothes factories and employed only six per cent of the total labour force in that industry. He nonetheless arrived at this surprising conclusion: "The Government fully realizes that if these uncontrolled factories were to expand their activities they might become a danger to the old-established factories . . . The factories in the uncontrolled areas are expected to ensure that they manufacture goods which will not endanger the employment of the White workers in the controlled areas . . . Where it is proved that the clothing factories in the uncontrolled areas manufacture articles which compete with those produced by the factories in the controlled areas, the existing industrial agreement will be applied to the area concerned."*

In other words, the one factor likely to attract industrialists to country areas (the lower wages) would disappear if their activities "endanger the employment of White workers".

In September, 1960, the Government published its "conclusions and decisions" arising from the meeting of the Prime Minister's Economic Advisory Council on July 26 and 27, when the development of the border areas was discussed. This document contained some positive decisions, but others that were opposed to large-scale decentralization: No tariff concession and no tax reduction would be automatically granted, so as not to compete with the existing industries; there was no question of the large-scale transfer of industries.

And Dr. S. P. du Toit Viljoen explained to the Executive Council of the Federated Chamber of Industries: there was no question of threatening the wages of the White workers by granting dumping wages to the Blacks; railway tariffs in peripheral areas would be "neutralized" in such a way that the decentralized industries would not be able to compete unfairly with the established industries.

The Economic Affairs Committee of the Associated Chambers of Commerce at the same time rejected the policy of decentralization: "With a static if not declining economy," it declared, "there is no justification for a policy of decentralization. All efforts should be

*House of Assembly Debates, 20 April 1959, cols. 4241-42.

concentrated on maintaining activity in the developed section . . ."

Judging from this example, are we not fully entitled to agree with the opponents of the policy of Bantustans who claim that it is nothing but a bluff and a smokescreen? When I said this to Dr. T. E. Dönges, the Minister of Finance, he replied that the Government was opposed to exerting any pressure on the economy of the country, which must develop freely, without state control and without protection. This is an astonishing reply from a member of a Government which applies the strictest state control in planning down to the slightest detail the lives of its Black citizens. And so in industrialization, as in every other sector of the building of the Bantustans, the problem is always the same. Does the Government really want to apply the policy it advocated with all its implications and consequences? Does it want to industrialize the Bantustans in a revolutionary way?

The Government institutions set up to turn ideas into facts do not, in my opinion, provide the necessary drive.

With regard to the industrialization of the border areas a "Permanent Committee for the Location of Industry" was set up in 1960 to co-ordinate the plans, advise industrialists about conditions of production in the decentralized areas and plan the necessary public works. Until now only a few industrialists have asked for advice.

In order to promote industrial activities inside the future Bantustans, a Government investment body has been set up, the Bantu Investment Corporation, which began to function on July 1, 1959. This Corporation aims at supplying capital and technical assistance to the Bantu for the establishment of commercial and industrial undertakings, encouraging all forms of development activity in the Reserves, and creating Bantu capital in the Bantu regions. Only, instead of endowing it with vast sums of capital, capable of assisting great undertakings, it has been given an initial capital of £500,000, of which only £126,000 was spent after 12 months of activity by means of 60 loans to 60 undertakings, of which the "biggest" were a wholesale business, a building concern, a cane furniture concern, a garage and a bus transport service. "A token sum," as Dr. Eiselen said to me. The decision taken in March, 1961—a healthy decision in principle—to allow the Corporation to buy up and to administer White undertakings in Bantu territory, will naturally be limited by the amount of capital available. But does the administration responsible really intend to spend even £500,000? The 60 loans were granted to less than 10 per cent of the applications received until the end of 1960. Out of these 606 applications, only 379 were investigated, and 320 of these were rejected.

Efforts on quite a different scale should be made. Even if all the applications had succeeded, they would have amounted to a drop in the ocean. Professor J. L. Sadie, a Nationalist, an Afrikaner, and a sincere believer in the policy of apartheid, calculated* that, between 1945 and 1953, the absorbing of a South African worker into industry represented an investment varying between £500 (at the beginning of the period analyzed) and £3,000 at the end. The capital necessary for industrialization works out at an average of £1,000 per worker. I am convinced that Professor Sadie's calculation is relevant, and that a financial effort of this magnitude must be made in the Reserves.

Then only could a movement be started, by means of another Tennessee Valley Authority, Hassi Messaoud, or Elath-Haifa pipe-line to buy up, all at once, not just a few White undertakings, but all of them, by paying for them above their value, if necessary . . .

When I asked to visit a Bantu industrial undertaking, all that could be found to satisfy me was a basket-weaving concern at Hammanskraal. Wicker-work is made there by hand . . .

I expressed my astonishment. "My friend," said Dr. Dönges, smiling at my astonishment and at Professor Sadie's figures, which I compared with what I had seen at the basket-weaving concern, "people must be taught to walk before they can run. In order to get into fourth gear, you must first of all get into first, second and third. The Government does not in any way prevent the Corporation from spending money. On the contrary, we want it to spend as much as possible. But if you were to decide, at this moment and in this office, to spend £10,000, I could not do business with you, because there are not £10,000 worth of goods in this office. It's the same in the Reserves. The rate of investment and development is related to the absorption capacity of the territory. The absorption capacity does not increase as one likes. It is the slow result of an effort, an accumulation of capital, an apprenticeship. It is like distillation: if you accelerate it, you will obtain a mediocre liquor . . ."

*"The Industrialization of the Bantu Areas", *Tydskrif vir Rasseaangeleenthede*, January, 1960.

The Minister of Finance did not entirely convince me. "Absorption capacity" for me was a familiar word and an idea I did not trust. Not long ago this capacity of absorption was one of the main arguments used against the Zionists. Commission of enquiry after commission of enquiry were set up in order to prove that in the "over-populated" and "over-developed" land of Palestine there was no longer room for even a cat. Without doubt many experts were genuinely convinced of the truth of their findings, even though dishonest politicians exploited their conclusions in bad faith. Builders and statesmen must know how not to take into account the conclusive arguments of the economists. People must do as the Jews did in Palestine. "The immigrants are bringing their absorption capacity with them in their suitcases," was the reply given in Tel-Aviv to the verdicts of the specialists in London. Faith can move mountains.

This does not mean that I believe that the Government in Pretoria is acting in bad faith. As in the other sectors where the positive side of apartheid is being developed, they are only starting and the industrial towns of the Bantus and their industries are things of the future. Being in its infancy, the whole idea of the Bantustans offers the widest opportunity for the "terrible simplifiers" to shape their future in any direction.

The problem is how to select the right direction.

In my opinion, the opposite course to current doctrines should be taken. Fortunately there are South Africans who are conscious of this necessity, and I believe I can apply the word "revolutionary" to the Organizing Director of Industrial Development for Bantu Areas, Dr. F. J. de Villiers. He will forgive me for using this word. The revolution that we plotted in our conversations is the revolt of faith and enthusiasm against *laissez-faire* attitudes, against the obvious folly of half-measures which will bring about a catastrophe.

"In South Africa," he said, "the obstacle to planned industrial development is first of all a question of psychology. Our industrialists prefer to go slowly. In this respect they are very English in their approach; and the English do not like to plan because they are pragmatic.

"Next there is our famous peasant mentality: it's that of the men in the Government, who are Afrikaners like myself, and who calculate the price industrialization will cost. They realize—and it is a fact—that industrialization costs less on the borders of the Reserves, in the White territory, than inside the future Bantustans. And so they say that the border regions must be industrialized. But the problem is social *and* economic, not *only* economic. The interior of the Reserves must be stabilized. Instead of this happening, the very real migration of hundreds of thousands of Blacks to Johannesburg is being replaced by the still theoretical migration of Blacks to the borders of the Reserves.

"This half-migration is a half-measure and only half of a solution. If you really want to settle the population inside the Reserves, the Reserves themselves must be industrialized—whatever the cost. See what is being done in Porto Rico: the government is building factories, and it is exempting those who want to run them from taxes for 15 years! In England, all sorts of ways are used to attract industries to regions where there is an excess labour force.

"It is quite clear that Black industrialists do not yet exist. We must, therefore, find White industrialists who possess the pioneering spirit—migratory industrialists who will be prepared to work among the Bantu for some time in order to establish Bantu industries. It would be the exact parallel of the Black labour force which comes for a time to the White territories: they would be provisionally established, without lasting rights in the Reserves.

"Neither films, nor books, nor speeches at Lake Success will convince the world of the honesty of our intentions. Words must become deeds. The world will understand only when it sees something big and practical and working. We have gone beyond the stage of mere theories and statements of policy."

Is there anybody to take up the glove? One of the members of the Economic Council which is at present planning the industrialization of the Reserves, Mr. Viljoen, has the same ideas, only less passionately.

"I am not against the use of Whites for industrialization of the Reserves, since it is quite evident that Whites are needed for this work. However, from the outset they will have to accept the obligation to sell their business concerns, at some stage, to the Bantu Development Corporation. If the prices are fixed in such a way as to make these retreats attractive, you will find industrialists for the Reserves. The only remaining problem is the acquisition of these industries by the Bantu—the aim of the whole scheme. In order to encourage the growth of Bantu capital, the Bantu employed in the border industries must be allowed to reach the highest levels of specialization. They will earn more, they will spend more, and you will have a class of Bantu traders capable of investing their money. Later on, an important loan from the Republic to the first Bantu State could serve to finance a nationalized industry in that state."

Does the Republic have "revolutionaries" in all the most responsible posts? A movement of awareness is growing stronger, also in the ranks of the National Party, and it is becoming a kind of urgent appeal, a summons to do something. S.A.B.R.A., the organization of the Afrikaner intelligentzia, is increasingly echoing these ideas. The failures and the weakness of our policy of separate development, writes Dr. P. S. Rautenbach,* must be attributed to the unduly slow rate of development in the Bantu regions, and he asks the Government for a series of practical measures:

1. A second Magna Carta, similar to the Charter of 1925 which started the industrialization of South Africa by means of protectionist measures, and which must this time organize positive measures at all levels, in spite of opposition from all sectors of the population.

2. The gradual retreat of the White traders in the Reserves, either according to an evolutionary process, as the Blacks can afford to buy up the businesses of the Whites, and the Whites feel threatened by their competition and lose their social status, *or through a process accelerated by positive State measures.*

3. The encouragement of a Bantu "Zionism", using the ability of the 11,000 odd Bantu traders and artisans who are working in the White regions, who acquired their skill in contact with the White population, and who must be encouraged by every means and by all the forms of assistance possible to transfer their economic activities to the Reserves.

Dr. Rautenbach mentioned the example of the best-known Bantu industrialist in South Africa, who today employs about 50 Bantu, and who is now being helped to move to a Bantu area, near a village planned for this purpose. It is essential, he writes, for such Bantu leaders, who can start industrial development, to be helped and encouraged to introduce industries in the Reserves.

This example could be multiplied by as many Bantu industrialists and artisans as there are. The Republican Government is proud of the

*Tydskrif vir Rasseaangeleenthede, October 1960.

142

Bantu who have succeeded. It did not fail to make me meet the directors of the Vendaland Trading Company, a big wholesale business which controls 30 shops and supplies 184 retailers, and whose directors are Bantu "Zionists" who one day decided to leave the big town, to "go North", to return home: Mr. P. M. Negukhula, a former labourer in Johannesburg, who could not succeed in business there; Mr. Mutsila, a former teacher in Orlando; Mr. Lukoto, a former golf-club caddy in Johannesburg, who to-day drives a Cadillac, and has his private golf-course ... I also met Eric Ben Ngobeni, who formerly worked for fifteen shillings a month as a garden-kitchen-boy in the smarter suburbs of Johannesburg, who had seven years' apprenticeship in a grocery shop in Tzaneen, saved up enough money to buy two oxen, became a butcher, and today is one of the richest men in the North Eastern Transvaal. I visited his principal shop in Thabina, and I saw a queue in front of his store, a kind of Bush Woolworths where they make you a cotton dress on the spot, where they sell all the necessities of daily life, and even the "coca-colonizing" Coca-Cola, as Koestler would put it.* I was happy to go for a drive in the luxurious Chevrolet owned by Ephraim Tshabalala of Mofolo township, who possesses a shop, a restaurant, a hairdressing saloon, a pharmacy, three butcheries, and a garage which sells 60,000 gallons of petrol a month—the biggest sales for a filling station in South Africa.

Mr. Tshabalala said to me: "I am going to build an air-conditioned cinema for my people. It will cost me £60,000, and it will be called "Vusabantu" (Bantu, wake up)."

But if I were the Minister of Bantu Administration, I would make more effective use of these magnificent Bantu than by relating their success stories in booklets on "the progress of the Bantu peoples towards nationhood". I would build a bridge of gold for these 11,000 Bantu traders and artisans who learnt their job as businessmen with the Whites; I would make the most intelligent amongst them leaders of a "movement"; I would get them to move to the Reserves, to start business there, to teach their brethren.

Far from discouraging decentralized industries by preventing them from competing with industries on the Rand, I would encourage them by every imaginable means to be more competitive than the industries in the White areas, because this is the only way of

*Arthur Koestler: *The Lotus and the Robot*, the MacMillan Company, 1961.

inducing private enterprise to move its capital from the Rand to the veld. If necessary, I would go so far as to drive certain industries to the threshold of bankruptcy in order to oblige them to move—because this is a war effort, an attempt to save the nation. The industrialists who arrogantly claim protection against "unfair" competition, might be massacred to-morrow in the ruins of their burnt-out factories by those very workers who are prevented, by the criminal short-sightedness of the owners, from finding employment in the Reserves. It is not a choice between evolution and revolution (who would hesitate between such alternatives?) but a choice between revolution and revolutionary evolution. And, in any case, is not competition the very heart and life-blood of all economic development? In the name of what principle of strict economy does one claim to arm oneself against competition when it is that of the Bantu?

After all, a government has to choose, from amongst the divergent theories of the lobbyists who besiege it with their demands, the theory which best corresponds to the general interest. Today it is in the general interest of South Africa to solve its Bantu problem—at whatever cost to the State and the pockets of the Rand industrialists.

Even if the Government were to fail, and even if the Bantustans were never to see the light of day, the setting up of industries in the Reserves would have lasting effects on the social structure of the Republic. If the artificial "ceiling" which today prevents 82 per cent of the Bantu workers from rising above the rank of labourer or semi-skilled worker, is broken in some spot or other, the breach will sooner or later widen. Once the Bantu worker has acquired a taste for skilled work, which leads to initiative, promotion and responsibility, his whole psychological approach—today limited to his weekly pay—will be enriched with all the motivations indispensable to man in order to rise through work: an interest in the work accomplished, a feeling of participation. This is true of the Bantu individual as of the community. An under-developed people best acquires the culture of a higher civilization in the melting-pot of the towns. When the migratory worker returns home after his encounter with civilization in Johannesburg, he only brings back its least useful elements to the community of the Reserves: the taste for a living standard that he can no longer find on his lands; eating, clothing and social habits that he cannot satisfy. He literally brings back an element of disorder. Industrial towns, situated in the Reserves or nearby, would organically link all the Bantu nations to urban civilization. They would also give agriculture a life impulse, encouraging the growth of crops which could be sold in the markets of these towns. They would provide a harmonious medium of transition between the old tribal traditions and the twentieth century. Something real, not simply the stories, the legends brought back by the migratory labourers, those Bantu "troubadours" who long for a golden age, returning with their illusions and marvellous memories of the town to the native kraal in order to sow their fields and give children to their wives. From the political, psychological and human point of view, the industrialization of the Reserves would be one of the most positive contributions to the progress of Africa.

"Once we subordinate our economic aims to social and political objectives," wrote a South African economist, "and allow ourselves to disobey the test of an accountant's profit, we will have begun to change our civilization."* It is a marvellous programme. To save South Africa, I would subordinate everything to political and social objectives.

VI

When the Bantu becomes an industrial worker and businessman, he does not cast off the heritage of his milieu. The opponents of the Bantustans use this as an argument to claim that the Bantu are incapable of supplying the technicians necessary for a modern industry. To what extent is this true?

The Bantu economy was traditionally a subsistence economy. The family or clan provided for daily needs, but scarcely for anything beyond them. The history of the Bantu bears witness of very rudimentary traces of manufacture and trade: the making of assegais and other arms, the export of a few scarce raw products, like palm oil, ivory and skins. But there was no really diversified organization of imports and exports, and no division of labour in the way we understand it.

His past did not predispose the Bantu towards industry. The White man has, of course, changed the Bantu by teaching him the habits of a money economy; but the old traditions have remained

*Samuels: "The Tomlinson Report analyzed": *The Cape Argus*, May 2, 1956.

more deeply rooted and active than is commonly thought. The Bantu in the Reserves has an urge to obtain the necessities of civilized life, even if he dreams of the luxuries. If he has a good harvest, he will allow himself four or five months' rest, as his father and grandfather used to do. If the harvest was bad, he will go to the town in order to earn enough to make up for the shortfall—but hardly anything more. He has not been brought up in a tradition of permanent work. Work is for him only the means of procuring the maximum amount of leisure. And sometimes migratory habits (never forget that the Bantu are an immigrant people in South Africa!) are deeply rooted. The tribe of Chief Makapu, thirty miles north of Pretoria, provides a curious example of this habit. For two generations, nearly all the men of his tribe have worked in Johannesburg and Pretoria, but since 1910 less than 10 families have established themselves permanently in these cities.

This tradition has endowed the Bantu with a certain lack of adaptability to industrial life with its risks and efforts whose rewards are sometimes good and sometimes poor. In short, he lacks a spirit of enterprise. Is it not significant that even in the United States, where contact between Negroes and Whites in industry has been closer and older than in Africa, there is practically no class of Negro industrialists?

Old traditions have, for most Bantu, retained a romantic flavour. The Bantu generally feel that they lost a great treasure when they lost the golden age of pastoral life, and they hold the White man responsible. This explains their attachment to their chiefs: they represent the past. Of course, this does not always apply to the Bantu in the towns.

On the other hand, certain traits inherent in this psychology make for valuable industrial aptitudes.

The Bantu is courageous in the face of disaster. He readily suffers famine for months—and rejoices at better times when they come. If he does not do much to bring about these better times, it is because the impatience and the imagination of the European are lacking in him. This lack of imagination and impatience makes him a very good worker in all the jobs which would seem unbearably monotonous to a European. On the other hand, this lack of imagination can cause a long series of mistakes when the foreman does not immediately spot a mistake.

This faculty for repetitive work, this imperviousness to boredom, make Bantu brick-layers highly productive when they put up hundreds of standard-type houses: as soon as there is a diversity of form, their output immediately drops. Their capacity for adaptability is lower than that of the Whites. The effects of the Bantu's ancestry are sometimes amusing. In their homelands the bricklayers knew round huts, and their eyes are not used to straight lines. When they build a rectilinear wall, they have to check their work with instruments all the time. In the same way, the old tribal habit of a long rest with the security provided by a good harvest has its effect on the behaviour of the industrial worker: for some of them a work bonus is not an incentive to work more, but an occasion for additional leisure corresponding to the additional pay in the pay-packet. They disappear from the yard or the factory for a while, and come back to the yoke when the windfall has been spent. Then the cycle starts again . . .

These are merely observations. As an American writer said: "What the author intends as description may appear to the reader as evaluation, and condescending evaluation at that."* The observations I recorded in South Africa do not indicate any kind of incapacity. With regard to industrialization, they merely underline the necessity, as in every other field, for more education and more training. Industrial "geniuses" are to be found amongst the Bantu as with other people: for example, Petros Radebe, an almost illiterate Zulu I met in Hibberdene, who had made, with his bare hands, from some barbed wire, some wood, bits of rubber tires and odd pieces of copper, a sewing-machine which sews regular stitches, and a reciprocating steam engine. Without any training, he instinctively repairs bicycles, gramophones and watches at the rate of twenty a day!

"He has the hands of a fairy," said Patrick J. Farrell, the wealthy sugar-farmer who discovered him. "He can do anything. I showed him and his turbine to an engineer in Durban who just could not get over it . . ."

The innate characteristics of the Bantu people therefore neither indicate nor preclude any particular direction with regard to industrialization.

*Samuel Sandwel: *A Jewish Understanding of the New Testament*, University Publishers, New York, 1960.

What about their country?

The nature of the first industries as well as their location are suggested by the resources and equipment of the Bantu territories.

Modern industry needs water. Industrial development will have to be concentrated chiefly along the eastern escarpment, the Ciskei, the Transkei and Natal, where there are several rivers.

The Reserves are not badly off as far as electrical potential is concerned. A large part of the Transkei, the Ciskei and the Northern Transvaal are situated in zones that can be served by Escom. Several high tension lines pass through the Bantu territories, or very close to them. At several places, hydro-electric current can be produced. Several Bantu territories are well situated with regard to the coal-mines, particularly in the Southern and Western regions, and in Natal.

On the other hand, the Bantu territories are not well served by the railway network. Certain secondary lines pass near the Reserves: the line to Umtata is the only one specially built to serve a Bantu region.

This also applies to the national roads. Some of them cross the Bantu territories, notably in the Ciskei and the Transkei. But the Reserves are mainly served by second class roads. This therefore suggests a form of industrialization based initially on local resources. Of course, this does not exclude all the later development if appropriate means are made to operate.

The local resources are mainly agriculture. As all the industrial potentialities of the Bantustans cannot be listed here, a few indications will serve as examples.

We know what industrial development can be based on sugar-cane plantations, the cultivation of fibres and afforestation. Adequate investments, and extension of the railway network and the roads, must allow for the creation of a sugar industry in Bantu Natal; the manufacture of ropes and sacks, an industry which easily develops from the artisan stage, is the very type of activity to introduce into an agricultural country in the initial stages of industrialization; it has been calculated that when the maximum development of reforestation has been reached, the timber industry will be directly or indirectly responsible, owing to the secondary industries (factories) and tertiary activities (trade), for the employment of 800,000 Bantu.

The exploitation of the mines has hardly been touched in the Bantu areas, which possess (especially in the North) platinum, lead, barium, lime, graphite, magnesite, beryl, gold, copper, coal, marble, asbestos, chromium, iron and kaolin. Natal produces coal, iron and titanium. The Transkei is poor in minerals, but it possesses several good deposits of nickel, copper and marble. In the Ciskei nothing has yet been discovered which could be economically exploited.

The first step would be to undertake a serious study of the mineral resources of the Reserves. Maybe another Kimberley lies sleeping in the country of the Tswana . . .

Another series of possible industries is indicated by the degree of social and economic development reached by the populations of the Reserves, and will naturally depend upon the exploitation of the natural resources. These are the secondary industries, which produce the full range of consumer goods, and the tertiary industries, which sell the goods and services. Most of these industries require a big labour force.

As the income of the population increases, the demand for food and housing will increase automatically, to the benefit of the bakeries and the building trade. Afforestation will bring about saw-mills, workshops for making flooring, furniture, paper mills and cellulose and cardboard factories. The cultivation of fibres will bring about decortication plants, sugar-cane cultivation, and refineries. If the cultivation of fruit and vegetables develops, it will bring about the manufacture of tinned fruit, and, in a similar way, larger dairies for the industrial production of butter and cheese, condensed milk and powdered milk could be stimulated. Grain-mills to process the cereals will spring up as agriculture develops. The creation of towns will bring about the opening of stone-quarries, the making of cement, and the exploitation of limestone layers. In general, the increase in purchasing power will increase the demand for clothes, shoes, spades, knives, forks, nails, bolts, plates, cooking utensils, dishes, etc. . . . thus creating the conditions for a light metal industry, and, after that, an iron-smelting industry.

Such industries producing models adapted to the tastes and the buying power of the Bantu will have an outlet on the markets of several neighbouring territories to the North of South Africa, where the social and economic conditions require similar goods. South Africans do not like the word, but it is in effect a dumping industry, capable of distributing on a gigantic scale consumer goods of fairly good quality.

Finally, an industry which is in no way developed, but which has countless possibilities, is capable of supplying the Bantu areas with endless resources: tourism.

People in Europe do not know what delight the South Africans take in Bantu folklore and to what extent this Bantu culture deserves interest. The mine dances organized every Sunday in which the young people, practically isolated from the towns (and women), give vent to their surplus energy, are always watched by crowds of people. What a clever businessman like Mr. Lister Hunter does in Umtata, or what Mr. Hugh Tracey, Director of the International Library of African Music, does in Krugersdorp, can be taken up on different levels and in many fields of the tourist trade in the future Bantu States. Mr. Hunter takes groups of tourists on a guided visit to the villages of the Transkei and sells them necklaces and woven mats made for him by a few artisans at home. The St. Cuthbert Mission in Tsolo has even started a school for making "souvenirs", where young girls learn to spin, to dye and to weave wool into carpets. Hugh Tracey is preserving the treasure of the musical folklore of the Bantu: his scholarly work is financed by the sale of his records. I remember a group of Bantu girls painted and covered in necklaces, who stopped my car one evening on the road from Butterworth to Idutywa to entertain me with a serenade on primitive instruments and to leave me a few of these love necklaces, of which every colour, every row, according to the patterns, contain a clear message. I took a few pictures of their jerky trampling, and left them a few shillings. Admittedly, they were not professional entertainers, but anything can evolve from this clumsy beginning: big hotels, filling stations, factories for making souvenirs, game reserves, etc. Ten years from now, in this Africa which is taking giant steps forward, one will probably have to go right into the heart of the Bushman country to find a naked man.

Tourism is certainly one of the valuable assets of the future Bantustans. Although modern Africa is wide open to the influences and troubles of the world—which come closer every day (seven months, seven days, soon seven hours and then seven minutes)—it still remains the tourist paradise of to-morrow.

There is room for many black Switzerlands between the Limpopo and the Kei . . .

CHAPTER 5

SELF-GOVERNMENT

I

Mr. J. H. Abraham, Commissioner-General of the South African Government in the Transkei, in other words, the Ambassador to the Xhosa "Bantustan", took me to one side. The large reception room of the Savoy Hotel in Umtata, the "capital" of the Transkei, was crowded with people. The waiters were passing glasses and trays in a relaxed, smiling and less correct way than in Johannesburg, giving one a refreshing feeling of the country and its placid ways. Their wide smiles encouraged one to drink; as they passed they joked with the guests. None of them were ill at ease or formal. It was very hot. A large fan was turning slowly on the ceiling. The chief magistrate was giving a reception that evening for all the V.I.P.s in Umtata, about fifty officials and their wives, and when I entered the room several of these gentlemen had got to their fifth or sixth whisky. With the first breath of hot air, mingled with sweat and alcohol and stirred up by the fan, I was back in the atmosphere of a colonial party: the flock of eager courtiers who cluster round the local big wigs; tentative but decorous flirtations; snatches of serious conversation where one continues to talk shop after office hours. ("And, of course, my dear chap, this report took three weeks to reach me . . .")

From the world of Great General Ideas which I had just been discussing in Pretoria for eight days—with the Minister of Foreign Affairs, the Minister of Finance, the Minister of Economic Affairs, the Minister of Bantu Administration and Development—I was plunged straight into a group of men who deal each day with the down-to-earth realities that are to be modified by these ideas. In Pretoria I had had talks about Big Plans, Quick Decisions, Justice for the Races. In Umtata I was plunged into the problems of implementing schemes, time running short, the races living together.

And so the Ambassador took me to one side.

"Mr. Giniewski, you came to Umtata to see how we teach people to rule themselves? I am going to tell you a story. It's a true story. One of our Commissioners of Native Affairs once saw a villager who had walked fifteen miles to come and present a report to him in his office. The carcass of a dog had fallen into the well from which his kraal gets drinking water. The water was polluted. The man had come to ask the Commissioner of Native Affairs for an order to have the carcass removed. Yes, my dear sir, government is an art . . ."

The Whites have only recently started to teach self-government. The reserves were traditionally regarded as reservoirs of labour; the Commissioners were told to keep order, but they were to interfere as little as possible in tribal life. All administrative matters were in the hands of the Whites. Under the new policy of apartheid and advancement of the Bantu, all this is to be changed officially. The Bantu are to be dissuaded from walking fifteen miles to ask a White administrator's permission to take a dead dog out of a well. They are to be accustomed to act by and for themselves.

"You must learn to develop your motherlands so as to make prosperous lands out of them," Mr. J. G. Strijdom, the previous South African Prime Minister, told the Bantu of South Africa.

"You must learn to govern yourselves in your own territories."

"And," said Dr. Verwoerd, "up to the most responsible Government posts, if you are capable of it."

"And," he added at the time of the ceremonial opening of the first Bantu "Parliament" in the Transkei in May, 1959, speaking in that picturesque style so often used by politicians when they address the Bantu: "Self-government is a fruit tree that the Government is giving to the Bantu of South Africa. The Government has planted the tree but that tree must be tended in order to grow. If it is looked after well, it will grow and bear fruit. If it is not tended properly, it will wither away.

"And the tree should not grow too quickly. The type of tree which grows too quickly also dies quickly and its fruit can only be picked for a short while.

"But the tree which grows slowly, and bears few fruit at first, gradually becomes very big. Then it will bear many fruit and people can enjoy the fruit from such a tree for many, many years. May the tree that has been planted for you be of this kind . . ."

Let us have a look at the tree that was planted, and the fruit that it is bearing.

The Bantu Authorities Act (1951) and the Promotion of Bantu Self-government Act (1959) set up a complete system of administration for the Bantu by the Bantu.

Traditionally, in Bantu society, the tribal chief had complete authority over his tribe. This authority, although regulated by unwritten laws, was sometimes arbitrary and sometimes conflicted with the "colonial" administration of the Whites. The basic idea of the 1951 and 1959 Acts is to restore the authority of the "chief in council", and to define its exact limits so as to bring it in line with the central government. In short, it defines the intangible dimensions of the State within a State which the Bantu now constitute.

The law makes the tribal chief the base of a pyramid, the man responsible for keeping order in his tribe. He has a right to the respect and the allegiance of his tribe and his jurisdiction extends to all the Bantu residing in or travelling through his territory. From my point of view it is regrettable and unjust that this jurisdiction does not also extend to the Whites, but such an extension may still come. The tribal chief exercises his privileges in consultation with his council.

These privileges are chiefly administrative: the enforcement of sanitary regulations, tax-collecting, registration of births and deaths, the struggle against epidemics, building hedges and enclosures, preventing unauthorized departures of Bantu to the towns, weed extermination, preservation of flora and fauna, public monuments and so on. The chief has to report crimes, the presence of unauthorized strangers and the illegal possession of fire-arms, munitions and drugs to the higher administration. He has to prevent the sale of poisons and love potions, impound stray cattle, and so on.

His council, raised to the status of tribal authority by the law, acts as mediator between the Bantu and the central authorities. The council has been given the powers of a court to settle minor civil matters, and is even a corrective tribunal. The council has to establish a treasury empowered to receive the customary dues of the tribe, the fines, the communal income and government grants. These financial attributions are considered to be the most important function of the tribal authority. People are not very imaginative in South Africa about financial matters, and so consider—wisely indeed—that a small, poverty-stricken tribe which possesses a hundred huts and a few emaciated cows, should have the same financial policy as the Minister of Finance: it must not live beyond its means, it must save money every year and it must draw up reasonable budgets . . .

"It is a school," they told me. "Its first task is to get these communities to discard the collective inertia by which they are characterized. Today you have five hundred chiefs and councillors doing this work. They manage well or badly, but they are beginning to understand what it means to draw up a budget, what responsibility they assume when they impose a local tax or when they decide to build a school, a clinic, a reservoir. And in the long run, what a rewarding satisfaction it is to a leader when he can give his community greater welfare and comfort."

Above the tribal authority there is a regional authority for every group of two or more tribal areas. This higher authority is composed of all the chiefs of the tribes thus federated, and controlled by a chief-president chosen by his peers. This authority is responsible in its region for schools, roads, water resources, forests, soil conservation, cattle vaccination, hospitals, and the budgets necessary to these tasks.

Above the local authorities there are the territorial authorities, the apex of the pyramid: the protagonists of apartheid see in these authorities the embryo of future "Bantustan" Parliaments. At the present stage, they supervise the judiciary powers exercised by the tribal authorities, decide when and where to build markets, dipping pools and buildings, and grant trading rights. They have a certain legislative power in these matters, but resolutions have to be confirmed by the South African Government acting through the intermediary of the Minister of Bantu Administration and Development. In actual fact their use in the plural is hypothetical, because so far there is only one of these Black "parliaments", the Territorial Authority of the Transkei in Umtata, which is composed of all the chiefs of the regional authorities of the Transkei.

This "parliament" meets for ten days in the year. In between sessions its affairs are controlled by an executive which meets at least every two months. The head of this executive body is a Supreme Chief, at present Chief Kaizer Matanzima.

It is difficult to predict what the other Bantu "parliaments" will be like. Six or eight at the most have been either foreseen or provided for, of which five at least have still to be established. The Minister of Bantu Administration, Mr. De Wet Nel, declared that all the "parliaments" would be functioning by the end of 1961. So far, they are not. There is to be one for the Zulu, one for the Northern Sotho, one for the Tswana, one for the Venda, and one for the Tsonga; but at present only the territory of the Venda has a geographical continuity which would allow a "parliament" to exercise jurisdiction over a homogeneous territory. All the other territorial authorities are, in fact, "ethnic authorities", exercising their jurisdiction over fragments of scattered territories which have not yet been welded together by expropriation or exchange of territory.

The specific character of the territorial authority lies in its special jurisdiction in ethnic matters, in its extra-territorial authority. The Government has, in fact, established the principle of grouping the Bantu resident in the "White" territories of the Republic under the reserves of which they are supposed to be the ethnic citizens. This is to be done through the intermediary of "ambassadors" that the Zulus, the Xhosas, the Vendas, will elect in the towns where they live. These extra-territorial citizens will enjoy complete political rights in their homelands and, as a result, the representation which the Bantu enjoyed until recently in the White Parliament has been abolished.

To fulfil the spirit of the new legislation, the functioning of these Bantu administrations must lead to:

—a regrouping of the scattered members of the different Bantu national groups into a national unity, forming, wherever possible, a country with territorial continuity;

—the Bantu becoming gradually drawn into the problems of soil conservation and mixed agriculture due to the gradual replacing of all White agricultural officers of every grade by Bantu;

—the Bantu becoming gradually drawn into education through the gradual and systematic replacement of primary and secondary White schoolteachers and the school administrative staff by qualified Bantu;

—the legal training of the Bantu, aimed at setting up a Bantu judiciary system which will apply its own customary law, within the framework of the civil and criminal legislation of South Africa, through the gradual withdrawal of the White judges;

—the creation of a Bantu public service;

156

—and finally, the setting up of Bantu legislative authorities, enjoying limited prerogatives at first, but with the declared intention of regularly extending their powers.

In short, the "creative withdrawal" of the Whites from the Black regions is being contemplated. In order to organize this retreat, a Commissioner-General with the title of Ambassador has been accredited to each of the great Bantu "nations". He has direct contact with the Government in Pretoria and does not have to use the intermediary of any other authority. These Commissioners-General are in fact the Proconsuls of the "Power". They indicate to the government what stages can be omitted, what powers can be transmitted to the Bantu authorities functioning within their Empire, and at what rate the Black regions can be decolonized. Everything can depend on their personality and their dynamism. "They are really anti-administrators", said Mr. Van Rooyen, of the Information Service of the Department of Bantu Administration. "The aim of any civil service is not to transform the rules which govern it, but to apply them. It goes in for red-tape. Our Commissioners-General have the statutory duty of doing away with the existing state of affairs; they must look for new ideas and new plans of action. In short, they must bring about a revolution."

III

To what extent has this policy been applied?

The highest degree of self-government reached in South Africa is to be found in the Transkei. It might appear ridiculous, but it must be judged in relation to the Stone Age in which the Bushmen of South-West Africa are still living. Then it assumes its real proportion . . .

The pediment over the entrace to the Parliament of Umtata will one day bear the coat-of-arms of the Transkei Republic. At the moment it is still bare; the coat-of-arms does not even exist.

When I went through the porch beneath this virgin stone, the promise implied by its incompletion filled me with deep happiness. There were two flag-poles in front of the Parliamentary building, and from only one floated a flag, the South African flag—blue, orange and white against a Mediterranean azure sky. The Union Jack had been taken down. When will the colours of the Transkei fly from the other pole? What will they be? The black-green-gold banner of the African National Congress? A more "savage" tribal emblem? We are very far from a Bantu national flag, but steps have been taken in this direction, and steps which are irrevocable, no matter what the opponents of the system have to say. In the portrait gallery, the group photographs of the Transkeian General Council for 1941 show two rows of White councillors seated, and several rows of Bantu standing behind. The photograph for 1959 shows only Bantu, seated and standing. Near by are the portraits of all the governors of the Transkei. They are all White. When will the first Bantu hold the highest office in this territory which is supposed to be proclaimed the first Bantu State?

When I went through the Hansard of the Transkei, the "Proceedings and Reports of Select Committees at the Session of 1959" of the Transkeian Territorial Authority, I came across very interesting information about the degree of self-government that has been reached. The smokescreen of propaganda and the hostile criticism cannot conceal it. The 150 large pages in small type contain the minutes of what was discussed, what the Bantu of the Transkei have the right to tell the Government, what they hope for and demand. This evidence, which was not put there to prove anything or to cover up the facts for outsiders, told me more than the dozens of inspired theses that have been written about the same subject.

It was first-hand evidence.

Of course one can smile at resolution No. 27, proposed by Councillor L. Ndamase, who moves "that the Health Department be respectfully requested to instruct its ambulance drivers, when fetching patients located in the district, to proceed to the patient's home whenever possible, instead of waiting on the road." Actually, the words reveal a laudable interest in the comfort of the patient, when one realizes that the huts, widely-scattered in the veld, are sometimes far from the road. One will probably stop smiling when one hears the reply of another councillor, W. Singata, who points out that "the reason why an ambulance is not allowed to go off the thoroughfare and go to the kraals, is because the tracks are often very bad off the roads, and the hospital authorities are put to a great expense repairing the ambulances because they are heavy vehicles and expensive to repair." This is a matter of petty domestic economy, a concrete example of the thousand and one down-to-earth problems which humanity in all its marvellous diversity has to solve day by day and which seem suddenly very much more real and important than great principles. Is it not better to begin with these primary degrees of legislative authority, rather than with the sophisticated discussions of the Parliament of Leopoldville in Lumumba's time, which lead to bloodbaths? Independence, like the grocery trade or orthopaedics, must be acquired through apprenticeship.

Motion No. 36, moved by Councillor Le Fleur Potwana, asks that "with a view to reducing the number of fights in the Transkeian territory, the carrying of two sticks be made illegal."

The motion shows a praiseworthy interest in assuring public order. "If," says Chief S. S. Majeke, in support of the motion "you are carrying something on your person which you realize can cause some injury to another person you always feel brave and bold. People who carry dangerous weapons like that are always irritable and lose their temper easily."

"But," Paramount Chief Botha Sigcau himself pointed out, "there may be occasions when these two sticks are carried for a legitimate purpose. I am thinking of our boys in Pondoland who use two sticks for dancing. I wonder whether it would assist if this were to be amended, for instance, to make provision for where these two sticks are carried for ceremonial purposes or with the permission of the headman."

And Councillor E. J. Sese had the last word with this philosophical remark: "When you see a man walking about with one stick, don't think he can't fight. He might have a sharp knife in his pocket. If we want to enjoy a happy life, let us not make many laws . . ."

The education of children is the object of numerous resolutions. Councillor L. Ndamase asked that all the chiefs of the Bantu Administrations should subscribe to the *Journal of Bantu Education*. A. Z. Maqungo, from Mount Fletcher, asked for the abolition of the rule that a Bantu child be required to leave school after failing standard II twice.

C. W. Monokali, from Butterworth, proposed that "first-aid should be taught in all Bantu schools". Another Mr. Ndamase asked for "the curriculum in the school for the sons of chiefs at Tsolo to be extended to matric".

The importance that the councillors attach to educational problems is shown by the very formulation of their resolutions. One often finds their habitual formula ("that the government be respectfully requested") replaced by a very much more imperative "earnestly" . . .

The councillors are not afraid to take a stand on the policy of discrimination:

"That the Transkeian Liquor Proclamation No. 333, 1949, on the sale of alcohol to Bantu be amended and that the holders of letters of exemption be granted the privilege of being served in licensed hotels and bottle-stores in the same way as the Coloured people . . ."

"That the South African Railways and Harbours should be obliged to employ Bantu bus drivers on the Kokstad-Umtata line, which serves only Bantu passengers . . ."

Sometimes the very privileges of the Whites are directly attacked and demands of a political nature are made, which are so many Bantu bricks brought to the building of an autonomous Transkei state. These are some of the motions:

"That the Government should incorporate the Glen Grey District into the Transkei, in pursuance of its policy of ethnic regrouping."

"That trading and mission sites in all rehabilitated locations be reduced to one acre in extent and that no traders or missionaries in such locations be allowed to run stock therein."

"That the Government be requested to accelerate the establishment of industries in the vicinity of the Bantu reserves."

"That the Territorial Authority of the Transkei, representative of the people of the Transkei, should have direct contact with the Government."

"That the establishment of the various Bantu Authorities be expedited, so as to enable the Bantu people to exercise full control of their own affairs."

"That the judicial powers granted to heads of tribal authorities be extended, so as to cover the following cases: 1. abduction; 2. faction-fighting; 3. stock-theft; 4. fraud; 5. indecent assault; 6. public violence; 7. incest; 8. receiving stolen property; 9. defeating the ends of justice in the chief's court."

"That within the framework of tribal administration posts should be created for prosecutors, Bantu Administration Commissioners of all grades . . ."

"That a 'Transport Committee of the Territorial Administration of the Transkei' should henceforth deal with all transport problems in the territory . . ."

"That proclamation No. 26 of 1936, as amended, should be again amended in such a way that certificates of land tenure should henceforth be issued by the tribal administration and not by the (White) administration . . ."

"That all forests should be fenced-in . . ."

"That all dams in the territories should be used as far as possible for stocking of fish so as to increase the resources of the land . . ."

These minutes reveal a positive desire to advance. Every now and then the habitual formula, the "respectful" solicitation addressed to the government, is supplemented by an innocent little phrase which means a great deal: "The time has come" . . . "the time has come" . . .

The time has indeed come to transfer more and more power from the White authority to Bantu authority, to end various forms of discrimination, to fence in not only the forests but the spiritual jungle as well. Perhaps the time has come to present a "Bantu States Independence Bill" to Parliament . . .

The councillors of Umtata think so, and said so in plain words during the last session of the Territorial Authority in 1961. All this, of course, is rather timid and rather limited. One has been accustomed to more aggressive tones, to another concept of national independence and sovereignty by the speeches of the Black leaders who have access to the forum of the United Nations and whose words are splashed on the front pages. But when I arrived in Umtata in the midst of the scorched veld and the scattered huts with their thatched roofs, I measured the harmony, the reality of a degree of legislative power adapted to local conditions, to the local capacity for autonomy and I began to think that these councillors are at the right school. A great philosopher of the struggle for independence, Aggrey, has formulated its golden rule: "Never stop asking for what you want; take what you are given, use it, and continue to ask for more." I don't know if Kaizer Matanzima has studied Aggrey. But he and his councillors are making history. Like Chief Luthuli, like the leaders of the Pan-African Congress, like Dr. Nkrumah, they will in the end be satisfied only with independence. No nation, no people is satisfied with less. In the meantime they are laying solid foundations for it. Luthuli or Kaizer Matanzima: one of them must one day have his official portrait in the town halls of the Transkei . . .

These are the merits of the system of Bantu Authorities. What are its faults? My list is not exhaustive.

1. First of all, the system is in its infancy. A Territorial Authority has been established only for the Xhosa nation in the Transkei (31.8 per cent of the Black population of the Republic). No other territorial or ethnic authority exists for the Zulu nation (27.5 per cent), the group of Northern Sothos (10.4 per cent), the Southern Sotho (10.1 per cent) the Tswana (8 per cent), the Swazi (2.8 per cent), the Venda-Tsonga (1.8 per cent). At the basis of the administrative pyramid, there are no tribal administrations in most of the reserves in Natal, Zululand, in the districts of Glen Grey, Queenstown, Stutterheim, Komga, Fort Beaufort, Sekhukhuneland, Pilgrim's Rest, Nelspruit, Lichtenburg.

2. The system is not democratic. The chiefs and councillors, members of the tribal and regional authorities, are chosen by the Minister of Bantu Administration. Only one third of the members of the Territorial Authority of the Transkei are elected. The others are nominated. One can readily accept that administrators should be nominated, but a Parliament must be elected. The Territorial Authorities should be elected by universal suffrage.

3. It follows that political functions must be entrusted to the Territorial Authorities. At present the Territorial Authority of the Transkei has only administrative powers. The Minister of Bantu Affairs must approve all its decisions and promulgate them. He can countermand them and himself take, in the name of Bantu Administration, any measure that he thinks useful and the Parliament of Umtata will be considered to have voted it. The head of the White administration in Umtata can suspend any action of the executive committee which meets in between the sessions of Parliament and which is supposed to carry out its policy.

4. In actual fact, the real powers of this Parliament, as of any Bantu authority, tribal and regional, are in the hands of Whites. No chief can leave his territory without permission from the White administration, any chief can be deposed "in the general interest of the Bantu", and the Minister of Bantu Administration decides without appeal what is the "general interest of the Bantu".

Only a reversal of this principle, whatever the degree of *technical* perfection of Bantu authorities, can lead to independence. For every law of apartheid which is to the benefit of the Whites in the White regions, there must be a similar one to the benefit of the Bantu in the reserves. The Territorial Authority of Umtata must control the whole life of the Transkei. It must control the White administrations which still function there. The White official must become more and more of an adviser and the Bantu must become the actor.

"The moment has come," an important Bantu civil servant said to me—a man subordinate to Whites who have not half his merit— "the moment has come when the man sitting in the sun calmly watching the passers by, must be the White official, not the Bantu."

If there are no capable Bantu on the spot then they must be recruited through competitive examinations from amongst the Bantu administrators, students, teachers and lawyers in the White regions. It will be a *natural* means of getting the Bantu in the urban regions interested in settling in the reserves. The two problems, that of the reserves and that of the towns, would be harmoniously solved. Once a prominent Bantu lawyer in Johannesburg is eligible for a position of, say, Secretary of State in a real independent Bantu State, the Bantu States will command political attention.

The Government insists on the ethnic tie between the Bantu in the towns and those in the reserves. It wants the Xhosa in Johannesburg to have political rights only through a "consul" of the Xhosastan. This must be a two-way link. The Xhosa in Johannesburg must be able to contribute in Umtata to accelerating the autonomy of their race. If this right is denied, and if the principle does not work both ways, then it seems to me to be impossible to agree with this policy, and it can be associated with a smokescreen. In this connection the Government of South Africa makes, in my opinion, a very serious mistake in maintaining without any change discriminatory laws of apartheid inside the territories of the future Bantustans, in the very capitals of these future independent states.

I have already said that there are locations in Umtata and that there are separate public facilities for Bantu and Whites. With regard to the resolution we have mentioned before, that of authorizing Bantu bus drivers on the Kokstad-Umtata run, the Government replied through its official who deals with transport matters in the Transkei: "Mr. Chairman and Councillors, it is unfortunately not the policy of the Administration to authorize the employment of Bantu drivers in positions usually held by European drivers, and at this stage, it is not possible to agree to such a step."

5. One must also observe that the inclusion of five-and-a-half million Bantu scattered through White territory in the potential Bantustans by means of an ethnic link is an ideal more than fruitful reality. The five-and-a-half million Bantu scattered outside the Reserves (three million in agriculture, two-and-a-half in the industrial suburbs) form the most developed section of the Black community. In the towns these Bantu have received a relatively high degree of education. Owing to their numbers, the wages they earn make them an economic factor. In contact with the Whites they have a real knowledge and a long experience of Western civilization. It is in this part of the population that the political tendencies and demands have germinated. Many of them are followers of the African National Congress and the Pan-African Congress, opposed to the Bantustan idea, and partisans of Black integration. This most developed part of the Bantu people will in fact enjoy the least political rights, since it will be foreign in the midst of a White state and attached to the Bantustans by the frail link of consular representation. Much has been done, and more is still to be done for the benefit of the Bantu in the reserves. But will the Bantustans satisfy the demands of the Bantu in Johannesburg? Giving two coats to one man and leaving his brother without any, is wrong in two ways.

The abolition of Bantu representation in Parliament has been justified by the argument that it would encourage the political growth of the Bantu within the framework of "parallel development": the Bantu élite who no longer have a possible outlet in the political institutions of the Whites, would turn to the only institutions open to them. It has been argued that the British Empire, for similar reasons, never allowed the territories earmarked for autonomy and independence to send representatives to the British Parliament, and this discrimination by not allowing talented natives to seek a metropolitan career, had a decisive and positive influence on the formation of local élites. India and Ghana, in different ways, bear this statement out. This is true in theory. But it is only valid in the perspective of a "Bantu Zionism", in the event of an enthusiastic movement among the five-and-a-half million "expatriated" Blacks towards the Reserves, in the case of a great Bantu trek towards the

Dr. W. W. M. Eiselen, (right) former Secretary for Native Affairs and at present Commissioner-General to the Sotho, Venda and Tsonga peoples. Dr. Eiselen is the father of the Bantu Education Act. With him is Mr. M. D. C. de Wet Nel, Minister of Bantu Administration and Development

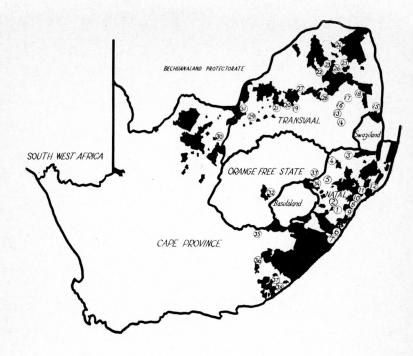

This sketch-map of the Republic shows the Bantu areas in Black. The most important potential centres of industrial development on the borders are shown in numbers

Bantustans and a desire to put all their energy into making them prosperous. As long as these millions of miners, labourers, errand-boys, agricultural workers, maids and nurses spend all their sweat and toil in serving the Whites in White South Africa, the illusion of their ethnic incorporation into the reserves, and their political muteness, are dangerous trouble factors, and the theory which gives rise to them is wrong.

6. Finally, the system of Bantu Authorities is in no way accepted by the whole Bantu population. It is impossible to determine exactly the degree of consent of this population, since the Bantu are not consulted when laws are made for them, but the debates of the Parliament of Umtata are very revealing in this respect.

Councillor R. W. Soshankano asked for the chiefs to be authorized to carry fire-arms.

"As things are today," he said, "there are certain laws which have been enacted by the Government, and certain policies and schemes are introduced. (We) have accepted those schemes but the people are objecting so that the officers concerned are in danger of losing their lives . . . The Paramount Chief has on occasion had to go and live in the bush because he found that his enemies were surrounding him in order to kill him . . . People dare not come into my yard because they know I am armed; and it is that same privilege I am asking for the chiefs and headmen who are co-operating with the Government in what they consider progressive steps, but which the general public do not understand as such."

And councillor M. Salakupatura added: "We people who are in the service of the Government have found we are in great danger . . . It is the opinion of the general public that we have come here in order to make laws which are going to be an oppression to the people . . . When dogs bark at night you find it difficult to go out. You ask your wife to blow out the lamp and you sit there in darkness . . . Even in the Kentani district the headmen have been rounded up and shots fired at their kraals . . . At night, when the dogs bark, you do not even open the door . . . You take an axe and when you open the door you are ready to deliver a blow, because you do not know who is waiting there for you.

"We shall all be killed if the Government does not take notice of our request."

Quislings? Collaborators? Oppressors who have made common cause with the White enemy, to help him—in exchange for a meagre salary—to keep their brothers under the yoke of oppression?

The criticism that is most often levelled against the system of Bantustans is that it perpetuates the old tribalism, and seeks to thwart the desire of the Blacks for emancipation by using the power of the backward, reactionary and uneducated tribal chiefs at the expense of the educated and of democratic development.

Is this true? Who are the tribal chiefs, and what political and social doctrines do they represent?

The kraal of Paramount Chief Victor Poto, in Pondoland, is about an hour's drive from Umtata. I had been informed of the necessary ceremonial behaviour to adopt when meeting the Chief. He had been telephoned to ask for an audience, and he agreed to receive me. Victor Poto is a very civilized Chief. In his village he lives in an almost European-style house, with a Dutch facade similar to the beautiful white Dutch houses of the Cape. When I went there, they were preparing the "town-hall" for the expected arrival of the Minister of Bantu Administration: that is to say the corrugated iron roof of a tiny brick house was being painted blood red.

When our car stopped in a great cloud of dust in the beaten earth square of the village, we had to observe the rules of protocol and wait with our doors shut until one of the Chief's councillors came to invite us to get out and to lead us to the Chief, who was waiting on the threshold of his town-hall and who welcomed us with a marvellously radiant smile. He invited us into a room which was furnished with a table, a typewriter, and a few chairs, and which was fiilled with files and books—on the table, on the chairs, and even on the floor.

"Gentlemen, I am listening to your questions," said Victor Poto, and he pointed to a subordinate, humbly seated on a bench and who, like himself, was dressed in European clothes—old second-hand clothes, though. Not like his, which came from an excellent tailor.

"This man," he said, "is my councillor, and will translate your questions and my answers."

Victor Poto thus very diplomatically had my questions—which he understood perfectly well—translated so as to give himself time for reflection. I found all his fancy frill a little silly and, together with the cheap protocol, I had the painful impression of being present at one of those parody-displays of the power given to the Blacks. I was right in the middle of the smoke-screen, with my eyes full of smoke . . .

However, as the conversation with Victor Poto developed, my first impression was changed. I had my own interpreter who translated into English the melodious sentences, full of clicks and soft nasal sounds, that Victor Poto and his man were exchanging. I gradually realized that the chief and his interpreter were consulting each other, discussing my question and the reply to be made, and that I was not getting back the opinion of one man, with his subjective approach and the stamp of his temperament and interests, but that the average opinion of the tribe was being formulated for me. This was why his answers were stereotyped and impersonal, as though they were being read: declarations were being made to me, policy was being formulated, and they felt responsible.

Eight days earlier, at the kraal of Chief Mohlaba Shilubani, near Tzaneen, I had the same astonishing experience. Shilubani is a minor chief. He rules over 25,000 people. He did not speak to me of the wonderful ideas about the Bantustans that Victor Poto developed for me, in the name of his people, but of the problems of his village, of the school he wanted to build, the strips of land which were being redistributed in the district.

Chief Shilubani had received me in the hall of the Tribal Authority, a large bare room, with fifteen raw wooden benches and the portrait of his father, the late Chief, clothed in a lion-skin, above the platform. Nine councillors surrounded him. He translated my questions to them and the replies came back to me—well pondered replies representing collective opinion. After an hour or two of conversation, I found myself enjoying a novel experience and one which I had not yet had in South Africa: I was not interrogating a man, but a group. A choir was replying to me, although it was only using one voice, that of the Chief. This was true collective action. Authority was not being delegated, permanently or for a given time, to a spokesman or a leader: it invested him permanently with this mandate and renewed it permanently, and it was only valid for the present moment. It was a kind of "raw" democracy. Later, in Durban, the "ambassador" of the Zulus in the capital of Natal, Prince Sithela Zulu, of the royal blood of the great Dingaan and the blood-thirsty Chaka, welcomed me in the same way. He received me in the office of the superintendent of the urban location of Somtseu Road. He is a cultured man, a journalist; he has written a book on the disruption of family life and migratory labour. I could easily picture him naked and gleaming with oil, proudly bearing the weapons of the Zulus. He had that kind of warrior beauty, without a trace of fat and without a single wrinkle. He was also escorted by a councillor in rags, Sidwell Mopeli-Paulus. They questioned each other at length about my interrogations and they said to me: "We speak in the name of the Zulu people of Durban . . ."

The tribal chiefs are in no way unchecked autocrats. It is a fundamental error to see Botha Sigcau, or Kaizer Matanzima, Chiefs of the Xhosas, or Cyprian Bhekuzulu, the Chief of the Zulus, as potentates who rule autocratically, and according to out-dated principles. Not even succession is automatic. The son of a deceased Chief must be elected by the majority vote of the general assembly of the tribe. In the exercise of his statutory powers, the tribal Chief is assisted by a great number of people. He has his representatives in the different parts of the territory that he administers: if they act in his name, he is also obliged to take into account the local interests they represent. The Chief nominates councillors during his reign, but there are a certain number that he cannot designate because the unwritten tradition of the tribe gives them fixed rights to certain privileged positions owing to the blood which flows in their veins, or the relations between their families and the royal house. The Chief is obliged to have a certain number of councils, or "ministeries". The Chief of the Tswana has a council for soil problems, grazing-rights and irrigation; a second for family-affairs; a third for schools; a fourth for war. Often the Chief has a "private council", and a principal councillor, a kind of Prime Minister. He has messengers, tax-collectors, a police-force and guards. But, over and above all this, there is a popular assembly which controls his acts and those of his councillors. Unfortunate is the Chief who strays from the paths of tradition, which are the narrow paths required by the simple and difficult life of the tribe: summary justice, meted out on the outskirts of a wood, has ended the career of many an "absolute monarch" of the past who had forgotten the interests of his people and the spoken tradition which curbs his power.

This direct democracy places the Chief in a real position of dependency with regard to his tribe. The tribe really considers that the Chief belongs to them. It is indeed the tribe which pays the dowry or *lobola* of the Chief's mother, and the children of the "queen-mother" thus belong to the people. As the elders of a village in the Transkei told me: "The Chief is our child."

The considerable powers exercised by the Chief—political, administrative, executive, military and religious—are thus essentially nominal. He gives the signal for the fruit to be gathered by tasting the first offering, but he can perform this ritual gesture only at the precise moment when the elders decide that the fruit are ripe. He chooses the time for circumcision, but according to criteria of which he is not the master; his authority does not reside in himself, but in the principles of order of which he is the guardian. The allegiance that the people owe him is of the same nature as allegiance to a national flag in "civilized" states. The flag and the national hymn are symbols and have no reality in themselves. Allegiance is in the heart of the citizens, and concerns cultural, political and sentimental values which make up the tribe, the city and the state. The tribal Chief is a symbol. In himself, he might be a mediocre or evil man: the allegiance which is owed to him is given to something more than himself, because he represents an idea and an ideal in the eyes of the people. Like the Queen of England, he is the living link between the past, the present and the future of the nation.

VI

Is it right to rely on the tribal system? It is certainly easy for the generous diatribe-writers of Fleet Street to decide that backward tribalism must be abolished through the sudden substitution of the perfect forms of Western administration. But, on the spot, ideals are corrected by the hard facts of reality.

Sithela Zulu and his ragged councillor opened up new perspectives for me. I learnt a great deal from the hours we spent together in the sad location of Durban, in the midst of a colourful throng of Bantu clothed in blankets, faded greatcoats and sacks, feathers or battered old hats on their heads. Sithela Zulu is one of the finest men I ever met: a man who thinks and suffers, and believes in the power that has been entrusted to mankind over events and evil.

I asked him (and I was prejudiced against him, too, before we met): "Why did you agree to be the representative of the Zulus in Durban, and to be paid by the Whites for it? You are helping to enslave your people. Why don't you work to free them . . . ?"

Sithela did not reply to me in strong terms. He replied with real diplomacy, and perhaps it was his royal blood, the blood of Chaka the conqueror, which spoke through him.

"I was proud to accept this task," he said. "To represent the tribe outside the reserves is an honour. The Paramount Chief is obliged to care for the welfare of the members of the tribe, just as you are obliged to look after the members of your family. The law of the Whites, when it provided for a Zulu ambassador in Durban, respected our custom."

"But will the Zulus in Durban, who are far away from their kraal, accept the authority of Cyprian Bhekuzulu, the Paramount Chief? Have they not learnt in the towns to follow other chiefs?"

"We are no more united than you Whites," said Sithela. "Some of us obey the Black chiefs who have arisen in the towns. Others look towards the country of the Zulus. I am one of them. My party is the Zulu party, and I do not prevent any of my brothers choosing as their party the Liberal Party of the Whites, or the Pan-African Congress. Although we have black faces, we have our ideas, like you Whites, and they are of many colours. The council of the Paramount Chief in Durban has powers. When there were disturbances in Durban, the Chief was informed. He consulted his councillors, and he ordered us to calm the Zulus, and the Zulus in Durban listened to us. When I visit factories in Durban, and I have to carp at wages, work conditions, and hours of work, I inform the Chief, and his advice is invaluable to me when I have to consult with the employers and the authorities about improving the lot of the Zulus. When one of our people is tardy about sending back to his village the wages that his family are waiting for, I intervene."

While listening to Sithela, I realized that this system, fashioned and adapted to changing realities through centuries of tradition, had a certain perfection as things stood, and it was right to use it. Of course, it could be used in a better way and systematized, but

170

it was no dark secret plot on the part of the White Nationalists. The day after my first visit, Sithela spoke to me even more openly. The evening before, the White superintendent had withdrawn to the adjoining room, but nevertheless his presence was felt by both of us and his typewriter was clicking away while, from the barred windows of our office, we could see the never-ending files of Bantu in front of the tax-collector's desks where their passes were being stamped.

I met Sithela for the second time in his tiny office, the corner of a room, where, on top of his cardboard case, he had piled some dirty old files, a few newspapers, and a hide shield, the symbol of his position. I started dreaming of a Sithela installed in a real embassy, not necessarily an embassy just for the Zulus, but a "Bantu States House", where Sithela of Zululand, M'bongo of the Transkei, and T'choso of Vendaland, would together control the affairs of their brothers in Durban.

"The tribal system is contrary to progress," I said to him. "You are an intelligent man, Sithela. You must realize that the tribe must be broken up."

Sithela rose and, taking the note-book in which I was jotting down his words, made a drawing: a square—the cattle-kraal—with graves on one side; on the opposite side, in a semicircle round the kraal, five dots, representing the house of the head of the family in the middle, and, on either side, like the wings of a palace, the first house which is called the "big house", that is to say that of the first wife, and the second, third and fourth houses, those of the three concubines.

"You see," he said, "it is not as simple as that. Our tribal system is not simply obscurantist. I'm sure they told you about our resistance to agrarian reforms. This opposition does not stem simply from ignorance.

"When a man has three or four wives, he keeps up three or four houses. He must provide milk and bread for each household and all the children. That is why we have a number of heads of cattle, and four small fields of mealies, instead of one big one, for the same family: it's a guarantee for each of the wives and her children that they won't be left to starve. You come and tell us: 'You must cut down on the number of your cattle, and unite the strips of land. It must be done.' But, first of all, the wives must be convinced that one cow, which they have in common, is capable of giving as much milk as three different cows which have individual owners. It's a big change in their way of thinking, and the hunger of their children is a prudent counsellor!

"The tradition was not bad. It guaranteed milk to the children when there were no cows from Holland and no good instructors. It must now be replaced by a better tradition. But we won't manage to create a new Zulu tradition in the towns—only at home, in the heart of the Zulu country. I'm a Zulu Nationalist.

"Here, in Durban, the family is being destroyed, morals are becoming corrupt, and the culture of the people is being impoverished.

"The men who work in the town go back home for short periods. Some are lucky: they go for six months. Others go for a fortnight. It is impossible for a man to carry out all his duties in a fortnight. The roof of his hut has to be rethatched, the fields have to be ploughed, and each one of his wives must be given the hope of a new heir. When he leaves, they discover that they are not pregnant. They are unhappy. They follow him to the town, but they only have the right to remain there for three days, and besides, where could they stay, what means of subsistence would they have, what would become of the cattle and the fields in the village?"

"And so they settle in Cato Manor. They become corrupt. The *tsotsis* turn them into prostitutes, and they learn to drink. I want to live with my family in my own Zulu country, just as you want to live at home in your own country. I want to be able to take care of my family, and see to the education of my children. I want my daughter to call me *ndabezitha* (Sir), but in Cato Manor she will learn to stick out her tongue and pull faces. I want to tell my sons the history of the Zulu. All this is impossible in the towns of the Whites. I am all for progress; I am for cars and telephones: but I want them made and used in my country, and not merely so that my people should come and help the Whites make them in the White country . . ."

"If you try and eradicate their customs," people had told me in Pretoria, "you will have a revolution on your hands." I didn't believe it, but I slowly came to believe there is some truth in it. While it was necessary to rely on the tribal system, it was necessary to purify it and give it a new direction. There was no question of wiping it out with a sponge: it was deeply ingrained in the Bantu

172

people, and fulfilled the function of all cultures whether primitive or civilized: that of adapting the people to their environment and allowing them to survive.

The Chiefs can be made instrumental to promote changes inside the reserves because they have the benefit of the traditional allegiance of the great majority of Bantu. Progressive Chiefs can give a new direction to tribalism.

The Government understands this: they are busy training them.

The school for the sons of Chiefs, Jongilizwe College, in Tsolo in the Transkei, is the Bantu Eton of South Africa.

This school, the only one of its kind in the country, has set itself a difficult task: to form the characters of and give a sense of responsibility to the Bantu leaders of tomorrow, by basing its training on Bantu traditions, and yet modernizing them by adding the best in Western civilization. An under-developed people, in contact with a higher civilization, is the meeting-place for the obviously antagonistic forces of assimilation and conservative resistance. At Tsolo they are going to form men contemporary with their future, men who to-day are fifteen years old. Mr. Jansen van Rensburg, the young director of this college, must have the faith that moves mountains to have undertaken this task.

When I visited Tsolo, the college with its fine white buildings had not even been officially opened. Mr. van Rensburg was just ending a conference. It was a message of welcome to a group of future chiefs. I heard him say with the emphasis of deep conviction:

"Chiefs or headmen or councillors, by virtue of their birth, are confronted with the task of caring for the welfare of their people. If they do not feel this task, this compulsion, then they can never accept the ideals of leadership. These ideals are: acceptance of their duty to the welfare of their charges—a Chief or headman is in the service of the people and not the other way round—; acceptance of the idea that they are responsible for the welfare (spiritual or otherwise) of their people. That is what chieftainship, headmanship and councillorship means. If you can accept that then your credo in life will be: Yours Faithfully; if you cannot accept it, then you are not even fit to carry the name of 'has-been Chief, headman or councillor'. Live for your task, pray for it, visualize it, be with it."

Van Rensburg had not made up this speech for the occasion. It is written in the statutes that "the day a student becomes a fully

173

enrolled member of this college he no longer belongs to himself. He has then taken the first step in his dedication to duty to his people. He then becomes a leader in being."

"Our school," Mr. van Rensburg said to me later, "is entirely practical. I don't believe in separating doctrine from technique. Life is a mixture of ideas and deeds. Teaching must be too.

"Nowadays, a Chief is not merely a symbol. He is an administrator. He must act in all kinds of complex fields. He must maintain law and order, administer finances honestly, undertake useful development work, promote education, and create sanitary services. And to do this, he must surround himself with the councillors he chooses, or directs. In a primitive milieu, all these problems are complicated by prejudices, supersititions and resistance which would not occur in the West and which must be overcome. Consequently, we have introduced a curriculum which reflects the complexity and the density of real life, under real conditions."

Van Rensburg showed me this living, realistic education. The day I visited Tsolo, a group of students had been set to work on "a scheme for enclosing a communal field." All the problems of arithmetic, economy, book-keeping, and the social and psychological complications entailed by such an undertaking in a village in the bush, were set and analyzed. The quantity of barbed-wire necessary was calculated and ordered. Accounts were kept. The reactions of the farmers and villagers were imagined, discussed, and their objections met by arguments about collective interest. At the end of the afternoon the very simple problem of arithmetic had brought us to a discussion of social anthropology, which revealed, with all the variety of individual temperaments, the moral stature of these chiefs of to-morrow. Some were dynamic people with a fervent desire to enclose not only a communal field but the whole fetid jungle of backward traditions, at the same time eradicating all the moral weeds. Others were indifferent or just good enough to become unimaginative but painstaking bookkeepers for a small town-hall. I was deeply interested in these games, which may determine the whole future of the Bantustans.

"We want to be down-to-earth," said Mr. van Rensburg, "without forming monkeys who will blindly imitate the games we practise here. We want to train them to understand the practical and moral implications of a problem, and get them to look in the texts for a

174

way of solving concrete cases. We want to form integrity and a sense of responsibility, and not just stuff their heads with theoretical knowledge. We are not teaching laws, but the desire to exercise justice with integrity."

He showed me one of the questions asked at the second-year examination in administration:

Write an address on the proposed establishment of Bantu towns in Bantu territories. Set out your address under the following headings:
a) *How a town is planned.*
b) *Advantages and/or disadvantages of towns in Bantu areas.*
c) *The effect of such towns on Bantu social and economic life.*
d) *Your own evaluation of this project.*

"You can imagine that these essays clearly show us which of our students have the temperament of town-builders, and which don't want to lift their little finger . . ."

When I went over the Tsolo School, where plumbers and masons were still at work among the young Chiefs, I found myself in the South Africa of to-morrow. On the dining-room wall I read the unknown names of these potential leaders, the Libengas, the Ntantala, the Ndemase, the Ntulis and the Ludidis, who will one day perhaps become famous, and who will be known throughout the country, some perhaps throughout the world, for their services. Some of them are not even sons of Chiefs, but praiseworthy commoners, signalled out by their superiors, and ennobled through circumstance, in conformity with the custom which allows a Chief to create his peers . . . At Tsolo, the purpose is not the continuation of an out-dated and parasitical aristocracy—on the contrary.

"Our programme is very heavy," added Mr. van Rensburg. "After five years of study, they reach the level of a special matric which they pass at the school itself. They learn English, Xhosa, Afrikaans, social studies, Bantu administration, law, commerce, agriculture and typing. The lectures are given with the aid of films, and every effort is made to direct attention to the problems of history, administration and development in the underdeveloped territories. We attach importance to a knowledge of the great men of history, so as to give the Chiefs the conviction that man must dominate and mould the course of events. All our lectures are typed and bound at the end of the year, so that when the pupil leaves here, he is taking away practical documentation. He will just as easily find in it the approved type of report to be sent to the Department of Bantu Administration about a case of adultery—which he will have really judged, after having had a mock-trial here—as the complete series of formulae for ordering beams or cement, that the secretary of his village council is probably, even now, drawing up wrongly because he has not been taught. When these administrators are sent out into the world, they will obviously have much better training than their fathers . . ."

The special "matric" of this small but comparatively important centre of learning contains, with regard to Bantu administration, matters which one would like to see taught to politicians in our highly-civilized countries: the composition of a speech, complete with documentary research, logical exposition, oratorical attitudes and a comparison between traditional Bantu speeches and modern methods; the art of conversation, with warnings against irresponsible statements; the organization of a meeting, with the composition of the audience, the rules of the right to speak and the role of the chairman; the interpretation of information, with critical reading from newspapers, forming of opinion, evaluation of articles and summaries of various lengths; telephone conversations, demanding clarity, logic and brevity; the drawing up of reports, telegrams, offers of tenders, and all administrative formulae; translations into the three official languages; and, finally, criticisms of the lectures of the year . . .

When going through these programmes, I thought of Shilubani, Victor Poto, Sidwell Mopeli Paulus. None of them had had such a training in their youth as these people were receiving.

I thought that Mr. van Rensburg had a noble mission, and began to share his faith and to envy it. If South Africa could have fifty of these schools, and there is enough time for teams of new Chiefs to leave and practise what they have learnt, all its problems will perhaps be solved, because corrupt and illiterate Chiefs won't have a chance against the "young Turks" who will have learnt a love of their functions along with a technique of performing them.

CHAPTER 6

NEW FRONTIERS

I

What would be the frontiers of a partitioned South Africa?

On a map of South Africa the Bantu reserves appear as black spots on a big white field; they enclose the White territories, more or less in the form of a horse-shoe. This political configuration is the result solely of geography and the historical background of South Africa. The southern part of the horseshoe, with the densely populated east coast and the pasture lands in the plain between the Limpopo and the Orange River, corresponds to the penetration of the Bantu migratory tribes of the seventeenth and eighteenth centuries. In the south this penetration followed a line parallel to the sea because it was a natural thing to trek down the coastal plain: it was stopped in the extreme south on the Kei River by the military victory of the Whites who were trekking in the opposite direction from the Cape. To the north this penetration took place beyond the Limpopo and down towards the future Witwatersrand because these regions were then virgin land which the Whites had not yet reached. It stopped on the Orange River in the middle of the nineteenth century because the invading Whites had then reached this natural limit.

Looking at it very roughly and ignoring the haphazard straggling of contours, the Bantu horseshoe, the future territorial base of the Bantustans, surrounds White South Africa with a vast circular arc of 1,500 miles from East London on the Indian Ocean to Kuruman and Griquatown in the north of the Cape Province, following all the while the outline of the international frontiers of the Republic with Mozambique and Rhodesia. These territories cover about 12 per cent of the total area of the Republic (56,000 square miles). They form 16 more or less compact blocks: in the extreme south the Ciskei, separated by the White spots from the most important block, the Transkei; very close to it in Natal, the region of Umzimkulu— Harding; going up the coast, the regions of Tugela, Nugoma and

Maputaland; in the northern part of the horseshoe, to the extreme west, the blocks of the Kalahari, Kuruman, and Taung; and in a north-easterly direction the blocks of Rustenburg—Pilanesberg, Hammanskraal, Bochum—Potgietersrust, Letaba—Chingwedzi, and finally, welding together the two arms of the horseshoe, the Olifants—Steelpoort—Blyderivier complex.

Operation number one of partition and the regrouping of territories consists in adding to these territories, in removing the uneven contours and in forming territorial units corresponding to the great ethnic formations. Specialists have studied this problem and have mapped out ideal frontiers for the Bantustans of tomorrow. They agree with remarkable unanimity on a blue-print of seven territorial units:

— the country of the Xhosa (or Nguni), with the Transkei and the scattered Reserves in the Ciskei;

— the country of the Zulu, comprising the reserves of Natal and Zululand, which will have to be generously linked by land belonging to the Whites;

— the country of the Swazi, a small region bordering on British Swaziland;

— the country of the Venda-Tsonga, made up of the reserves in the region of the Sebasa in the northern Transvaal;

— the country of the Southern Sotho, the district of Herschel, bordering on British Basutoland;

— the country of the Tswana, made up of the "ethnic dust", the small clans and tribes scattered to the south of British Bechuanaland;

— the country of the Northern Sotho or Pedi in the Transvaal.

These seven territorial units can form the framework for the creation and federation of the seven Bantu states.

II

There will, of course, have to be several steps.

Partition must coincide with the reintegration into the Bantu states of the High Commission Territories, which, economically, geographically and ethnically, form an integral part of the Republic of South Africa. These territories are Basutoland, Swaziland and Bechuanaland, which are today British Protectorates.

These three countries were placed under the direct control of the

British Crown at the time of Union in 1910 because they were already countries with homogeneous Black majorities (Bechuanaland: 300,000 Blacks and 2,500 Whites; Swaziland: 237,000 Blacks and 6,000 Whites; Basutoland: 650,000 Blacks and 2,000 Whites) and could consequently anticipate the creation of Bantustans by removing them immediately from the authority of the Cape and Pretoria. But the frontiers traced between the Union and the Protectorates have left Swazis in the Union, who logically belong to Swaziland, Basutos who belong to Basutoland, Tswana who belong to Bechuanaland. The frontier often cut across lands belonging to the same tribe.

The case of Bechuanaland, which even lost its capital, Mafeking, to the Union, illustrates the arbitrary nature of the division and of the close interdependence of the three British territories and South Africa. The arguments that the Republic puts forward to claim these territories would be equally valid to justify the integration of Basutoland, Swaziland, and Bechuanaland in the future Bantustans. These arguments are economic, historical, legal and political.

Economically, the three territories are an integral part of the Republic—Basutoland is completely enclosed by South Africa. They have practically no economic outlets other than in South Africa, both for their products, and for the whole of their surplus labour force, fifty per cent of which come to work in the Republic (more than 100,000 a year). The citizens of these three territories are purposely excluded by the 1937 Act from the category of "foreign Natives," whose entrance is prohibited into the Union, and each year they send home to their families more than £1,000,000 earned in South Africa. If the Republic were to establish an economic barrier against these territories, they would become bankrupt at once. The Republic grants a fixed percentage of its customs revenue to the three territories, freeing them from the necessity of setting up their own customs barriers; the railways belong to the South African network, air transport is in the hands of private South African companies, and the roads are under the supervision of the South African Ministry of Transport.

Bechuanaland, Swaziland and Basutoland have two guardians: Great Britain for political and South Africa for economic affairs. But this is an anomaly, as if Scotland and Wales were to be French

179

Protectorates while benefiting from economic integration with England.

Historically, as we have seen, the removal of the three mandated territories anticipated the creation of Bantustans. The Zulus are a nation in the same way as are the Swazis, and if the Zulus are to become independent, the Swazis have to become so too—the Swazis in South African Ingvavuma, as well as their Swazi brothers in British Mbabane.

Legally, the transfer of these territories to South Africa was provided for in the South Africa Act whose preamble states, *inter alia*, "whereas it is expedient to provide for the eventual admission into the Union or transfer to the Union of such parts of South Africa as are not originally included therein", and enumerates the conditions under which the Crown can order this transfer (notably "that land belonging to the tribe will not be alienated to the detriment of the Natives of Basutoland, Bechuanaland and Swaziland.") These texts show that the transfer was envisaged. The Governments in Pretoria and London started to implement this policy, by negotiating about the conditions of incorporation.

The Government in Pretoria is certainly right in maintaining that these negotiations, even if there are no results, are ample proof of the original intention of the British Government to grant the request, and that the South African policy of putting aside land for the Bantu, introduced in 1913, was aimed at creating in a part of the Union the very conditions which already existed in the three High Commission territories; that is to say, conditions of ethnic homogeneity which allow for the incorporation of these territories in the Union.

Last but not least, *politically*, the existence of three weak territories, adjacent to the Republic (or, in the case of Basutoland, enclosed by South Africa), certainly constitutes a military danger to South Africa or to the Bantu states which will be created by partitioning the Republic.

One day, these territories might serve as a basis for subversive activity: their long frontiers with the Republic (and, tomorrow, with the Bantu states) cannot easily be supervised. The former South African Minister of Defence, Mr. F. C. Erasmus, rightly pointed out that they represent a breach in the advanced system of radar control through which attackers by air could penetrate, thus gaining several hundred miles undetected, when approaching the industrial Witwatersrand.

From the point of view of the defence of South Africa, from the point of view of the interest that the West has in ensuring a strategic position in the South of Africa, there is an urgent need in stopping-up these gaps, which will be all the more dangerous as the British make their presence less felt—or withdraw.

None of these reasons have persuaded the British Government to agree to the transfer. Obviously, Britain could not, under present conditions, agree to transfer another million Blacks to a régime abhorrent to all the members of the Commonwealth. But I do not see why these territories could not be joined to the South African Bantustans when these states have been created: Bechuanaland with the country of the Tswana; Basutoland with the country of the South East Nguni; Swaziland with the country of the Swazis. The seven "great" Bantustans will then occupy an area of 348,000 square miles, that is to say forty-five per cent of the combined areas of the present South Africa and the three protectorates.

In order to hasten this evolution, why does not Great Britain take the initiative and proclaim a conditional transfer?

Why does not the South African Government invite the British Government to pool Bantu territorial resources so as to realize immediately a great and viable Bantu federation of Southern Africa?

CHAPTER 7

HOW MUCH INDEPENDENCE?

I

In 1955 a group of English students from the University of Hull addressed words of thanks to a talented speaker who had come to explain to them the point of view of the South African Government on the policy of apartheid: "We were indeed very pleased to have the opportunity of hearing you speak. We were all impressed by your power as a public speaker. We learned a lot about the problems facing South Africa, whilst some of the audience now believe apartheid is the correct policy. Perhaps the main remaining doubt is as to whether the Union ever intends to give the black African a separate state with true independence."*

The students of Hull have posed the problem correctly. Does apartheid aim at real independence or does it put up a smokescreen of parallel development and self-administration?

When presenting to Parliament the Promotion of Bantu Self-Government Bill in 1959, Dr. Verwoerd made a clear statement about his "ultimate aim". Parallel development implies the Black nations of South Africa can become "as free as Ghana is today... If the different Bantu national units show the ability to attain the required stage of self-sufficiency they will eventually form part of a South African Commonwealth together with the Republic of South Africa, which will during the intervening period act as the guardian of the emergent Bantu self-governing states."

To explain his idea Dr. Verwoerd used the example of the British Commonwealth system "based on the systematic political emancipation of the dependent and national units following on proof being furnished by the different units of their ability to govern themselves in a progressive manner."

This declaration did not mention any "timetable" for the march towards independence. What it means here, said Dr. Verwoerd, speaking on the motives for the Bill, is a process of internal growth

*Thomas Boydell, *My Beloved Country.*

182

for the Bantu communities, "and it is not possible to anticipate the rhythm of growth by establishing a precise timetable". In addition Mr. Eric Louw, Minister of Foreign Affairs, told the General Assembly of the United Nations in 1959: "There is scepticism in South Africa about timetables for independence fixed by international resolutions. Because international resolutions cannot create conditions for independence, where they do not in fact exist: firstly, a degree of reasonable cultural development; secondly, a political system which has come from the people and which has their enthusiastic support; thirdly, a degree of real economic independence."

These reservations are sound and we have seen how far the foundations of independence have been laid in the cultural, administrative and economic domains that we have examined.

But passing from the principle to its application one meets not only contradictions but disturbing indications of a real desire *not* to turn administrative autonomy into independence.

During this very debate in 1959 the Minister of Bantu Administration and Development, Mr. M. C. De Wet Nel, stated that the Bantu states would gradually be given independence in all fields, except defence, foreign affairs, posts and telegraphs and railways, which affected all sections of the community and had to be handled by the South African Government on a national basis. Asked about the future citizenship of the Bantu, the Minister replied that they would be members of their communities but that everybody, in the Black and White states, would be considered as South African citizens. These statements by the Minister are not taken from press reports which might have distorted his ideas. They are to be found on page 97 of the *State of the Union Yearbook for South Africa* for 1959/60.*

There are even more disturbing statements.

The Promotion of Bantu Self-Government Bill was tabled in Parliament on March 24, 1959, by Mr. De Wet Nel. At the same time Dr. Eiselen, Secretary for Bantu Administration, published in *Optima*† a study of Bantu advancement which contained this categorical statement of policy:

"The utmost degree of autonomy in administrative matters that the Union Parliament is likely to be prepared to concede to these

*Da Gama Publications.
†Publication of the Anglo-American Corporation.

183

areas will stop short of surrender of sovereignty by the European trustees and there is therefore no prospect of a federal system, with eventual equality among members . . . The maintenance of White political supremacy over the country as a whole is a *sine qua non* for racial peace and economic prosperity in South Africa." The year before, the Director of the South African Information Service in London replied in still more categorical terms to a series of articles which had appeared in the *Sunday Times* in January, 1958:

"The policy of the Government," he said, "is not and never has been a policy of total territorial separation . . . the first concern of separate development is not geography but people . . . it is not the sign that stands at the forking of a road: it is represented rather by the two lines of a railway track. These, though separate, are essentially interdependent and they carry towards a common objective . . ."*

And he added an illustration which is very relevant indeed: "One of the primary purposes of the Group Areas Act of 1950 was to make long-term provisions for a place of their own *within* the White areas for non-White groups. Scores of millions of pounds have been spent on building non-White townships in the White areas and on amenities for their people, such as schools, community centres, hospitals and transport. The railway development programme for Bantu townships in the industrial regions is, alone, estimated to cost £22m. This solid evidence in the form of homes, buildings and railways, together with legislation such as that which provides for the future local government of Bantu both in their own and in White areas is unmistakeable corroboration of what, in fact, apartheid is: namely a policy for the development of Bantu as Bantu and Europeans as Europeans *wherever they may be in the country.* The evidence is there for all to see who wish to see it."

II

What *is* going on?

What *is* the policy that is being followed? What is the real ideal which inspires the men who have such an overwhelming responsibility in years to come in South Africa? What is their real purpose in respect of the political future of the Bantu?

Dr. Eiselen's article in *Optima* disturbed me a great deal.

Reports on the State of South Africa, No. 11.

184

"As I said to you," I wrote to him, "I think that the Bantustan policy is just if it is seen through to the end, that is to say to partition and to the independence of Bantu states. I thought when we spoke about it in Pietersburg that you were of the same opinion. I have just read *Optima*. I was very upset by this article because if it truly reflects the doctrine of the Administration, then I fear that the policy based on this doctrine will inevitably fail. You know what efforts I am making to understand and to explain the political situation in South Africa objectively, and how I believe in the necessity for Bantustans which must be created at once and, if necessary, by means of great sacrifices. I ardently hope that the quotation from *Optima* will take on another meaning in a more complete context and I beg you to send me this journal so that I can get a clear or idea of things."

Dr. Eiselen gave me an explanation. "I am glad," he wrote to me, "that you have raised the question of complete or qualified independence.

"The position is that my article was written and submitted to the editor of *Optima* as early as November, 1958, at his request, although eventually it was only published in March, 1959. In November, 1958, approved Government policy did not enable me to forecast anything going beyond qualified independence. In January, 1959, the Prime Minister made his first comprehensive statement in Parliament concerning this matter, and on that occasion he promised ultimate complete independence.

"When soon after that my article appeared it was in this particular respect already outdated. As a matter of fact, this point was immediately spotted by the parliamentary Opposition and the discrepancy between the Prime Minister's statement and my article was raised in debate. The Prime Minister, in his reply, explained how this had come about and what the correct chronological order of the two statements was.

"He made it perfectly clear that Government policy had now been officially defined in his general statement and there would not be a ceiling of any sort imposed on the general development of the Bantu territories, but that this would be encouraged in every way and that this applied in particular to their political development."

Is this explanation satisfactory?

Did a dramatic, spectacular and fundamental reversal of political thinking take place amongst the leaders of South Africa, between the end of 1958 and the beginning of 1959? I would like to think so, because I desperately hope for such a change, but where are the signs of it? Where is the timetable of independence for the Bantu states? General Smuts saw things clearly when he asked his fellow-citizens to take care "that one day little Black children do not play in the ruins of the Union buildings." In 1961 the acceleration of political progress in Africa makes this apocalyptic image both realistic and anachronistic. There is no need to reduce the Union Buildings to ruins. Other government buildings have to be erected elsewhere in South Africa for separate Bantu states. As early as the nineteenth century a missionary, Dr. John Philip, asked for Bantu states in order to protect the Blacks against the extermination which threatened them because of the Whites. The wheel of history has turned. It is no longer the Blacks who must be protected in this changing Africa which has upset all the calculations of the White man . . .

With regard to the degree of independence South Africa is ready to grant the Bantu states, the report of the Tomlinson Commission contains a remarkable paragraph which reveals more of the psychology of the White man of South Africa than a whole library of reports and analyses:

"The Commission wished to refrain from suggestions in connection with further political developments; but if it may permit itself a prophetic look at the future it *would be inclined to regard* the proposed development plan as a means of bringing about *a degree* of political development which *might* serve as a *forerunner* of an *eventual* configuration of Southern Africa under which certain parts of the continent would be reserved for Europeans." (My italics, P.G.)

Such a cascade, such a collection of qualifying statements, of evasions and half-tones would be a comic masterpiece if written by Molière or Courteline. The effect is tragic when one thinks that the political mentality which is revealed here—and I think I can vouch for this—is characteristic of the thought of the average South African, of the man in the street who really feels himself inclined to consider that, eventually, a certain degree, could, as the forerunner . . . etc.

"If it should happen," said Dr. Verwoerd,* "that in the future they progress to a very advanced level, then the people of those

*Hansard, January 27, 1959.

186

future times will have to consider in what further way their re-lationships must be re-organized . . ."

And yet the future is knocking at our doors!

In London and in Cairo a persistent rumour is circulating about a P.G.R.S.A., a "Provisional Government of the Republic of South Africa" in exile, which will be directed by Dr. Yusuf Dadoo, one of the leaders of the South African Indian Congress, and whose Minister of Foreign Affairs will be Mr. Mahomo, a member of the executive of the Pan-African Congress. What problems would be created for the Government of Pretoria if a P.G.R.S.A., recognized by a certain number of countries in Africa and Asia, succeeded in bringing about in South Africa a genuine movement of revolt, thus creating another Algeria for the international organizations which would have automatic support from certain countries. The formation of a united front between Indians and Africans, enjoying African and Arab and Indian support, would be to India like a finger in a political pie of which she definitely wants a slice. If a P.G.R.S.A. were to be set up in and act from a capital less notorious for sub-versive acts in Africa than Cairo, would it not have support even in the camp of the Western Powers who never stop condemning South Africa for its racial policies?

Would not the most substantial gain go to the camp which was the first to brandish the flag of independence, and would the Republican Government allow itself to be irremediably outdistanced?

Can the South African Government, even if it wants to do so, really allow itself to delay the publication of a timetable for Bantu independence?

CHAPTER 8

COLOUREDS AND INDIANS

I

A few years ago an incident took place at the Cape, and the way it was exploited by the Press abroad was motivated neither by a prejudice against South Africa nor by sensationalism. In fact a prominent Afrikaans poet, D. J. Opperman, has written a moving poem about the event, entitled "Draaiboek". A young Coloured boy of sixteen had hanged himself from the beams of a barn for the simple reason that his brothers were White enough to be admitted to a White school from which he had been excluded because of the colour of his skin.

There are even darker dramas (no atrocious pun is intended): more blood and more tears have hardened us to even greater sufferings. But within the framework of the great South African tragedy, the suicide of this Coloured child is a symbol of a more desperate situation than that of the Bantu, who are protected by a shell of simple-minded indifference and a great political hope which they share with 250,000,000 Black Africans. The symbol represents the case of the one-and-a-half million Coloureds, who are alone in the world.

The definition of "Coloured", according to the Census Act of 1950, indicates the difficulty of stating positively what these people are. It is completely negative. A Coloured man is a person who is *not* by his appearance a White man, and who is *not*, in fact, *generally accepted* as belonging to one of the aboriginal races or tribes of Africa.

One can see the enormous arbitrary powers that census officers and officials derive from this classification. What are the irrefutable characteristics of the White man? What criteria establish general acceptance in a context which varies according to time and place? The regulation of March 23, 1959, which sought to make the law water-tight by drawing up seven groups of Coloureds, did not succeed. They enumerated the Coloureds of the Cape, the Malays of the Cape, the Griquas, the Chinese, the Indians, those who "having their country of origin in a place other than China, India or Pakistan," are classified as other Asiatics, and, finally, the exceptions who do not fall into any of these groups and who are "other Coloureds."

In fact the dramatic situation of the Coloureds stems from their marginal position. They have no tribal context; they do not live in a reserve; their languages are those of the Whites, English and Afrikaans, and 90 per cent are of Afrikaner culture and language; they do not have and do not claim any other civilization but that of the West. If they are different from the Whites only by reason of colour, in many cases this difference is very slight. A Coloured man is often turned away both from the counter for the Whites and from the Counter for the non-Whites at the Post Office because of his "appearance" which clearly has nothing about it which can be "generally accepted" without discussion, and in many families one child would be entitled to go to a White school, while his brothers attended the Coloured school.

The little schoolboy had cause to hang himself! Those who cross the fateful line are condemned to a clandestine crossing or to an anguished conscience which destroys personality. If they want to venture into the domain of the Whites when their skin allows them this chance, they are reduced to lying, to dissimulation, to fleeing their families. The slightest accident can upset everything. According to the caprice of nature (in politics one cannot trust biology) a Coloured man fair enough to live as a White man can have children who are definitely Coloured, and who will be registered as such. And, on the other hand, a Coloured man can have children with a White skin whose whole lives will be ruled by an inscription which describes them as Coloured. When in 1955 30,000 Coloured people were scrutinized minutely in Johannesburg a good number were crossed off from the Coloured group, and placed on the footing of the Bantu. Crinkly hair could make all the difference. The criteria were completely arbitrary. For example, one brother could find himself on the list of the Whites, another on the list of the Coloureds. For the latter it was a degradation for life, whatever merits he might have had.

What are the Coloured people really?

The popular and sketchy biographies of Jan van Riebeeck, the father of the South African nation, whose head adorns the bank-notes, coins, the steles, the frontispieces, the dadoes of South African drawing-rooms, bring out one detail of his family life which throws light on the situation of the South African Coloureds. Van Riebeeck introduced into his own family a young Hottentot woman, whom his wife herself baptized Eva, and who before her twenty-first year gave birth to two illegitimate children, one of whom was the first of all the Coloured people in the Cape Colony. It is symbolical (and this symbol has today the value almost of a political signpost) that the Coloured people of the Cape originated in the very house of the founder of the new White nation. This was the beginning of a new nation of Coloured people, with at least as many rights to the country as the Whites had, and certainly more rights than the Bantu, who were still a century away in time and 1,500 miles away in distance. No official document states who the father of the Van Riebeeck servant's child was. But the East India Company, when later generously rewarding a certain Pieter van Meerhoff for making an "honest woman" of Eva, indicated that they attached some value to the regularizing of this situation, and that the father must have been someone highly placed.

Van Meerhoff was made the Company's surgeon. Van Riebeeck was a witness at the marriage. Eva's children were sent to Batavia after the death of their father, and Eva herself, the first baptized heathen, became the first "famous woman" of South Africa. A domestic problem had been solved, and a social problem had been created for South Africa. This problem was, therefore, present in embryo in the conditions of the occupation of the Cape.

The first batch of Van Riebeeck's companions included only a few women, all married, and one of the first messages that the directors of the Company received from the Cape was a laconic "send us a few solid farmgirls". In reply to this only a few arrived, and to remedy the situation, Van Riebeeck introduced a custom which was traditional in the other establishments of the company: the mixed marriage. "A historian of the old and respected family of de Villiers," writes the French journalist Anne Marie la Barraque, "even dared to express herself thus at a large family gathering: two brothers de Villiers arrived in South Africa in the seventeenth century; one married a black woman, the other died single. Take your pick of ancestors."

190

The indigenous population—the Hottentots, cattle-breeders, and the Bushmen, bush hunters—were already mixing between themselves. The war that they were forever waging against each other supplied both groups with spoils, notably women. The Whites found their first concubines amongst these local races.

But an economic factor—the Hottentots, who were the most hard-working of the indigenous peoples, showed little enthusiasm for the organized work desired by the Whites—caused the Dutch almost from the beginning to import Black slaves from West Africa. The first shipload arrived in Table Bay in 1658. Later on they imported slaves from Ceylon, India, Indonesia and Madagascar. A few marriages and a host of extra-conjugal relationships followed, in a general mixing-up of all the colours. Ships of all countries anchored at the Cape on their way to and from the Indian Ocean, and sometimes they remained at the Cape for weeks and months. The Coloured people of the Cape had come into being. Owing to their origins (and no doubt also to their constant contact in every form with the Whites) they have kept not only the pride, as we have seen, of "belonging to them", but also all the outward signs of their origins, notably that which most closely defines a man—his name. Many proudly bear the names of van Wyk, Maasdorp, Erasmus, Smith, de Villiers, Petersen. These names closely indicate their blood-ties.

One group amongst the Coloured people, the Malays, has retained its original identity to a remarkable degree. They are the descendants of the Moslems, brought by the Company to South Africa from Malaya, India, Ceylon and China. In the beginning they had amongst them political exiles, who were sometimes of noble birth.

Estimated at 70,000 today, they still follow the faith of Islam. They neither smoke nor drink, and they have a reputation for high moral standards and a professional conscience.

II

The man who welcomed me would have made no particular impression on me in Paris or London. I would perhaps have noticed his slightly bronzed complexion—but he could have just come back from the Riviera or the winter sports—and his dark eyes. If I had any reason to think about it, I would have placed him as a Lebanese or an Italian. I do not think I would have thought of him as a man at all *different*. If I had, I would have seen in George Golding what he is —a man who stands out from the crowd because he is rich, a powerful man, an influential member of the Union Council for Coloured Affairs, the respected leader of the moderate section of the Coloured people, who, if things become more logical, would be a member of Parliament, even a Minister in the South African Cabinet.

The Coloured Affairs Department and the Coloured people themselves had told me that Golding would speak without hate or fear about what was going right and what was not.

"What is going right and what do I strongly applaud? Well, my young friend," said Golding to me with assurance, while he gave a signal to the Coloured Affairs official who had introduced me to serve tea and to pass the biscuits.

"The State builds fine schools for us. They will certainly show you the University College of the Western Cape," (the next day this was done) "and it is not just eyewash. In twelve years the Nationalist Government has done more for the education of the Coloured people than all the preceding Governments put together, and this is a very good sign. When one becomes educated, it is something. Knowledge is power.

"As far as housing is concerned, there has also been progress. There was a complete change in policy six years ago. Before that the municipalities built houses which were let to us. Now they are lending money to our people so that they can become owners. It is the opposite of their Bantu policy, under which Natives are not encouraged to have roots in the White areas.

"They have created a Department of Coloured Affairs. This Department serves as a link between the Coloured people and the Municipality, the Provincial Councils and the Government; it gives subsidies to our cultural institutions, it helps to train professional men, it gives land to those of our people who wish to become farmers, and it helps us with housing. It centralizes everything. If the head of the department is competent and sympathetic to our cause, good work is done on all levels.

"For the past three years there has also been great progress as far as administrative jobs for our people are concerned. In the Post Office, in the Railway administration, in the Department of Coloured Affairs, from the top to the bottom of the ladder, careers are open to the Coloured people. It is the Government, I must repeat, which is doing this. There are more and more Coloured doctors, artisans, skilled workers and teachers.

"And then there is the Union Council for Coloured Affairs which has been in existence since 1959. It has 27 members, 15 of them nominated and 12 elected by the Coloured people. The Government *may* consult it on all matters concerning Coloured people. It is not obliged to do so. The Council meets four times a year *in camera* and this allows councillors to speak freely.

"The Government can also delegate administrative functions to this Council. Up till now this has not been done."

Golding stopped. He has a pencil-thin moustache and two deep lines from the nostrils down to the chin. His eyes burnt intensely. He was silent for a while.

"I am now going to tell you what really is not so favourable.

"Take, for example, job reservation. It is a completely unacceptable measure. The wonderful education that we receive is useless if we are excluded from many jobs.

"We Coloured people want to collaborate with the Whites, but not with the Job Reservation Act. This law means that people who are in certain positions are down-graded, that their children will be trained only up to a certain level in certain occupations. For example, in the furniture industry, there is no economic justification for this because there are not enough Whites to fill the jobs. I know an engineer. He has done a certain job for forty years. But he must be down-graded.

"There is a danger for Whites in this horizontal stratification. If work from a certain level in a factory, for instance, can only be done by Whites, what happens to that work if the Coloured people, who are below this level, strike?"

Golding stopped once again. The tea and biscuits were passed a little more nervously.

"I was a prosperous man," he continued, "and now there is the Group Areas Act. Before we had this law, there was a gentleman's agreement between the Whites and the Coloureds. Individuals had the right to build anywhere, but the Coloured people had always built their houses away from the Whites. It was the custom for years.

"Take myself, for example. I have been here for thirty years. But they have built houses for Whites around me. The law gives me two years to leave. I will be ruined because I will only be able to sell my house at a ridiculously low price and I will need a lot of money to build elsewhere. It is persecution.

"I am going to explain to you how it works. The municipality values my house at £4,300, the Group Areas Board at £2,000. The true commercial value of my house is £5,000. They want to force me to sell it at £2,000: because if I sell at £4,000 I must pay the Government a fine totalling fifty per cent of the difference. It is true that if I do not get £2,000, eighty per cent of the difference will be made up to me . . .

"A victim of this naturally feels frustrated. And even then it would be accepted if they let the people who were already there continue to live in their houses, and they segregated in the future. That could be reasonable, and we want to remain reasonable."

Golding stared hard at me.

"I mean what I say. A reasonable policy, a policy which wants to meet us half-way. We are a force. We reproduce much more quickly than the Whites. We have 3,000 students at universities. The Whites must understand that we must govern the country together.

"We have played many parts, and if the Government co-operates with us, we can do much for it in many fields. I repeat, I am a moderate and I believe in the power of a reasonable policy, and I am not afraid to be involved in such a policy, although extremism is the fashion. I proposed to the Government that they should send Coloured trade union leaders to the countries which are boycotting South Africa to explain to them that the boycott makes the Coloured workers suffer, and that it is better that the Coloured people should themselves tell the Government of South Africa what is wrong. Because I do not think that it is for the Government of Ghana to dictate to us. I would like to send envoys to the Philippines, to the West Indies, to the United States.

"My government has not yet replied to my proposals . . ."

The next day, as forecast, I did visit the Western Cape University College for Coloureds, a young university then six months old, from which one could not reasonably ask more than could be shown from a few months of existence.

What it had to show was very fine, and as Golding had said, it was not eyewash. Dr. J. G. Meiring, one of those Afrikaners who have made me like the Afrikaner intellectuals because they are direct and practical, explained to me why he had preferred the principalship of an embryonic university to more brilliant posts.

"It is because I do not in any way believe that I am here to carry out measures of discrimination but, on the contrary, to help the Coloured people to get back on their feet again.

"In the mixed universities, the Coloured man did not receive his due. First of all, from the academic point of view: a Coloured man could never teach in a White university. The Whites wouldn't have accepted him. At Cape Town there were two Coloured people capable of lecturing. They were not accepted. Now, in the separate universities, they will have the possibility of reaching the highest university posts.

"Socially, the Coloured people were excluded completely from university life. Sports and all the extra-curricular social activities, which are so important, are reserved for Whites only. Now, for the first time, the Coloured people will have a complete university life.

"Above all, I believe that I am working to make happy citizens of these students. The Coloured students in the White universities were losing contact with their own people. They had a tendency to despise the Coloured masses. They were forgetting that they formed the élite of the community, which cannot do without an élite, and that one must serve one's own community. If the Whites had only integrated them it would not have been so bad. But after their studies most doors were closed to them. They had no place in the White community. A Coloured barrister or doctor could not build up any practice amongst the Whites. And they had lost contact with their own community. Many felt frustrated, and took refuge in extremism.

"This university therefore has a social task: to give Coloured students the ideal of serving their own community. If we succeed in giving them this ideal, there will be better relations between Whites and Coloureds.

"There will be better relations because this élite will work with the Whites for the advancement of the Coloured people, and also because it will be a true élite, occupying in its own community the place taken today by the Whites."

I did not entirely agree with his ideas. I think that it is right to grant the Bantu races independence, and I think it is wrong to separate the Coloureds from the Whites. But perhaps in this period of formation of élites one must do what is most urgent, and wholeheartedly welcome all that is being done in every field to educate as many Coloured people as quickly as possible.

Mr. Adam Small, a lecturer at the Coloured University College, endorsed these views:

"The university is working towards a good, not a bad, ideal—that of integration. Ninety per cent of the Coloured people come from a family background where the culture and the language are Afrikaans. The Afrikaans universities were closed to them.

"The half-open universities were English-speaking. Now there is a university run in our language which is completely open."

He also told me (and each of the Coloured students was later to reveal the same hurt) of the shame they had felt at being excluded from social contact in the White universities.

"They didn't want us on the rugby field. It's absurd. If a man is fit enough to be with you on the bench of an amphitheatre he must be admitted to the other fields of university activity. If we are not admitted it is better to be apart. It would perhaps have been better to have given the Coloured students a choice between the open and separate universities. I think that in that case most of the Coloureds would have chosen the separate university for the reasons I have just given.

"Above all," he added, "when the sports fields and the swimming bath have been built . . ."

Later on, at the D.F. Malan Airport, another influential member of the Coloured Affairs Council, Sarleh Dollie, told me almost the same thing in his own terms. Dollie is the only Coloured pharmacist in the Republic. He is a very clever politician who affirms his religion by a black fez.

"Under the old colonial system the White was the master," he said. "The others were servants. That must change and that is going to change. As far as we Coloured people are concerned the change must consist in making us feel that we are not inferior. It must put each class of Coloured (the workers as well as the privileged classes) on a level with the corresponding class of Whites. To bring about this equality the level of instruction of the Coloured people must be raised."

Dollie pulled a letter out of his pocket.

"Here is a letter from the Mayor of Cape Town asking me to

Sisal growing plays a major role in the agricultural development of the Bantu territories

Chief Kaizer Matanzima addressing the Fifth Session of the Transkeian Territorial Authority, of which he is chairman. Seated on his right is Mr. J. H. Abraham, Commissioner-General to the Transkei

visit her. To me that means nothing. I *feel* I am her equal because I *am* her equal, and there is no problem. What does count for me is to know how many of our people will be accepted on this level as soon as they have reached it. The political problem, an extension of our social problem, is to have our people accepted on a certain level when they have reached it. That is to say, to have them recognized for what they are.

"And that," Dollie said to me after a pause, "is also in the interests of the Whites, because we will in any case be more numerous than they in the year 2000. Thus it is in the interests of the Whites to work it in such a way that we will be *really* identical with them . . ."

III

To my mind, there is only one solution to the problem of the Coloured people: purely and simply, integration into the White community. Linguistic and cultural integration is already accomplished. Economic integration is on its way. Biological integration—practised every day to a slight extent—will neither increase nor diminish when it is legal. There only remains political integration. It is not only just, it is indispensable to the survival of White South Africa.

This will shock many of my Afrikaner friends. I regret it. But one of their great statesmen, Gen. Hertzog, who was Prime Minister of the Union from 1924, thought the same way. He believed in apartheid, but he wished to exclude the Coloured people from it. He thought that the Coloured people belonged to the White side of the barricade, and that it was irresponsible to push them into the arms of the enemies of the Whites. That is just common sense. The more liberal ideas that have always prevailed in the Cape are threatened by the ideas and laws from the Transvaal which has political dominance. But I am convinced that there is a dangerous error there, and that the psychology of the Afrikaner people is the cause of it.

The Afrikaners have become rich, of age, and politically free only a short time ago. They are not used to relying on the normal play of economic laws to keep the classes "apart" residentially, socially and even sexually. They must learn this. Bad laws are above all bad for those who make them.

It is necessary to fill the gap between Whites and Coloureds, not to make it wider.

For political reasons, first of all. There are no Bantustans possible for Coloured people. No-one can seriously envisage the re-settling of the Coloureds in a so-called "national" territory and Dr. Verwoerd's declaration of January, 1961, announcing a "national home" for the Coloureds in the Northwestern Cape, is incapable of fulfilment. It therefore is inconceivable that one can permanently impose on one-and-a-half million citizens unequal rights based not on a difference of colour, which would be the external sign of a different nationality, but on nuances of colour, and when the level of civilization is the same as that of the Whites.

Consequently the Afrikaners must follow a policy which shows that the people born at the Cape at the same time as their own nation was born have been separated only superficially, owing to the colonial régime which they claim to be abolishing. The Coloured people have accepted the culture and standards of the Whites too completely for any going back on this.

Apartheid, as regards the Bantu, has a positive side: The Bantustans, which constitute the final goal. But there is no equivalent to this for the Coloured people. It would be extremely dangerous to allow a people to develop separately in the midst of another people without the escape-valve of a "Zionism". The Coloured peope find themselves between two stools, one occupied by the White man, the other by the Bantu. One day they will have to choose one of them, because their position is uncomfortable. Room will have to be made for them peacefully—or they will take their place less peacefully, and against one party they will mobilize the person sitting on the second stool.

Besides, of all the races who make up the population of the Republic, the Coloureds have (from a sociological point of view) the most legitimate right to live there. The Whites came from Europe, and the Bantu from outside the Republic. As we have pointed out, their invasion coincided in time and their claims are strictly equivalent. The Coloured people did not come from any-where. They sprung from the meeting, the amalgamation and the cultural mixing of the Whites and the Blacks. If one really wants to, one could, by denying three centuries of history, accept the theory that the Whites and the Blacks have other home countries than the

Republic, but the Coloureds have none. One can perhaps see in this fact—for the very distant future—the real justification of the point of view of the most liberal Whites, who believe in a multi-racial state and the inevitable biological mixing which will ensue.

The Coloured people must also be integrated for economic reasons which will benefit the Whites as much as the Coloureds. The South African economy as a whole needs such a normalization. The absorption of the Coloured people into the professional hierarchy will put an end to the immoral and uneconomic protection given to a certain number of Whites for whom the law reserves certain jobs. The State and the consumer pay heavily for subsidizing the inefficiency of foremen, simply because they are White. They are found asleep on all the roads of South Africa. There are also painters who are helped by three men who do nothing but dip the brush of the master into a pot of paint . . .

Economic and professional competition must eliminate the differences in the wages paid today on the basis of pigmentation, not according to skill and talent. Greece, Spain and Italy have poor Whites, even poorer than the poorest Coloured people of South Africa, and sometimes less educated and less civilized. These poor Whites have no Coloured people to serve as super-poor people for them. Each one must be made to earn his due, and the country would then be spurred on towards greater prosperity, when the withdrawal of job reservation throws into a common market the brains and the brawn of the Coloured people. When the Bantustans have been created—and they will be created, either for the Whites or against the them—the Coloured people will, more than is possible now, hold the balance of power.

George Golding, in his Cape Town house which had become familiar to me and where I found calm and reason after days of investigations and interviews during which the most controversial ideas had been hurled at me, said to me one evening:

"The Whites must understand that we must govern this country together . . . The Coloured people have never been in conflict with the Whites. During the two World Wars we fought for the country. During World War II they put us into the auxiliary services, without arms and with a special uniform. But outside the frontiers of the country we took arms and we fought. Such was our loyalty. But if this loyalty is rewarded by the Group Areas Act, the moderates like

199

myself will lose their popularity and will be replaced by extremists."

With the kind of calm which impresses one, because, after all, this man represents 1,500,000 people capable of marching as one single man, Golding added:

"We are not merely a potential political force, but a real one, a force which has already acted on the Whites, and the Whites remember it, you can take my word for that. The riots at the Cape last year show this clearly. When 45,000 Bantu marched on Cape Town in April, 1960, the Government asked me, Golding, to see that the Coloured people remained calm. I spent a whole night with trade union leaders. We published a proclamation, requesting the Coloured people to remain calm. They did. Do you realize that a proclamation calling the Coloured people out, or a neutralist policy, would have set Cape Town to fire and blood? Do you think that one can neglect such a force?"

Perhaps the solution to the Coloured problem lies in their self-emancipation, in their acquiring such a cultural, economic and social stature that the Whites will no longer be able to deny them political equality. The Coloured people will not, as no other people will either, get a present on a silver platter, and they must achieve their emancipation through sweat and tears.

Richard Ernest van der Ross is one of the young leaders (he is forty) of the Coloured people. When one listens to him one realizes that a whole generation is caught up in a frenzy of combat, getting ready for the struggle, flexing its muscles, choosing with care the cudgels and the swords suitable for this particular battlefield and for the capacities of the fighter.

"It is the inferiority of status and the denial of rights which today goes with being Coloured which we must reject, not the being Coloured as such," he wrote.*

"In the second place, economic advancement will not come willy-nilly. Or, if it does come, it will not come at the desired or maximum rate of its own accord. We must work for it. This we do in a variety of ways, but we must work harder. We must press for the opening up of more and better job opportunities, for better training facilities, for better remuneration. But these demands must go hand in hand with another very necessary factor, namely, that we must stop economic wastage. We must not only work to get more money,

*South Africa, the Road Ahead. Howard Timmins, Cape Town, 1960.

200

but we must resolve to let the money which we get serve our interests and not counteract our interests. Although I tread on dangerous ground here, I feel grave warning must be sounded against such money-wasters and life-wasters as drink and debt. It is no use the worker working if he uses his wages to undermine his own welfare and that of his family. We are in a stage of development when we need to promote the welfare of the home and the child. We dare not allow the worker—at whatever level he may be—to drink to an extent where he prevents the full development of his home and of his children. This must be seen as a social and as an individual problem. And it must be so seen by us, for it is no use asking the oppressor to stop us from doing that which is in his interests. We must stop it, for the loss is ours. The same may be said of debt, if it is incurred in acquiring needless luxuries. A higher spending power may be a blessing; it can also be a curse in the hands of the wrong people. We must prove ourselves to be better and wiser spenders as well as better earners.

"The third requirement, that of better education and leadership, can be obstructed if this leadership, this 'intelligentsia' or 'talented tenth', allows itself to become so embittered and frustrated that it refuses to identify itself in fact with the upward struggle of the people and becomes selfish. I say 'to identify itself in fact with the people', because the intelligentsia will never admit that it does not so identify itself, and may expend much energy and even more money in the process. But it may be no more than lip-service. The test is whether the people know them, accept them, follow them, and this will only happen when they are prepared to make sacrifices in the cause."

And Van der Ross's conclusion is like an echo of the warning words of Golding:

"One of the most encouraging positive signs of the last decade has been the manner in which Coloured people have become ever more willing to communicate with the African. Not, I would warn, that there has been a great deal of increase in this direction yet, but there has been a great deal done in preparing people's minds for this increasing communication. I predict that we are now entering a time when we shall see more of Coloured meeting African on the level of education, political discussion and co-operation, sport, art and entertainment.

"Such communication generally takes place most easily and with most lasting results at the higher levels, and the gradual development of Coloured and African over the past years in these fields, as well as a feeling of common suffering due to a common cause—colour—has helped to prepare the ground. Also as we Coloured people lose our childlike dependency on the European and learn to stand on our own merit, as we learn that we have a bargaining power, we shall be more willing to undertake joint ventures with less fear of loss."

Can the Whites allow themselves to neglect this degree of political awareness? Is it really in their interests to throw the Coloured intelligentsia with its professional and political leaders towards the eleven million Blacks who perhaps tomorrow will be seeking a ready-made élite? Is it in their interests to favour united action between Bantu and Coloured when everything is favourable for Coloured and White unity?

Is it not in their interest, not only to grant the Coloured people Coloured members of Parliament, but to put them back immediately on the common electoral roll from which they were brutally removed in 1956 by the Separate Representation of Voters Act? There should be no distinctions other than age and property, which should be the same for all, so that tomorrow on the benches of the representatives of the people in Cape Town and even in a ministerial office in the Union Buildings in Pretoria, we should be able to see, in their rightful places, the Goldings, the Swarts, the Dollies and the Smalls, South Africans whom their country needs.

This is a revolutionary demand, yet it is beginning to take shape. In Stellenbosch one of my Afrikaner friends confirmed this to me in the following terms:

"There is a tendency to integrate the Coloured people. It is not yet official policy. For the moment the word integration is dynamite in South African politics, but S.A.B.R.A. has reached the stage of thinking that the Coloured people must be given Coloured representatives in Parliament, and that they must then be put back on the common electoral roll.

"The White M.P.s who represent them today are, in any case, more extremist than the Coloured people would be. S.A.B.R.A. believes in the progressive integration of the Whites and the Coloureds, especially in the Cape, because the policy of apartheid which has come from the Transvaal is too severe for local conditions. In international politics, what a gain it would be for South Africa."

Will South Africa go along this road or will the radiant hope which was given to me at Stellenbosch be denied by the recent declaration of Dr. Verwoerd which said that no form of integration was envisaged for the Coloured people "nor any mixing of the political structures of the Coloureds and the Whites, neither at municipal level nor in a higher sphere?" Will they really be so mad as to pursue to the end this disastrous ideal, which means suicide for three million Whites? In their search for allies, friends and people who understand them, do the Whites of South Africa not realize that within their national frontiers, in the heart of their civilization, there is another Western people, a million-and-a-half potential allies? The *Burger*, the big Afrikaner Nationalist newspaper, has itself admitted that too much useless ballast is carried in the suitcases of apartheid.

I would like to say to my Afrikaner friends and to Dr. Verwoerd: Under the pressure of your catastrophic policy, the traditional admiration of the Coloured man for the White man will very soon change to frustration, resentment and hatred.

Politicians have only two choices—amending their policies or completely contradicting themselves. Great architects of history have never feared to change.

Change your gun from one shoulder to the other while there is still time, or it will be wrested from you, it will be turned against you, you will be killed with it, and the world will cry out that justice has been done.

IV

The Indians are a problem within a problem, because while one has the hope of national independence for the Bantu, and for the Coloured people the hope of final integration into the White community, none of these categorical perspectives seem to suit this mass of 500,000 ambassadors from India, endowed with a strong national individuality, who have not the slightest desire to be assimilated in a non-Indian civilization.

Only two per cent of the Indians in South Africa have adopted the familiar use of English or Afrikaans. This statement seems unlikely but when one walks through the Indian market in Durban one finds there, in the colours, the smells, the forms and the atmosphere, the Far East transposed, the decorative and suggestive illustration of these unlikely statistics.

The market in Durban is a great coloured bazaar. In the adjoining streets the crowd jostles in front of the gaudy shops with their windows full of trash, displayed everywhere as bargains, as sale goods and wonderful second-hand opportunities: materials from Madras, plates and dishes from China, huge assortments of cheap silverware, second-hand clothes and endless piles of food. Tempting prices in big letters are painted in orange or green or in brilliant-coloured inks. All the women wear saris.

The bazaar itself is dark, deeply impregnated with the perfume of spices, leather, the kaffir-beer which is sold there, sweat and boiled mutton: the crowd is even denser than in the street, and the foreigner, easily picked out by the cameras which he carries, is hailed, and his sleeves are plucked at by the merchants.

India is inside the bazaar. Vegetables, fruit, and, especially, mountains of curry of a wide variety of colours, ranging from snow-white to black, the nutmegs, the varieties of rice, reveal to the Westerner, who is not used to them, the infinite diversity of eastern condiments whose nuances we do not even suspect. Beyond the knick-knacks and the materials, beyond the opulent Indian vendors, there is the African market. The odours there are even stronger, nauseating near the tanners who work in the open air and who hang up freshly-quartered skins on wooden slats to dry in the air. In fragile street stores vaguely witch-like herbalists sit motionless at the back of their shops, waiting for the customer to choose, from dusty flacons, dark powders, greyish debris, dry herbs and strips of skin hanging from strings; the vendors of souvenirs display sculpted figurines, daggers, assegais, masks, and pieces of ebony. Tailors, under their plank shelters, work on the spot with their ancient sewing machines. It has the atmosphere of a flea market, a magician's den. Little piccanins with pathetic eyes beg for alms. This display of culinary riches and brilliant silver from the East in the very heart of Durban, and this market of Africans seated in the dust and the revolting smell of tanning, is the image of India, transported, grafted with colour and exuberance in the slow, earthy Africa, and flaunting its saris, its curries, its dialects and the architecture of its terraced houses with their pointed cupolas and their verandahs, just as they are in the suburbs of Delhi.

It was in 1855 that the growth of the sugar industry in Natal caused the City Corporation of Durban to ask the Government of the Cape Colony "permission to bring in a limited number of Coolies and other Eastern workers to help the new industry, for the success of which sufficient and reliable labour is absolutely necessary". There was opposition in Natal to this project, but the "import licence" was granted in 1860 by the British authorities, and the rapid expansion of the sugar industry between 1860 and 1865 was due to the Indians. Indeed, everybody profited. The planters, that goes without saying; the Government of India which received £10,000 a year as compensation for the loss of a few thousand useless mouths; the recruiting agents who visited Indian villages where the crops had been bad and also the pilgrimage centres where thousands of illiterate and extremely poor people collected together and who received £3 per male immigrant and £3 13s. 6d. per female immigrant; and, finally, the Indians themselves, who were engaged by contract and who were for the most part the untouchables from Madras and the southern provinces, half-starved agricultural workers whom emigration freed from the caste system and from hunger.

One shudders when in the Archives at Pretoria one glances through the collection of identity photographs of these strange workers, posing, half-naked, with all their ribs jutting out, and a number on their hollow bellies. An "historical error" was perhaps committed by the shareholders of Natal Sugar Plantation Limited when they opened the doors to Asiatic immigration. The winding course of history is made up of errors of this kind. But one can only live history as it is made by men, urged on by the impulses of their psychology, and, in any case, the Coolies of 1860 foreshadowed a century in advance the still more urgent problem before India today, and which will tomorrow be before the world : where to send her millions, her tens and hundreds of millions of excess mouths.

From 1870 to 1891 the Indians in Natal grew from 6,000 to 41,000. The families of the indentured workers accompanied them and soon became merchants. Few made use of the free return ticket which was given them after ten years' work. There were 51,000 immigrants between 1891 and 1903. There were 46,000 between

1904 and 1911—a total of 143,000 until an official stop was put to immigration in 1913.

Natural increase brought this figure up to 367,000 in 1951, and 500,000 in 1960.

The problem set by the Indians in South Africa is shown in the example of Durban, where they are now numerically equal to the Whites—but where the pitiless law of figures shows that they will be double the White population at the end of the century. The Whites detest them because they see in them dangerous competitors in commerce and industry, where they succeed all the more because they are satisfied with much simpler living conditions than the Whites, and lower profits. The Bantu see in the Indian grocer or small proprietor, who sells dearly the necessities of life, and who rents out at an exorbitant price slum dwellings on the outskirts of the towns, the only apparent obstacle to their well-being, without realizing that the Indian, like the Jewish usurer at the times of "Jewish" usury, is only the instrument of an infinitely complex political and economic system over which they have no more control than their victims. The bloody incidents of 1949 in Durban, when the Bantu masses savagely murdered all the Indians they came across, had the same basic origin as the pogroms.

The distribution of the Indians in economic fields clearly shows a lack of balance: 50 per cent of their income is derived from trade, 25 per cent from small-scale industry, 29 per cent from rent in various forms and transport undertakings; and only six per cent from agriculture.

To this must be added the undeniable fact that the Indian immigrants have refused to abandon their Indian identity of which their houses, their clothes and their eating habits are but the exterior signs. The "double loyalty", Indian and South African, for which they are reproached, is often a single loyalty, felt towards the mother-country beyond the Indian Ocean. And it is certain that South Africa feels uneasily the existence of this badly-assimilated bridgehead, faced as it is with the human antheap of India herself, who unequivocally takes sides with her outposts on other continents. And did not Mr. Nehru state clearly at Bandung that there is nothing more horrible than the tragedy of Africa . . . and that Asia must help Africa, its sister continent? Africa, with its vast resources and its virgin lands (and South Africa has an overabundance of under-exploited riches and arable lands), must almost inevitably figure largely in the minds of the millions of Indians who each year increase the population of India, itself each year more hungry and starving. Is not the whole eastern coast of Africa being repopulated by Indians? Is not Uganda already an economic satellite of India? Does not Kenya have four Indians to one White man? Is not Mauritius already an Indian "colony"?

Is there no solution (which will be immediate and not put off for generations to come) to this social and political problem? In spite of the tenacity with which the Indians of South Africa wish to preserve their Indian traditions, 90 per cent of them were born in South Africa. South Africa is their homeland. Their fathers also, owing to the keen economic competition that they have stimulated, have played a role in the development of the continent and the conquest of virgin lands by civilization, and the words that Churchill wrote in 1910 are still valid:

"It is the Indian merchant, penetrating into territories where no White man wished to risk his life or could earn his living, who has, more than anyone else, set up the basis for trade and opened up the rudiments of our communication lines."

One feels that the repatriation encouraged by the South African Government has contributed but little to decreasing the Indian population, and one can be sure that illegal immigration since 1913 compensates for the number of Indian emigrants.

An agreement, signed in 1927 between the Governments of India and South Africa, organized state-subsidized repatriation; but between 1927 and 1931 the departures for India exceeded the arrivals by only 7,000; and most of those who left were elderly people.

The Indian traders showed little desire to leave, and the birth rate rapidly made up for emigration. In 1949, after the Zulu riots which cost 149 Indians their lives, the Government increased the repatriation bonus from £20 to £40 per adult and from £10 to £20 per child, but only 290 people (188 adults and 102 children) made use of it. Since the end of World War II only 750 Indians asked for the Government immigration subsidy.

Voluntary repatriation does not work. The legal pressure which is exerted on them through the laws of ethnic regrouping will not solve the problem of the Indians in South Africa either; even if it seems abnormal that, for example, in Athlone, where the Coloureds outnumber the Indians by 80 to one, the Indians possess 113 out of 121 commercial enterprises, what will happen to the 113 Indian traders when they are obliged to leave their present living places? I have been told that the economic development of the Bantu, and the Coloureds achieving commercial careers, would in any case remove the Indians from their semi-monopoly; but the ruin or the impoverishment of the Indians or the transposing of their problem to another place in South Africa, or to another field of human activity where they would perhaps excell owing to their dynamic qualities, and from which they would once again have to be dislodged—are they solutions?

What is the solution?

Can the Indians of South Africa continue to exist without an adequate recognition of their South African existence in the political sphere?

Much more imagination is certainly needed than in the case of the Bantu and the Coloureds, and perhaps the solution of "the Indian problem" is to be found more on the other side of the Indian Ocean than on the coast of Natal. Perhaps an economically-developed India, free from the spectre of famine, will exert the same attraction for the three million Indians who settled outside the mother country, as the neighbouring continents where bread was to be found, exerted up till now. Perhaps, then, the Indian immigrants will go back to the mother country who will no longer be a stepmother obliged to defend the portion given to her hungry children. In the meantime, whether these prospects are real or not, one has to hope for more freedom and for more rights to be granted to the Indians as to all the other inferior "castes" of the racial mosaic of South Africa. But if rights are essentially a reward for duties, have not the Indians of South Africa, to the extent to which they see themselves as South Africans, a duty to incline their double loyalty more towards the country they live in today?

CHAPTER 9

SOUTH AFRICA AND THE WIND
OF CHANGE

*For better or for worse, the old
Africa has gone, and the White
man must face the situation which
he himself created . . .*

General J. C. Smuts

I

Tense as South Africa's internal situation is, her international
position is even more tense and dramatic. In a study limited to the
problem of the Bantu, I have no intention of examining all the
international difficulties that the Republic has to face, but I will try
to isolate those elements which stem from the policy of apartheid.

I am convinced that the problems of the coloured races in South
African can be solved. When the problems have been solved, all the
secondary effects of this infectious sore which to-day poisons the
South African way of life, both internally and externally, will
gradually disappear: the conflict with Great Britain about Basutoland, Swaziland and Bechuanaland; the conflict with the United
Nations on the administration of South-West Africa; the more
general conflict with the rest of Black Africa, and the moral gap
between South Africa's racial philosophy and the more liberally
inclined philosophy of the free world.

A list drawn up in 1959 of the White diplomatic representatives
accredited in Africa shows that the U.S.A. had nine ambassadors on
the continent, 11 consuls general, nine consuls or vice-consuls, and
11 press attachés. Great Britain had seven ambassadors, nine consuls
general, 14 consuls and vice-consuls. South Africa had one Minister
in Cairo, two High Commissioners (in Salisbury and Nairobi) three
consuls general, and only one consul. Since the wave of African
independence which marked the years 1960 and 1961 the differences
in diplomatic representation have become even more noticeable.
The gap has widened. A South African journalist, Mr. W. van

Heerden, was right in saying that "for White South Africans this is undoubtedly a tremendous adjustment, this transition from three hundred years of Western and White domination, from an Africa under Western masters, to a continent of free Black and White people who have to deal with one another as equals."*

The limited number of South African diplomats in the free countries of Africa shows that the transition has not been accomplished. The Republic has not yet assimilated this new Africa, which is contrary to its traditions, and the new Africa has not agreed to live on good terms with a "racialist" state—or even with a White state which stands too clearly for the political hierarchy of yesterday.

The Republic has, of course, a clear African policy, and one which clearly defines its desire for friendship with the new states of the continent. My visit to the Commission for Technical Co-operation in Africa South of the Sahara convinced me that the South Africans are not just paying lip service to a policy, but are actively participating in a series of concrete programmes of Pan-African interest, including the Inter-African Bureau for Animal Health, the Inter-African Tsetse Fly and Trypanosomiasis Permanent Bureau, the Inter-African Pedological Service, the Inter-African Committee on the Mechanization of Agriculture, etc. South Africa is certainly doing her duty in all these fields, and bears her share of the heavy burden of the White man.

But apart from these fields of work, the political no man's land is widening between Pretoria and Accra, Pretoria and Leopoldville, Pretoria and the 20 other new capitals.

In the Africa of yesterday, South Africa had direct relations only with Southern Rhodesia and Mozambique. The rest of the continent was for her a series of "possessions", with primitive populations, subordinate, barely productive, only useful for manual work. South Africa thought along the same lines as the rest of Europe (a continent of which she is in so many ways an integral part) that after centuries, these peoples would perhaps reach a high level of civilization and political consciousness. But within the six short years (six years and not 60 or 600) between 1939 and 1945 the Africa of yesterday changed into a completely new continent, where one could

*The study of reports on Africa and South Africa by W. van Heerden from which I have taken several of the ideas found in this chapter, appeared in the *Journal of Racial Affairs* (S.A.B.R.A.), October, 1959.

already foresee the growth of the future independent African states. Overnight, South Africa found herself in a completely new situation: she had only had contact with the "possessions" through the great European capitals; this contact was now severed and it had to be replaced by direct bilateral relations with the suddenly emancipated "savages", or otherwise she would find herself without contact, that is to say, in the awkward situation of being a kind of political backwater at the extreme tip of the continent. In other words, she had to stop being what she had always been—a European state in Africa— and become an African state among other African states, or be a foreigner and condemn herself to isolation.

Has she done this? South Africa has certainly acted as a conscious and praiseworthy African state when, together with other African nations, she studied the problems of the distribution of water which thirsty Africa needs so much, and the problem of the fishing-industry which could supply the necessary proteins for a continent which has been hungry for 3,000 years. In South Africa people think that this is enough. "South Africa has a policy," Mr. E. H. Louw, Minister of Foreign Affairs, stated to me without hesitation, "of friendship and co-operation with all African countries. We have given proof of our sincerity through the technical and scientific aid which we have provided. We are an African state and our 'colonists' have been rooted in the soil as solidly and for as long a time as the Bantu." Four years earlier, Mr. Louw had told the students of Pretoria: "We must act in such a way that the Union is accepted by the other states and territories of Africa as their link with the Western world." But South Africa has completely failed in this policy; she has *not* been accepted.

Quite the contrary, Black Africa is at daggers drawn with South Africa. Of course one must not think of Black Africa, in its present state, as a monolithic block—no more than of the "Arab world", which is just a mosaic of conflicts. The countries of Africa, although allies in the struggle against those colonial powers who refuse to abdicate, have their problems and dissensions. Morocco has her Mauritanian problem, Egypt her Sudanese problem, Ethiopa her Erytrian problem. Mali has broken up. Nigeria is likely to break up. The Congo is divided into Kasai, Katanga and Kivu, and the former unity has not been restored. A united Maghreb will have its Sahara problem. But, in spite of all these existing or potential

211

divisions, the African giant is united against the Black policy of South Africa. Ghana has instituted a boycott of all South African goods which will cause the Republic a loss of three million pounds a year in exports of machines, and £800,000 in exports of tinned fish. In 1960, Ghana demanded that South Africans in transit through Accra sign a declaration directed against their own Government. To do so would be degrading and (quite rightly) expose them to complications at home. Other countries have joined in the boycott. On top of this came South Africa's voluntary withdrawal from the Commonwealth in 1961. If this had not happened, she would in any case probably have been expelled at the instigation of the Black members of the former British Empire.

South Africa holds that her policy of apartheid is really directed towards "parallel development", that is to say, towards the promotion of the Bantu; and that her policy of discrimination is an internal affair. To support this stand she invokes the Charter of the United Nations which forbids any interference in the affairs of member states. But for the new Africa which takes the broad view, as befits its vast spaces, the future of the Bantu in the Republic is just that: an "internal" affair of the *continent*, which some of its leaders are already dreaming of unifying. And can one really blame them for refusing to accept a policy which would not allow the Ambassador of Ghana or the Congo or Mauritania—because he is black—to meet whom he likes, to shake hands with whom he wants, a policy which makes him run the risk of being arrested on some caprice? Such an envoy would only be able to enter a café owing to a clause which exempts diplomats from discriminatory laws.

It is true that South Africa is not really vulnerable to this boycott. At present only one per cent of her external trade is affected by Ghana's and Malaya's boycott. Gold, uranium, diamonds and wool cannot be boycotted effectively: the world needs them too much. And in the case of a more severe boycott, South Africa, with a certain complacency, envisages finding the necessary remedy in a new stage of industrialization exactly as she did during the Second World War. But she is nonetheless being cold-shouldered—and by the nations which count most for her: the nations of Africa.

What are the possibilities of this hostility developing into a real threat in a more effervescent Africa, an Africa, for example, where not only a Nasser reigns in the North, but also two or three

Lumumbas elsewhere, launching out together in a new adventure? In Africa the Republic has the reputation of being a strong country. The Mau-Mau, during their revolt, never attacked the farms of the Afrikaners in Kenya: the defeats inflicted by the Boers on the valiant Zulu warriors are still alive in all African memories. In case of physical aggression the White South African nation would retaliate with all the force at its command, but one must still consider such an eventuality in the list of actual and potential conflicts in which the Republic is involved.

The *Revue Liberale* envisaged this in its study of the question published in March, 1960.

"Everywhere in Black Africa," wrote Charles Leopold Mayer, "one must expect struggles between the extremists and populations which are ordinarily more or less passive. After these struggles the extreme nationalists will more often than not be victorious, whether through terror and rigged ballots, or by peaceful means; in any case, terrorism and popular enthusiasm will join hands to silence those who hesitate, those who are more reasonable. Whoever predicted the success of a Hitler in 1920, would have been regarded as a crazy prophet. However, what might have seemed impossible with a people as cultured, as reasonable in its habits as the German people, need not be regarded as impossible amongst the masses of Africans, still half-barbarian and endowed with only a limited measure of critical intelligence. How can one be sure that the Blacks of Ghana, or the Cameroons, or the Congo, will not form a vast confederation under the leadership of Sekou Touré or another, and that, spurred on by this display of power and by the enthusiasm which their leaders would arouse in them, they would not undertake a racial crusade against South Africa?

"Amongst the new states, born from what until recently was French colonial territory, and now under the guidance of remarkable men such as Sekou Touré in Guinea, a powerful Black confederation will be built up whose motto will be 'Unite for the Defence of all the Blacks.' It will be a rallying cry which will have to be accepted willy-nilly by the lukewarm sympathizers, the frightened and those who otherwise would specifically be denounced in Africa and pilloried by all the Blacks as collaborators and traitors . . .

"The secret ideal of several African leaders is to turn Black Africa into a vast and powerful confederation, setting out with a popular

213

theme in which the old feelings of racial inferiority will be stirred up freely. The Black confederation of Central Africa will very soon come into violent conflict with the Union of South Africa. What would the role of France be in such a conflict? This is an extremely embarrassing question because one need not be a prophet to see that part of French public opinion would support a vast movement of rebellion and an *open struggle of the Blacks in South Africa and Rhodesia and Nyasaland against the Union of South Africa*, whose policy of apartheid would be attacked by the majority of people in Britain and the United States as the cause of all the evil . . .

"One man only, Hitler, was capable of obtaining the support of, and indoctrinating, millions of people. If that could be done with the German people, who are no more bloodthirsty than their neighbours in the Western world, how can one imagine, and I ask you to think seriously about my question, that this situation could not recur with millions of Africans or Asiatics, that a new Black or Yellow Hitler could not use magic words to stir up strife, in the name of a desire to revenge the past, in the name of equal possession of the goods of this world? What a wonderful motive for a new crusade of Blacks, united under one leader in a vindictive attack to the sound of drums . . ."

But if something like this were to happen, if a Lumumba mentality should transform central Africa into a springboard for aggression, could South Africa depend upon the unconditional support of the West? The Middle East, the "soft underbelly of Europe", as it has been rightly called, is vulnerable to the dictatorship of Nasser-like régimes, and yet this did not deter the West from leaving its only democratic bridgehead, Israel, unprotected against the raids and the boycotts of the Arabs; and they disarmed Israel when she tried to push the Arabs from the Sinai and to break the blockade in the Gulf of Elath.

South Africa rightly believes that she is the "underbelly" of Europe in Africa. This was shown at the time when the Suez Canal was closed and the old route around the Cape of Good Hope had to be used. In case of violent political conflict, when the Suez Canal will again be closed, in case of war, South Africa would once again become the only half-way station to East-West traffic. But the West, which is pinning its hopes on peaceful co-existence, is likely in the coming years to conciliate the régimes in the new Africa, through appeasement, concessions, and sacrifices, as it did in the case of Nasser: it pays to be Lumumba and to send "volunteers" and "suicide fighters" to massacre and to plunder. Dictatorships, provided that they are Arab, have the unconditional support of certain nations at the United Nations, and tomorrow, perhaps, one will only need to be Black in order to benefit from the same privileges . . .

Prof. C. W. de Kiewiet, a South African at the University of Rochester, U.S.A., drew valid conclusions from these prospects. "World opinion is against us," he said to me in Durban. "Destiny is marching to the borders of South Africa. It will cross them in ways unseen, and we cannot prevent it. The pressure which is being exerted on our northern neighbour, the Federation of Rhodesia and Nyasaland, is increasing with the growth of Ghana, Nigeria, the Congo, Tanganyika.

"There, too, a White minority holds the reins of power. But we can hear the Federation cracking—and for us it is a very disagreeable sound. We must envisage the collapse of our neighbour. Probably Southern Rhodesia will, for some time, be saved from ruin, and she will turn to us. Then the Zambezi will become the dividing line between White supremacy and Black supremacy. And one day the Zambezi will be replaced by the Limpopo, which is our northern border . . ."

II

But the deepest and least perceptible conflict, which is also the one least likely to be solved, is the conflict between South Africa and Asia on a level which is neither political nor ideological but simply biological.

When one speaks of Africa, in no matter what respect, Asia has to be taken into account.

First of all Asia Minor.

Asia Minor has left a deep mark on Africa through the Arab conquest of Northern Africa, the deep penetration of Islam and the establishment of its slave trading stations along the whole eastern facade of the continent, from the Delta of the Nile right down to the Cape of Good Hope.

The impact of Asia on the African continent is much older still than the infiltration of Islam. The archeologist Professor Raymond

Dart has attempted to prove that none of the aboriginal peoples of Africa invented its meagre cultural equipment and its techniques, however primitive they were. The Bushmen's bow and arrow, his rock paintings, his weapons of stone, and his skill in making fire, the Hottentot's cattle and dogs, his weaving techniques, his whole mythology, the Bantu's fishing equipment, his hollowed-out log canoes, his domesticated animals, his pottery, his assegais, his hoe and even his huts—all this is owed to Asia. The natives of Africa did not themselves discover the technique of basketwork, the art of smelting iron for weapons and tools; they did not build the stone terraces and temples whose ruins are to be found in Tanganyika, Rhodesia and the Transvaal; the great towns along the East Coast of Africa, Sofala, Kilwa, Zanzibar, Mombasa, Malindi, the urban centres along the caravan route in Western Africa, all were built by the traders in slaves, gold and ivory to serve as relay stations. During the thousand years between the fall of Carthage and the colonization of Africa by Europe in modern times, the most intense activity on this continent was the trade in its sons, its ivory and its gold for export to Asia.

Compared with this impregnation by Asia, European presence in Africa seems superficial. During the greater part of the history of Europe, its conquerors and traders by-passed Africa. It was in order to establish a simple half-way house between Europe and the Far East that the Dutch established a base at the Cape, and not to settle colonists there. It is because of its strategic importance, and in no way because of its hinterland, that the Cape was a stake in the struggles between the great Powers. Is it not significant that for 150 years the Cape was governed from an Asian town, Batavia, the headquarters of the Dutch East India Company?

Africa has never been "old" European land. Once the continent has been finally decolonized, Europe will have only the memory of a brutal and, moreover, clumsy occupation. The mercenary and mercantile nineteenth century was never either delicate or impassioned. Twentieth-century Europe, turning away from its civilizing mission in pursuit of intellectual and technological adventures, perpetuated the mistake of the nineteenth century in its attitude to Africa; and so Africa will turn, as before, to the most demonstrative suiter—and Europe, for the time being, is no longer eligible.

This suitor is Asia.

Asia is the power of tomorrow. Asia means half the world, half of humanity. We, Europeans, do not realize that Africa will recognize in her—as soon as Europe withdraws—the master of former times . . . Western Asia has already made its mark on Africa through the political influence of Islam on its masses and through its conferences, whether they are held at Casablanca, Accra or Cairo.

It is not only Mediterranean Africa with its millions of Moslems of ancient lineage, but Black Africa which has been Islamized. Half the population of Nigeria (thirty million) are Moslems; so are two-thirds of the Sudanese, a third of the Ethiopians, and all the Somalis. Even in Tanganyika there are one and a half million Moslems, and there are already 250,000 in Mozambique. The simple principles of Islam are very attractive to the Bantu. Islam does not discriminate on the basis of colour. Missionaries also think that the most important reason for its success lies in the fact that Islam has no competitive sects and churches (as in the case of the Christians), each preaching doctrines which to the non-initiated seem to differ fundamentally.

But Islam is not the only "tradesman" of Asian philosphies in Africa.

Eastern Asia, a giant felled by secular hunger and nourished by the ideal of resurrection, is rising to its feet, and as its sun rises towards the zenith a disproportionately bigger and bigger shadow falls over the West. With its 650 million Chinese, its 96 million Japanese, its 350 million Indians, Asia has already established its vanguard—its hard-working and rapidly-growing populations—in Kenya, in Tanganyika, in Rhodesia and South Africa.

In 1921 there were 142,000 Indians in South Africa. They increased to 365,000 by 1951. In Tanganyika there were 9,000 in 1925 and 56,000 in 1952. In Kenya, they increased from 23,000 in 1921 to 150,000 in 1956. They control ninety-five per cent of the retail trade in East Africa. There are 750,000 in the whole of Africa south of the Sahara. They have an unswerving loyalty to their motherland and can act the Trojan horse, for good or bad, in their adopted countries.

These statements do not imply any political stand. It is quite certain that Asia can free herself from her dreadful distress. In 1947 the annual national per capita income was £470 in the U.S.A.,

£244 in Britain, £8 10s. in China, £12 in India and £13 in Indonesia. In other words, the chances that a Chinese would not have enough to eat, would die of cold or would succumb to a simple infection due to lack of medical attention, were then fifty times greater than for an American. Indeed, the average life-span is 69 years in Britain, 32 in Java, 30 in China, and 27 in India.

"Asia is the land of hunger," notes Josue de Castro. "No other social fact has conditioned human behaviour so radically as the chronic and collective hunger of the Far East."

Drastic agrarian reforms, radical modernization of agriculture, vast irrigation schemes will naturally bring some relief. But India notes with distress how her progress in food-production is immediately cancelled out by the increase in her population—four million a year. China has an excess birth rate of ten million a year. Until now only their death rate, the highest in the world, has saved India and China from complete catastrophe. But thanks to progress and international aid, this rate is rapidly declining. Where will India and China find the *Lebensraum* for their breath-taking expansion? The Western world is exhausting its energy in acquiring more freedom, more wealth. Will it have to fight tomorrow simply for its right to breathe? After China will have spread out towards the south-east and towards the vast continental spaces of Soviet Asia where Russia has no *biological* right, where will she turn to?

There is virgin Africa—Africa which no longer belongs to its former masters, which barely belongs to its fragile masters of today—with its uncultivated vastnesses, its sparse population, and its buried and unexploited wealth. Can Asia keep her mind off this land of Cockaigne for long, even if she wanted to?

In 1919 the East African Indian Congress decided to ask the League of Nations and Britain, who was the mandatory power in Tanganyika, to reserve this territory for Indian immigration. In 1946 the Indian Parliament discussed the possibility of inviting the Government to negotiate with Britain about the transfer of the mandate to India. In the same year Sir Maharaj Singh recalled to his compatriots that sixty-seven per cent of the inhabitants of Mauritius were Indians, and he added: "I firmly believe that Mauritius will become, in the present generation, a colony of India."

These statements are moderate and reasonable. They point to the tacit conflict, the battle of shadows wedged day after day as the population of the biggest third of the "third world" increases, as the disproportion between the two continents, now neighbours, is emphasized, as greed grows.

South Africa, an El Dorado, the richest, the best equipped and the most generously endowed country on the continent, is the symbol of the prize to be won. It is a logical objective.

But if the Government of Pretoria should open its unexploited spaces to the peaceful and fruitful invasion of the nine million Bantu who are vegetating within its frontiers, it can perhaps forestall a less peaceful invasion than biology is preparing for it.

Perhaps it can also, and must—in this land where its interests are intertwined with those of the Governments of Addis Ababa, Leopoldville and Accra—form a pacific African front to oppose Asia in pacific competition, in pacific co-existence: a front of development, repopulation, and exploitation of these enormous resources which will disallow the obviously legitimate claim which otherwise, and sooner or later, the thousand million Chinese and Indians will put forward against this underdeveloped, undeveloped, unexploited and spoiled continent. For Africa not only belongs to the Africans: it belongs to humanity.

CHAPTER 10

THE CREATIVE WITHDRAWAL

I

What can be done in practice?

I am convinced that the only way of avoiding a violent clash which would decide whether the Whites or the Blacks are to be the masters of the country, is to stake everything on real, vertical apartheid. Apartheid must be taken to its logical conclusions, because negative apartheid, with its endless period of incubation, only causes suffering and disappointment to the present generation of Blacks, while it holds out to the present generation of Whites the hope of a reprieve which blunts their political consciousness—and their conscience. Apartheid must be applied honestly because, if apartheid were only discrimination without any partition of the country, it would be a fraud, a dangerous ideology, a delirious racialist camouflage, and it should be fought until all its protagonists are defeated. The Black man in South Africa is not interested in freedom, in dignity and in political rights for generations to come. The White man in South Africa is not justified in enjoying the exorbitant rights he has over the Blacks, and there is no reason why he should leave the bill to be paid by future generations. Consequently the men of the present generation must solve their problems and settle their accounts.

There is no room for half-measures.

Certain Whites think that the Bantu will accept pseudo-independence in the form of eternal under-aged satellites of the mother country. They will not.

The following words appear on the base of Dr. Nkrumah's statue in Accra: *Seek ye first the political kingdom, and all other things shall be added unto it.* This is the new law of Africa, and South Africa will not be able to break it.

Other Whites, again, think the problems of South Africa are unique, and that experience and truth from the other side of the Limpopo or from Europe are not valid between the 22nd and the

35th parallel. They are also making a mistake. Race and colour have ceased to be the distinguishing marks of a degree of civilization; an arbitrary classification according to these categories is anachronistic. The distances and the time which separate continents and civilizations are daily being reduced, and South Africa, which, in many ways, is still thinking along nineteenth century lines, must think, together with other great nations, of entering the twenty-first century, and must be careful not to miss the important road along which the African continent is travelling. Brutally thrown, barely ten years ago, into the cruel game of the struggle between the great Powers for world control (a game whose rules she does not yet know well) South Africa must learn that no alliance is automatic; that the U.S.A. sacrificed established French and Israeli moral and legal rights when they considered it necessary to appease Nasser; that her three million White citizens are not assured of unconditional aid in the case of a conflict with two hundred million Blacks.

Those responsible for South Africa's new deal, which must be put into practice *in the months to come*, have to recognize the irrational factor which governs the collective consciousness of peoples. The knowledge that we have of the history of the past, oversimplified by dogmatists and makers of systems, usually obscures this nonlogical aspect, and reduces the meanderings and the unexpected deep changes in the lives of nations to "laws" of cause and effect. The Whites would like the Blacks to "behave", to evolve slowly according to an evolutionary pattern. They would like them to understand for what reasons (and very cogent ones, too) the Black needs to be protected against a premature acquisition of independence. But against all logic the Black does not admit that political independence can only come after economic independence. To most countries of Africa the need for a flag was more important than the instinctive desire for a full stomach. This wind of change sweeping over the continent is one of those illogical events, unaccountable by the "laws" of history. It is as regrettable and as useless to the march of civilization as cancer is to the health of a human being. But nations, as well as individuals, must live with their bodies—and their diseases. A Cartesian demonstration will not convince the wave which is bursting its banks to run against the tide, nor will the eleven million Bantu in South Africa accept the many reasons which could necessitate temporization and a deceleration of the process of emancipation.

Consequently, complete vertical apartheid must be applied: the South Africans must have the courage of their convictions and cut the Gordian knot. Apartheid has for too long been a political platform, a philosophical excuse for inefficacious half-measures. Apartheid must be what it is in the mouth of its theoreticians and its advocates: the separate development of the two peoples, White and Black, the "creative withdrawal" of the Whites from the Black territories, the abdication of the master for the benefit of the servant.

Apartheid can only be a technique of enslavement or a technique of deliverance—the delivery of a new-born child to the reality of life. Nationalism is a factor of disorder only when it is thwarted. Steam seeks an outlet and dynamite is dangerous only under pressure. If nationalism is canalized and given space to realize itself, it is a vital force which urges peoples on towards their mutual and profitable destiny.

II

The engine must be started. Starting is the trickiest but the most decisive operation. When a plane is started, great care is taken because the point of no return is 2000 yards from the point of departure: one either takes off or one crashes. Everything depends on the starting power. For the moment, South Africa has lazily begun to fiddle with the starter of a cold engine, without seeming to realize that there is no fuel in the tank. And yet so much fuel is needed in order to pass the point of no return.

As long as the potential Bantu states remain tied to the mother Republic, an unhealthy period of gestation is prolonged, and unfortunately nature cannot here impose an obligatory end to the birth pangs: we are in the completely irrational domain of history and not the comparatively rigorous domain of physiology.

South Africa must have the courage to cut into the living flesh of the country and to declare the independence of the Bantu states, implicitly contained in the six territorial or ethnic authorities which have been set up or provided for in the Reserves: the territorial authority of the Transkei, the ethnic authority of the Zulus, the ethnic authority of the Sotho in the north, the ethnic authority of the Tswana, the territorial authority of the Venda and the ethnic authority of the Tsonga. The frontiers of these states must be generous. The map of the reserves in the Republic today resembles a map of Germany in the eighteenth century with its countless fiefs, counties, duchies and free towns, arbitrarily thrown together. The Reserves have territorial continuity only in the Transkei, where great stretches of unified Bantu land are to be found. Not only must the so-called "White spots" be integrated into the Reserves; the boundaries of these future republics must also be enlarged so as to give them the completeness that true countries have on maps. They should form a horseshoe, open to the south-west, which will surround the remaining White South Africa from the frontier of Bechuanaland to Natal, and along the frontiers of the Federation and Mozambique. Whether these Bantustans federate between themselves, or whether each one federates itself separately with the Republic, or whether they all federate with the Republic, is irrelevant.

I think that such a federation has a very strong chance of coming off. But it must not be the condition, that is to say, the prerequisite, to independence.

The solution by partition is the only realistic and moral one. Marriage is an example of co-existence in its most obvious form; but without the possibility of divorce—in spite of all the difficulties of separation—it would be slavery.

Partition is the answer for human groups whose sentimental—and therefore irrational—aspirations diverge. Separate development (whether through violence, or resulting from the creative retreat of one of the parties) has solved most conflicts in history, including very recent ones. For a long time Scandinavia was one country with one king and one government. But the Danes, the Swedes and the Norwegians never lived in peace with each other until the territory in which they lived was divided into three states. A country cannot contain several nations: the Danes did not want the Swedes to govern them, the latter did not want Norwegian masters. Apartheid brought peace, only that word was not used. Since then they have lived together in harmony, their battle-scarred history forgotten . . .

Other conflicts of our time spring to the mind. On the Indian sub-continent a million victims had to suffer before partition brought peace between Hindu India and Moslem Pakistan. In

Korea hundreds of thousands of soldiers fell before partition separated the country along the 24th Parallel. The same thing happened in Indo-China. In the Middle East new countries have sprung up through partition: Israel and Jordan. Can one be sure that the Algerian problem will not eventually be solved by geographical partition?

III

Partition does not merely involve the division of the country. A series of practical measures, conceived and carried out with imagination, must give life and substance to the new bodies which will be detached from the mother-Republic. Soon after birth, a child is infinitely more vulnerable, infinitely less viable, than in its previous condition of osmosis with the mother-body. But pregnancy must lead to birth; it has no other purpose.

Positive apartheid must be introduced. There has been enough talk. Once this policy is implemented, the Bantu states must be made as attractive as possible, for it is imperative that the Bantu states should attract the Blacks in the Republic.

Mr. Thomas Boydell, that ingenious "ambassador" for South Africa, said to me in the courtyard of the Cape Town castle, facing the sculptured eaves supported on their wooden columns—a delightful piece of seventeenth century Holland under a Riviera sun—"What we call the South African nation has been built with the help of Bantu labour. What harm is there in our helping the Bantu to build their own nation? The Bantu cannot do it alone. They do not know how. But if we do not help them to build their state they will one day take ours, as the Indonesians did to the Dutch . . ."

Mr. Boydell gave that mischievous smile which has endeared him to crowds on several continents.

"Many of our people say that our economy will not stand the blow, that it is irrevocably based on Black labour. But I say that is all to the good. We need a hard knock. When the Bantu begin their trek to their promised lands, those who remain in the mother Republic, Black and White, will have to double their productivity, and that will be a healthy thing. Statistics already show that our rate of production per head is one of the most mediocre in the world.

224

"Our agriculture will also have to be mechanized. We will concentrate less on extensive and more on intensive farming.

"We will have to rationalize our industries and to introduce automation.

"Instead of discouraging immigration as we do today, we will have to encourage it. We must do what Australia and New Zealand are doing. We must profit from the psychological effect overseas: once Bantustans are established, public opinion abroad will change overnight: we will become 'angels'. That is the moment when we will have to create a vast movement of White immigration. But, above all, we will have to be prepared to do a large part of the heavy work, the dirty work, which our 'boys' and our 'nannies' had to do for more than two centuries. There is a very simple way of achieving all this: double the salaries of the labourers and the semi-skilled workers. You will then automatically have White workers, South Africans or immigrants from Europe, wanting to replace the Blacks."

Very sound ideas indeed. They must form part of a psychological, social and economic master plan of decolonization and construction. The Tomlinson Report has not been implemented, but hundres of millions of pounds have been spent on the *integration* of the Bantu into the White towns, while the policy of "disintegrating" them was proclaimed. The time has come for deeds to be adjusted to official policy. Instead of bringing the Bantu to the towns, White South Africa must move the attractions and responsibilities of the towns to the Bantu territories. The Bantu have shown remarkable facility for adaptation among the Whites.

Once under way, the movement will gain an impetus of its own. But it must be set under way. The engine must be started!

Certain Whites still do not realize that it is their duty. It is not only their duty: it is in their interest. When a colonial power withdraws from a territory it leaves the new nation the dowry of the new state: the roads, the public buildings, all the state lands, all the invisible material and spiritual capital of the civilizing work that it has accomplished change hands overnight. There is no compensation except the satisfaction that the colonizing or guardian nation derives from having carried out its mission, its duty of having carried the heavy burden of the White man. Perhaps there is no greater glory for the White man, whatever the attacks, calumny and the bad faith, than the fact that he has carried so many and such

225

heavy burdens, on so many continents, in so many countries, and, on the whole, with decency and self-control. South Africa in its turn must endow the beginning of the Bantustans. Not having much to give as a dowry, as the Reserves are merely barren land, it must invent a practical and daring new formula for a huge transfer of capital to the Black community. A free gift would, anyway, only be justice. In a partitioned South Africa the jewels will remain in the hands of the Whites: the mines, the ports, the towns. The Blacks must receive compensation for this in the form of the initial capital for the industrialization of the reserves. This compensation is not only just, it is indispensable for the construction of the Bantustans.

And even if it were merely indispensable, without being just, it would have to be given, with a free hand and an open heart.

IV

Utopias?

I was bubbling with enthusiasm for these generous Utopias on the evening of my arrival in Pietersburg, the future capital of the Bantu nations in the Northern Transvaal. We were dining, my guide and myself, in the communal dining room of the Northern Hotel.

Pietersburg is a little town of pioneers. It breathes an outpost atmosphere. The hotel is close to the Post Office, a splendid building of the year 2000, like so many others in this country whose architects are far in advance of the most advanced ones in Europe. But I reacted violently when I saw the normal sign, *Slegs vir Blankes— Europeans Only*, indicating separate entrances for the two races in the heart of Pietersburg, the natural capital of the Bantu nation of the Northern Transvaal. I must confess that, in Johannesburg, these inscriptions had in the end left me unmoved. Keeping in mind the positive significance of apartheid, I obstinately wanted to see in it a temporary phenomenon. But until this first walk in Pietersburg on the evening of our arrival I had really believed that apartheid, which is a drawback to the Bantu in the White territories, would be to their advantage in the territories which are supposed to be theirs. I came down from the clouds with a bump!

If the apparatus of discrimination works against them in the heart of Bantu country, all that is being done, all that is going to be done, is drained of its psychological efficaciousness.

"It is today," I said to my guide, "that one must show the Bantu of Pietersburg that they are at home there. You tell them they are not in their own home in Johannesburg because their home is in the Reserves. All right. But in the Reserves you herd them into a location, you force a curfew and separate entrances on them, and they cannot enter this hotel! Well, I say they have no homes anywhere in South Africa until the day they enjoy in the Reserves *ali* those rights that you refuse them in your home . . ." I pointed to the notices in the post-office, and said: "I mean rights, not on paper, but in practice!"

My guide said nothing.

My reactions had been the same in Umtata, at the other end of the country, the capital of the future Bantustan of the Transkei. We were playing darts in the bar of the hotel; there was a separate counter for the Bantu. Beer was served there to the holders of special permits, and through the gap in a curtain that the barman sometimes moved when he was rinsing glasses, the Bantu customers darted a quick glance at us in our reserved room. I was very ill at ease.

A few hours earlier, in a big lounge of the hotel, we had been present at a reception given by the Commissioner-General, Mr. J. H. Abraham.

The only Bantu there were the waiters. Were there no important people—chiefs or high Bantu officials—to join a gathering of White magistrates, officials and V.I.P.s in the capital of their future state, the Transkei—the one furthest on the road to independence, the one which has a parliament, and M.P.s?

The laws of apartheid are the same in Umtata and in Pretoria! This is a state of affairs that I do not understand, that I do not want to understand. They told me that minds were not yet mature, that the people would not stand a radical change, that time was needed; I did not agree then, and I still do not agree. The hotel-keeper had put his personal office at my disposal to allow me to receive a few non-White people. There was no question of receiving them in my room or in a bar in Umtata! One of them, a Coloured man, Dr. T. Swartz, president of the Union Council for Coloured Affairs, fascinated me with his shrewd judgements. To the background of a noisy Viennese waltz from the floor above where the reception of the Commissioner-General was in full swing, I tried to make him express his bitterness at being excluded from this reception, and I apologized for receiving him in this borrowed office.

He told me he felt no bitterness.

"They cannot invite me to the reception. But I see the Bishop and the doctor. There are Whites who visit me. I do not care."

One of his daughters had passed as White before the introduction of identity cards.

"You see," (now there was not only bitterness in his voice, there was menace too) "what hurt me most, what, through me, hurts the whole community, are these words that a White said to me when my daughter was classified as a Coloured: '*You will see, everything will be all right one day. Our lower classes will end up by inter-marrying with the Coloureds and their children will pass the line.*'"

I thought of these *lower* classes of Whites who would one day condescend to intermarry with the Coloured people, perhaps with the daughters of Dr. Swartz, one of the most intelligent men I have ever met. And that evening at Umtata, the capital of the future Transkei state, I was ashamed of my White skin. For the first time in my life, I suddenly started to hate the colour of my skin, like a piece of clothing, unsuitable for the circumstance or torn or dirtied beyond all possible repair.

And now, the same experience in Pietersburg . . .

While we were dining, my guide pointed out to me Dr. W. M. Eiselen and his wife, sitting at the next table. I had already recognized him. He is a small, withdrawn man with rather deeply-sunk eyes, which have some charm, and that sad smile of men who live entirely for an inner ideal.

Dr. Eiselen is indeed a man of single purpose. He is the theoretician, the foremost intellectual of apartheid. He is a former secretary of Bantu Affairs. Politically speaking, he is one of Dr. Verwoerd's closest associates. It is said (but this cannot be verified) that he is one of the top men of the Broederbond, that free-masonry of the Afrikaner. Some critics of the Afrikaners, when speaking of Dr. Eiselen, compare him to Dr. Goebbels. In Johannesburg an intelligent friend said to me before I left for the north: "If you are going to Pietersburg you will see the *Gauleiter* of the Northern Province." At that stage I did not have much sympathy for Dr. Eiselen.

When dinner was nearly over, we made an appointment for the next day.

The following morning Dr. Eiselen received me in the big Bantu

Administration Buildings of Pietersburg. My first objection was going to be discriminatory legislation which affect the Bantu in their own territories. I was going to ask the Republic's "ambassador" to the Northern Sotho why it had not yet been abolished. To my great astonishment, Dr. Eiselen, without seeming to fear the publicity which I might give his statement, began to talk to me.

Coming from the great theoretician of apartheid, his statements assumed the value of a manifesto, and I considered them to be such, and I have implicit faith in them, and I believe, with presumption, naivety and pride, that they are binding on the government of South Africa, and I believe that they must be put into practice without delay by proclaiming the Bantustan of the Northern Sotho.

"The Government," Dr. Eiselen said to me, "would like to do precisely what you have said: give the Bantu full rights in the Reserves; but, my dear sir, you can't imagine the bitterness of our internal political struggles. The Opposition criticizes us when we put into practice what they demand in theory, that is to say, when we improve the lot of the Bantu. The farmers lose sight of our aim, they do not think ahead. When the State purchases land for the Bantu they say: Perhaps it is my farm that they are going to buy up to-morrow. Our people, even those who belong to my party, the Nationalists, the Afrikaners, only think of their daily comfort. They accept the theory. But at the same time they want comfort.

"Obviously a generous theory and unchallenged comfort are incompatible. Personally, I think that a beginning must be made in the Transkei. There are still 26 "white spots." They must be declared Bantu territory, and be purchased or exchanged. This must also be done in all the other Bantu areas. It is Government policy."

"How this is to be achieved?" I asked.

"Well, there is one thing we can do which will neither imperil our economy nor betray the justice that is due to both the Whites and to the Bantu: we must encourage the Bantu in the Reserves to take over the enterprises of the Whites. It may be said that the Bantu have neither capital nor experience. This is true. With regard to capital, the Government must supply it through the intermediary of our Bantu Development Corporation. This Corporation has a capital of £500,000. It is a token sum, of which only £150,000 has been spent. As for the experience, the Corporation could employ the dispossessed Whites to work as technicians and instructors.

The Corporation itself will act as a guardian of the Bantu community, as the World Bank does in the under-developed territories. When the Blacks have their own technicians they will take over."

I did not expect Dr. Eiselen to go as far, but he went further.

"At the same time that the Bantu are stimulated to acquire White undertakings, we must positively encourage the Whites to withdraw from the Black regions. This can be done by giving the Bantu social equality in the Reserves . . . Those Whites who do not want to see free Bantu around them will leave.

"One must not just prevent the Whites from buying land in the Reserves (which is our present policy). One must encourage their emigration."

Of course I entirely agree with all this. It is indispensable if one really wants to build the Bantustans.

The Europeans came to the historical regions of the Bantu for the same reasons that the Bantu came to those of the Whites: economic reasons. The Bantu are told they must cease to stream into the White country, or leave it for political reasons. Justice demands that the Whites leave the Bantu territory for the same reasons, and this creative withdrawal must be like a river, that leaves a fertile sediment when the waters retreat. The indispensable proof of good faith, in the context of the policy of apartheid, is to organize the handing over of power by abolishing discrimination and by removing job reservation throughout the Reserves. There the Whites must be the visitors that the Bantu are supposed to be in Johannesburg. There they must abdicate all their privileges and the signs in the post office of Pietersburg must be inverted . . .

The Government must have the courage to define the frontiers and to bring Bantustans into being. If the electorate is against it, let them say so, and they will bear the consequences. The test is necessary.

Ambiguity has lasted too long and the moment of truth has come.

v

To proclaim Bantustans is not enough. They must be made attractive. Dr. Eiselen said: "If they are not attractive, they will attract nobody."

That means political rights, which means independence.

The natural obligation fully to develop the Bantu states is evident.

South Africa must show the courage to go right to the end without waiting for the mass of the population to be transformed into a conscious electoral body. The era of electoral restrictions has come to an end because the printed word, the screen and television have made distances shrink. Modern techniques have completely changed international and internal politics. The secrets of chancelleries and ministries are discussed in buses and tearooms. De Gaulle speaks on television: this means that he personally explains to every Frenchman, comfortably seated in his armchair by his fireside, the details of his intentions. Khruschev takes off his shoe and hits his desk at the United Nations, and the whole world has a close-up of the scene. This popularization, this simplification of the ideas, the means, the making of politics allows one to consult millions of illiterates in Ghana and India and what is true for Ghana and India must be true for South Africa.

In Ghana, millions of primitives cast a vote by means of ballot papers that had pictures on them: Nkrumah's was a crowing cock. Nothing prevents South Africa from organizing a referendum of Blacks and Whites on the question of the Bantustans, by means of absolute universal and general suffrage, exactly as the Whites were consulted about the institution of a republic.

In addition one must grant the Blacks in the White towns and the countryside, where they form the bulk of the agricultural labour force, political rights which they have not got today.

These rights are refused to them and their representation in the central Parliament has been abolished in the name of a principle of which I approve: within the framework of parallel development this suppression could contribute to infuse political blood into the body politic of the Bantu. The Black leaders, who no longer have an outlet in the central institutions of South Africa, would find a natural outlet on the only institutions open to them: the administration and government of the Bantu States in the making. The British Empire, for similar reasons, never allowed territories destined to become autonomous to be represented in the parliament of the United Kingdom; this "discrimination", by turning away the indigenous élite from a metropolitan career, perhaps decisively encouraged the formation of administrative and political leaders in certain colonies.

But this deprival of rights within one public sector must corres-

231

pond with increasing rights in a sector where such rights could be exercized: in the field of real Bantu politics. If such a political domain is not called into existence, the withdrawal of rights is once again an abuse of authority; as Fouché said, "it is worse than a crime, it is a mistake". A national council, representative of the Bantu in the Republic and the Bantu in the Bantustans, must be established now.

As early as 1924, General Hertzog asked for the establishment of such a council. The Government was to discuss with it all questions dealing with Blacks. Progressive granting of legislative and executive powers to the Bantu administrations must be logically accompanied at all the intermediary stages by consultative rights. This cannot be honestly questioned. Because this "national council" would have powers limited to Bantu affairs, it is the very essence of the policy of apartheid to institute it. By granting the Bantu of the towns the right to vote for this council, one would solve the problem of their political muteness which it would be dangerous to prolong. By investing the Bantu in the towns and the Reserves with reciprocal consultative rights about their own affairs, one would emphasize and materialize the link between the Bantu in the Reserves and the towns.

The existence of such a link is an axiom of government Bantu policy. Why would one then hesitate to deduce the most obvious practical consequence of this axiom?

As early as 1936 Mr. Boydell, in one of his speeches to Parliament, imagined a mechanism of this type. "These public bodies," he said (speaking of the local district and provincial councils) "should be given limited powers at first; but they should gradually be extended as Natives show signs of political development and statesmanship, until at the top there is a responsible National body. This could co-operate with a corresponding body in the European political field. The National Native Assembly could have a select committee to meet a joint select committee from this and the other House to discuss matters of common interest. In this way you give the Natives a clearcut policy by which they can find political expression and aspire to political maturity. I do not want to take away the existing vote from the Natives in the Cape Province. I want to transfer it to their own body politic." These words are as valid today as they were twenty-five years ago. The problem of the creation of Bantustans

232

and of discriminatory laws are the typical problems of common interest between two communities. Is it conceivable that they should not be discussed together?

I repeat: discriminatory laws must be abolished. A state can use its power and the law (which is merely the opinion of a majority of voters) to dictate to citizens what their places of residence should be, to prevent them from doing the work they are able to do: a state has the power, but it never has the right to do so—if the state does this, an odium rests on it.

If this was the price the Bantu had to pay for their liberty and independence, it would be better for them to fight for it.

The whole series of discriminatory laws should be repealed. Not a single one should be kept. If the rhythm of Bantu development must be regulated, it can be done, and must be done, only with their consent, in agreement with their leaders.

As a compensation the Republic, after proclaiming its Bantu New Deal, will have the right to claim what she has claimed since the Act of Union in 1910: the inclusion of the High Commission Territories within the Black States.

It is logical and just that Basutoland, Swaziland and Bechuanaland should supplement the Bantu states, with which they are identical from all points of view. We have seen that their surplus populations are sent to South Africa: economically they would not exist without the industry of the Republic. They were set aside in 1910 under British guardianship because they already formed compact Black countries.

Dr. Eiselen said to me, quite rightly, on this subject:

"If there had been others as compact and as 'Black', they would have also been left outside the Union. When the Transkei achieves independence, Basutoland should be incorporated into it, Swaziland into Zululand, and Bechuanaland into the Northern Transvaal."

I cannot see for what reasons Britain would be opposed to a union whose territories would form an economic unit. A British-South African conference could define what guarantees of civil and political rights, of economic balance, of real independence should exist in Bantustans, so that fusion would be automatic.

Such a Declaration of Transfer would certainly encourage South Africa to grant her "colonies" their new status.

It has been said that if one formulated the problem of the Bantu in South Africa with daring, it is simply a problem not of knowing whether there will be Bantustans or not, but whether the Republic of South Africa will in the long run be one big Bantustan, or whether the White or mixed regions will remain White territory. The warning contained in this formulation of the problem should cause all politicians in South Africa—and all South Africans—to think seriously about the drama that is unfolding before their eyes, because if today they still hold the power to canalize events towards one of the terms of the alternative, for how long will there still be an alternative? Already South Africa is behind the rest of Africa. Changes have taken place on this continent much more rapidly than was foreseen. In 1939 the majority of the English responsible for the destiny of the Empire based their policy on five centuries of peace in certain African colonies. Most of these colonies today send delegates to the United Nations. In 1945 the Belgian Minister for Colonies thought there were 30 years left before the political future of the Congo would become a problem. All these calculations, and many others, have shown themselves to be false.

By what strange aberration do people in South Africa imagine that time south of the Zambezi will pass more slowly than in the north? South Africa must keep in step with the rest of Africa because the choice is not between revolution and evolution, but between revolution and revolutionary evolution.

This means that the development of the Bantustans must be accelerated. They must be accelerated as much as possible. It is true that independence cannot be improvised. A culture can no more be incalculated to a people through accelerated techniques, than one can cultivate a field at any other rhythm than the rhythm once and forever dictated by nature. The Bantu say *hamba kahle*— go slowly—and the Whites seem to have taken this as their motto. And from time immemorial, the rhythms of Africa have been those of the camel, the ox and the canoe. The Boers have a thousand reasons for preserving the gracious art of living which they practise with so much refinement in their beautiful white houses with their gabled roofs in the Cape. They make a sort of cult of the rhythms of the ox-wagons of their ancestors. But in the era of the supersonic aeroplane, South Africa has given itself the symbol of the springbok and should thus move at a different pace.

"Within three generations," Anton Rupert had said to me, one of the most "internationalist" South Africans, the most lucid that I have met, "a letter from Europe took seven months, then seven weeks, then seven days to reach us. Soon it will take seven hours. How can we neglect this challenge?"

Must the farewell message that President Kruger addressed to his country before leaving it to go into exile—"take from the past what is good therein, and build the future on these foundations"—be interpreted as an appeal to immobile conservatism or as an invitation to action? Did not the "conservative" Kruger have a medal struck to honour the first motor-car driver in his Republic, and was he not the first in the world to buy the patent of the submarine? Is not his message one of revolution? Is the past a tyrant who pronounces fatal verdicts, or the wisest of teachers?

Indeed, if timing and rhythm are not taken into account, all is lost in South Africa. Even the most attractive Bantustans, the most honest "decolonization" within fifty years, within five years (perhaps within five months), could come too late. The very significant example of the Congo, thrown into independence and anarchy, will be raised as an objection. But the example of the Congo, which clearly shows what must not be done, shows that last-minute concessions bring only catastrophic results. The psychologists know that groups are motivated by psychology in the same way as an individual. When a child wants a toy, and it is not given to him at once, the child begins to cry. When finally the toy is surrendered, he furiously throws away what he was crying for a minute ago. He takes time to calm down. Sometimes, in his rage, he breaks the object he wanted so much. It is necessary, therefore, to act *now*. One must give the Bantu who are claiming rights their full rights in the Bantustans; otherwise, under physical pressure, either internal or external, the Bantustans in the Reserves will no longer suffice.

It is not here just a point of historical justice to be satisfied.

The coldest and the most selfish calculations should move the South African Government to accelerate everything that can be accelerated in this direction. The present policy of *laissez-faire* is disastrous. A slow and gradual progress in the Reserves cannot but increase the desires of the Bantu and magnify their claims for more products and services and for higher salaries; and thus discontent will grow, and so will pressure be increased by the exodus towards the White regions.

The nature and the quality of the context must be changed: not simply the quantity that is given. The gap is widening more and more.

Every aspect of progress made by White and Bantu adds to the difference. When the Whites get television, and the Bantu have money to buy radios, there will be something more that the Bantu will not have, which they will want, which they have a right to. In a ministerial office in Pretoria somebody spoke to me of 25 years. And what if in 25 years the average White is to spend his holidays on the moon? Will one have to use the 1985 counterpart of the Saracens which took me through Cato Manor, to prevent the Bantu from reaching the moon? The relative progress of the Bantu must go faster than the progress of the Whites, the gap must be closed instead of being widened. Slow progress and gradation are not virtues in themselves. If a revolution can be accomplished through methods which do not involve injustice, hardship, intimidation, and lying, its speed has advantages. Is it not significant that in the Soviet revolutionary tradition a sympathizer who is slow to understand is likened to an enemy?

Before World War II the absolute *laissez-faire* attitude which prevailed in the South African political mentality took no account of the time factor in the evolution of the racial problem. It is certain that the rise of the Afrikaner people to the responsibilities of power and their awareness of the necessities of a solution can prevent South Africa from being a victim of the tumultuous awakening of the African giant.

But one must then rapidly adapt oneself and if man has been able—with the help of technology, will-power and necessity—to adapt his body without harm to the terrifying accelerations of supersonic speeds, then one must have faith in the idea that political processes are capable of acceleration. Through this faith techniques will be discovered.

VII

This cannot be achieved slowly, nor can one lull oneself with the illusion that heavy sacrifices will not be necessary. It has been said that a flag is but a rag nailed to a piece of wood; but it is the most expensive thing in the world. The White people in South Africa must learn to agree (and very quickly: tomorrow is now) to material sacrifice in order to build on a gigantic scale, and at the pace we have just described, the Bantustans it owes to the Bantu.

The White people in South Africa believe they do not owe anything to the Bantu. It is an illusion. The great mine dumps in Johannesburg and on the Rand, which are often called the biggest manmade monuments in the world, come from the sweat of generations of Black miners who have torn them out of the entrails of the earth.

One must now give them durable compensation; and the White farmers of Umtata and Pietersburg who organize protest meetings "to ask the Native Trust Fund not to buy more land for the Bantu in the district", are making a big mistake. Dr. Verwoerd is not a "Nigger-lover" when he wants to take from the Whites—timidly—a little money to finance Bantu development. Perhaps a Verwoerd with an imagination ten times more dynamic is necessary in order to take ten times as much from them.

The Whites of South Africa have not yet understood that in any case, whether they choose integration between Black and White or separate development, they will have to foot the bill: by the final liquidation of the right of Whites to dispose of themselves, by the loss of their identity, and by the loss of their survival as a nation if they choose integration between Black and White; by heavy financial sacrifices if they choose to buy a state for the Blacks who have built their country. They have not yet understood that they must attack the problem of the construction of Bantustans as an all-out war effort; they have not yet been forced to practise what they preach in their numerous churches, to practise the precept that there is no life without sacrifice and no victory without the burden of a cross.

But above all the White people of South Africa are also, because of their opulent existence, used to thinking that they haven't the means to making such a sacrifice.

This is the most dangerous illusion, because it clears their conscience, because it allows them to think and to say that they want to, but that they cannot. It is an objection which makes someone from Europe smile.

Because when something must be done, one can always do it. All my South African friends should think about the anecdote told by the great missionary, Dr. Samuel Zwemer. He was looking at a little Black girl crossing the road in front of a policeman. On her back she was carrying another child, bigger than herself.

"What a burden," said the policeman admiringly.

"Master," she replied, "he is no burden, he is my brother."*

Yet, the Whites in South Africa are far from carrying a heavy burden on their shoulders.

The Whites of South Africa have at their disposal a comfortable margin which would enable them to make the sacrifice. Like that of the Americans, their standard of living is one of the highest. In 1959, a group of Swiss (yes, Swiss) journalists called South Africa "the coffer of the world". She produces more than half the world's gold, more than half its diamonds (and she could produce even more), the coalbeds are so close to the surface of the soil that the cost of exploitation is the lowest in the world, and coal reserves are considered to be sufficient to last for two thousand years. The reserves of very high-grade iron ore come to 122 million tons. Its wool is the best; sugar, fruit, wine and wood are abundant. With salaries higher than the corresponding salaries in France, the White South African pays the equivalent of four new francs per kilo for the best meat, two new francs for a dozen grapefruit, 2.5 new francs for a 20-kilo pocket of oranges, 70 new francs as the monthly wage of a servant, five new francs for a good meal. In France, the price would be 18 new francs for the meat, 30 new francs for the grapefruit, at least 30 new francs for the oranges, 300 new francs for the wage and 15 new francs for the meal. It is no exaggeration. These are the facts.

These figures would be proof only of individual comfort if they did not in addition correspond to a national prosperity which has no equivalent in Europe. During the past 10 years the savings banks have seen their deposits rise from £1,023 million to £2,269 million, an increase of 100 per cent. From 1956 to 1958 private savings came to £500 million. Expressed as a percentage of national revenue these figures are amongst the highest in the world and reveal the capacity for investment of only the private sector. From 1948 to 1953 private savings constituted 67 per cent of national capitalization. From 1953 to 1958 it went up to 92 per cent which shows, in the indirect form of the saving of family resources, an extraordinary

*Blaxall: op. cit.

238

increase in the standard of living, consumption having at the same time increased in all sectors. This increase can also be verified through the increase in risk investment in the private sector. On this level there is no movement towards a slump. Dr. M. S. Louw, one of the best economists in the country, speaking of the economic future of South Africa, said:

"We have good reason to believe that during the years to come South Africa will continue to be the most prosperous commercial undertaking on the continent . . . Still higher salaries will increase our capital savings . . . a more and more important percentage of these savings will be devoted to the development of our industries and to the creation of new industries. Each year we will be left with capital to export to neighbouring countries."*

Are people in South Africa aware of the urgent necessity of exporting capital to the *Reserves* in order to build Bantustans?

The State is no less rich than the White citizens of the country.

The rate of income tax is the lowest in the world, the theoretically average family (comprising four people) enjoys a revenue of £1,000 a year. A head of a family in Britain or France, if he were to compare the amount of his income tax with that of the South African, would draw instructive conclusions. The fortunate South African head of the family pays £6 17s. for his £1,000, with three children he pays taxes only after he earns £1,250. With two children, the head of the family pays £44 13s. on £1,500. When he reaches £5,000 the taxes become "heavy"; he pays £870! A married man with an income of more than £10,000 a year pays £2,960 in taxes, and this category of taxpayer supplies the Treasury with a substantial revenue, since there are many of them. A car or two per family, one, two, three or four servants; huge flats with gardens: these are average privileges for members a social category who in France would start thinking about saving a little money to buy a very small car in instalments.

Dr. Verwoerd, when presenting to Parliament the Tomlinson Report on the development of the Reserves, said outright to the country: You have the means of paying. Here are his own words; and he is a man who does not go in for oratorical effects and who is prudent about his accounts:

"Anyone who says that unbearable burdens will be laid on the

*Conference of the Association of Commerce and Industry at Goodwood, Cape Province, May 24, 1960.

shoulders of the taxpayer does not bear in mind the facts. I want to mention various reasons for saying that the country can afford it.

"This country, during the war, for what hon. members called the struggle for existence, spent not £100,000,000 over a period of ten years, but spent £100,000,000 per annum for a period of five years . . . Will the struggle to safeguard the White race here not make it possible to pay £10,000,000 per annum, or whatever the amount might be?

"Ten million pounds per annum is not a large amount compared with the benefits which will be derived; it will promote the safety of the people when the country is in danger of being swamped . . .

"Those (Bantu) people will be in the country in any case. And in any event we will have to incur expenditure to provide for their housing and transport, and to supply them with work.

"But if these 11 million in the course of the next 50 years are to be housed in the vicinity of the large urban developments, the cost of housing them and providing transport will be immeasurably greater than anything which may be necessary if the development can be directed in such a way that use can be made of the Bantu areas.

"Will it not be much cheaper to have this development there than if it takes place in the White cities? Of course. Therefore I say that the country can afford it, and can even save money on it."

VIII

This is obvious.

Starting from this reasoning, which is in no way theoretical, the most realistic plans for financing the most luxurious Bantustans can be drawn up.

Who would dare to suggest that an increase in income tax of 10 per cent would harm the taxpayer in any way? Yet such a step would provide £14 million a year. In 1958 the South African gold mines, which paid dividends of nine per cent on their capital value, handed out £43,400,620 in *profits*. Has one thought that a dividend *reduced* to six per cent would mean a new resource of £15,000,000 a year? And that the beginning of real work on the Bantustans, on a scale compatible with the size of the problem, would open South Africa to international funds through the multiple, parallel, and generous channels of the specialized institutions of the United Nations?

Once they have achieved their independence, the disinherited Reserves of the Republic will take their place as underdeveloped countries. This is a very honourable position in the great family of nations. It is sometimes a position to be envied.

We do not want to go into this matter any further. Dr. Verwoerd could mobilize £1,000 million a year if necessary and if the will to do it was there. What must be encouraged above all, is the will to build the South Africa of tomorrow, to dare to go in for political investments, whatever their economic viability; to build *hassi messaouds*, as France did in the Sahara, even if oil is less expensive in the Gulf of Texas than on the shores of Algeria; to create with the feeling for stage effects that the Alexanders, the Napoleons and the Moses' had; to start digging the wells, regardless of the granite layers or the mental resistance through which one must drill.

In 1959, there was an excess capital of £90 million after finalization of the budget and the payment of the invisible imports (the dividends). This capital served in part to finance the industrialization of Rhodesia. Capital is therefore available, and more severe taxation is not necessary.

In order that the White people in South Africa should be completely associated with this war effort one must perhaps also, in addition to the "great" collective sacrifices, ask them for their voluntary and personal agreement and contributions.

To build Palestine and to help modern Israel, the Jews have their "national funds" collected throughout the world, thanks to daily propaganda which began with the children at school. Penny by penny, shilling by shilling and pound by pound, enough money was raised to build a state.

A popular movement upholding a great political idea is more powerful than the forces of a government, and when a popular movement is allied to state doctrine it can move mountains. One would like to see in South Africa a great national movement to help build the Bantustans. One would like to see the youth movements call out their members for a week or a month in the work camps in Umtata or in Pondoland. One would like to see on the postage stamps of the Republic a voluntary increase levied, which would be paid into a national fund for the building of schools in the reserves. This is done all over the world for the Red Cross, for the blind, for cancer research, for the "Winterhilfe" . . . One would like to see a

241

great national lottery, devoting its benefits to a trust fund for the development of roads for the Bantustans. There are hundreds of possibilities which could be suggested: they are not charity (charity can do nothing to solve the national problem of the Bantu); they would be the sign of an immense awakening, a spiritual investment, an enthusiasm for the realization of the Bantustans that I have not yet encountered.

Perhaps this spectacular movement could change reality as much as political initiative. It can and it must, in any case, go hand in hand with political initiative. In the early days of Zionism, the Jews in Palestine, in order to finance their promised land, sent their delegates throughout the world to sell to Jews abroad small plots of sandy terrain in Jaffa near the sea in exchange for a handful of pounds that was thrown at them like alms. One August evening, in front of the teletype in the foyer of the Carlton Hotel in Johannesburg, which at regular intervals printed the prices on the world's stock market, I thought of these dunes where the dream has become steel and concrete, of these dunes of Tel Aviv and Ramat Gan, where each square yard costs a fortune and which really made the fortune of certain of these generous donors of earlier days who had bought them for pennies. There are hills without value in the Transkei and in the Northern Transvaal which are perhaps the Tel Avivs of tomorrow. Will a movement be born from the Cape to Durban to enrol each South African through his personal gifts, through his personal interest, through his personal work, in the great work of the redemption of the Bantustans?

The people of South Africa, this legitimate race, these people who have been denigrated, who have made mistakes, like all human beings, do they understand that the giant is stirring, that nothing except full rights and complete independence can and *must* satisfy the giant and that they must lend a brotherly hand to the new nations which are in any case going to be born, whether with their help or in the face of their stubborn passivity?

IX

But the real masters of their future are the Bantu themselves. Nobody has ever given a state to a people on a silver platter; a state is acquired and freedom is earned. A flag might be but a rag nailed to a stick, yet it is the most costly object in the world. But with a flag, given the fascination it has for people, one can lead them where-ever one wants. There is no real independence as long as the pioneers of independence do not come from the ranks of the people to be freed. Pinsker spoke of self-emancipation: in the end it is the only valid emancipation because it implies both education and revolution. Real progress doesn't mean a handful of Bantu intellectuals learning to discuss in stylized English the virtues of a system of modern venti-lation. Progress comes when the people who produced this handful of intellectuals have got used to sleeping with their head out of the blankets and with their windows open, and when they no longer seal up the openings of their huts. Progress comes when large numbers of people are capable of assimilating and using the yeast formed by the intellectuals who have sprung from their ranks. But when these intellectuals selfishly flee their community and go and fructify foreign masses, the nation is impoverished, and with each man it loses a small piece of its resurrection.

It is in themselves, in Bantu Zionism, that the Blacks must find the means of emancipating themselves.

The example of Jewish Zionism, of the political movement it produced in the nineteenth century, and the Jewish state which it gave rise to is applicable to the situation of the Bantu.

Money alone cannot do anything if it is not used to back an ideology which bears on its immaterial wings the people who have been inspired by it. Building roads in the Transkei, planting trees in Vendaland, and creating industries in the country of the Zulus would be the most disastrous undertaking if the bush were eventually to reclaim the roads, if the Zulus did not see in these trees the robust columns which will support independence, and if the legitimate pride in goods "made in Zululand" do not for the Bantu take the place of the simple satisfaction of bringing back indispensable wages from the factory. The popular funds of the Jewish Zionist movement led to the creation of the Jewish state because the francs, the pennies, the cents, collected from the people, were used to plant trees, to build roads, and to construct factories where a new race of Jews, the *haloutsim*, with an ideology and a national ideal, worked.

They also came from the most despised and persecuted nation in history. They had been victims of all the apartheids, of all the curfews, of all the political vexations, of all the racial theories, and through the centuries they had carried all the special passports, all the badges of infamy. These Jews have shown, by building their country, that they were the opposite of what everybody said they were. They have given the lie to all the racial theories, they have become tall and upright whereas people used to mock at their puny size and their hunched backs. They have given their country the most modern agriculture, where formerly they were accused of avoiding agricultural work. They brought millions of immigrants to the land of Israel although successive commissions of inquiry and experts had affirmed that there was not room even for a cat and that the soil was worth nothing. It is this Zionism which must spring from the heart of the Bantu people. It is this flag that they must set up in their midst. From the Bantu people themselves must come the visionaries who will dream the Bantustans of tomorrow, who will take the people towards the resurrected country, as Herzl dreamed and realized the Jewish state. Nothing in the present political condition of the Bantu makes this impossible. It was in the darkness of the ghettos that the concrete aspirations of the Jewish state were born.

Man becomes noble, in his own eyes, and in the eyes of his persecutors, when he separates himself from his human brothers who do not want him to affirm his identity and his maturity, and when he achieves on his own soil the equality that is being refused to him. Then those who have despised and trampled on him will recognize in the slave of yesterday their equal.

True nobility lies in seizing the offered chance. The choice is no longer between emancipation in the society of the Whites, and stagnation in the society of the Blacks. Salvation must be found in the emancipation of all the Bantu, with a Bantu language elevated to the rank of an instrument of civilization, with social, economic and spiritual values and a Bantu flag. Did the Jews not learn that the only political rights, the only nationality which could not be contested, the only flag which could not be imputed a crime were their own, and that instead of being assimilated in foreign nations, instead of being German, English, French, anything but themselves, they had to be themselves, Hebrew, Palestinian, Israeli?

They had to relearn in all its nuances the past of their nation, all the moving and changing aspects of their genius, in order to live honourably and freely in the present. Is one worthy of the freedom one demands, begs, claims from one's masters today if one is incapable of willing it; if one refuses the call of a national flag, a national genius, all the mysterious and invisible voices from the past?

The Zionists also had their enemies within their own ranks. People talked of chimera. Rabbis held that God, not man, was to re-establish Jerusalem. The rich did not give a penny . . . *They wanted to be English, or German, or French—and not Jewish.* The realists with their cold reasoning and their figures laughed at the idea of fighting a great empire which was occupying the country. But a handful of idealists, a handful of fanatics wanted a state, in the name of the mass of the Jews, bowed down under the laws of apartheid and curfews, marked with the stigma of infamy sewn on their breasts and shovelled into extermination camps. This state is today universally acknowledged by its former detractors: people come there to learn how to live well and justly and honourably. I say to my Bantu brothers of South Africa that they must find within their ranks this handful of fanatical visionaries.

Failing this, their independence, their freedom, their prosperity, will be nothing but a nebulous dream.

CHAPTER 11

THE HEAVY BURDEN OF THE WHITE MAN

I

South Africa's problems are not abstract; they cannot be solved in a laboratory. The trial to which South Africa is subjected is not a mock-trial. South Africa is caught in the storm, in the whirlpool of the fundamental changes taking place among 200 million Black Africans. A short while ago, the African continent was solidly tied to Europe by a thousand and one invisible and nourishing ties—and also by heavy chains. Now it is suddenly crossed by new centres of gravity, contradictory pivots plunging into the loose earth of new ideologies, each trying to become the central axis of the whole of Africa. Must one follow the Accra line, advocating a haughty negritude? Or the Cairo line pointing, like a dagger, from the Maghreb to Mauritania and the Sahara? So many discordant voices tend to turn the head of the old, immobile continent. It is on this loose ground that South Africa will have to build her contribution to human civilization, the Bantustans, and if she fails to create them and to anchor herself on them, she will sink in the quicksands of African numbers. But, once she has played her role, she will have a legitimate right to a share in the control of the continent, and to continue in the name of the White man the magnificent work which he has initiated there.

II

The Whites who suffer from a guilt complex when they look at their deeds in Africa are wrong. In most cases, if they knew the truth, they could be legitimately proud of their achievements.

To be imbued with this pride, one has only to focus one's mind the right way to obtain an accurate picture of the African scene, and to forget the comfortable fictions of propaganda. Within fifty years, Europe has contributed more to the development of Africa than she herself has contributed in a thousand years to civilization in her own lands. Thanks to Europe, Africa has been able to jump without any intermediary stages from the first century to the twentieth century, literally, from the Stone Age to the age of the space-rocket. The young Africans whose fathers wore tiger skins, and who had no words to describe a date or a fork, have now become—thanks to the Whites— surgeons, lawyers, sometimes Prime Ministers. These are facts. It seems to me absurd that the White man should feel guilty, that he should accuse himself for not having squeezed a little more than a thousand years into fifty, and in a more efficient way.

The words of Philip Mitchell, a former governor of Kenya and Uganda, seem to me to be valid for the whole of Africa:

"The Africans had no wheeled transport and . . . no animal transport either; they had no roads nor towns; no tools except small hand hoes, axes, wooden digging sticks, and the like; no manufactures, and no industrial products except the simplest domestic handiwork; no commerce as we understand it and no currency, although in some places barter of produce was facilitated by the use of small shells; they had never heard of working for wages. They went stark naked or clad in the bark of trees or the skins of animals; and they had no means of writing, even by hieroglyphics, nor of numbering except by their fingers or making notches in a stick or knots in a piece of grass or fibre; they had no weights or measures of general use. Perhaps most astonishing of all to the modern European mind, they had no calendar, no notation of time . . . Before European occupation there was no way of saying 1st January, 1890 or 2.30 p.m., or their equivalents, in any language spoken from Abyssinia to the Transvaal, except Swahili along the coast . . . They were pagan, spirits of ancestor propitiators in the grip of magic or witchcraft, their minds cribbed and confined by superstition . . . They are a people who in 1890 were in a more primitive condition than anything of which there is any record in pre-Roman Britain."

What did Europe do to help Africa out of these deplorable conditions?*

First of all she abolished slavery.

The slave trade has been practised for more than two thousand years by the Arabs in Africa. The European countries began to

*We are borrowing the outline of this analysis from the excellent work by Dr. J. J. Oberholster: *The Contribution of the West to the Development of Africa.*

participate in it in the fifteenth century, but already at the end of the sixteenth century voices asking for its abolition began to make themselves heard in Europe, and the British Government abolished the trade in 1807. The practice of slavery, however, disappeared slowly in Africa, and Albert Schweitzer found vestiges of it in 1913 when he arrived in Equatorial Africa. There was a slave-trading scandal in Liberia in 1930. Members of the government were implicated. But in no country ruled by a European power was slavery able to maintain itself. In Paris or London, or New York this statement means nothing. But in primitive Africa the indelible marks of the slave merchants imprinted on the backs or thighs of old people are visible landmarks on the road travelled by Black Africa under White guidance. In contrast to what the Europeans did, Saudi Arabia, where the spirit of Europe has not penetrated in spite of the Cadillacs and the air-conditioned palaces, still practises slavery and takes part in the slave trade along the Eastern coasts of Africa. And yet we are on the threshold of the twenty-first century.

The White man also absolished inter-tribal warfare. War, for Africa, was a tradition, a pastime for the young warriors. Perhaps it had its roots in the biological necessity to get rid of hungry mouths in a starving continent. Tribal warfare kept Africa in a constant state of agitation. It caused the migration of the Bantu. It made the simple enjoyment of life and property uncertain. The White man has turned the troubled sea of the Bantu's social life into a calm lake. Cannibalism has been rooted out.

But the White man not only suppressed these positive causes of destruction and death; he also created positive sources of well-being and life. He brought with him sanitary services and medicine. The tropical climate produces a series of diseases peculiar to Africa: malaria, leprosy, yellow fever, dysentery, sleeping sickness, elephantiasis, trachoma, etc. Many of these diseases were unknown in Europe. Malaria was the worst killer, and still accounts for about three million victims a year. The Quinine Company of the ex-Belgian Congo, the Rockefeller Institute, the Pasteur Institute of Dakar, the West African Institute for Trypanosomiasis in Northern Nigeria, the Institute for Research of the American Foundation in Liberia, are among the hundreds of sanitation pioneers in Africa. Tens of millions of human lives are owed to them. In addition to the struggle against endemic diseases, the White man organized the struggle against infant mortality, which has brought about a spectacular rise in the population figures. This better chance of survival triggered off a demand for better living conditions: better lodgings, and more leisure-time, the very basis of a higher and just civilization.

Above all, the White man brought education.

Before the White man came, the Black man lived under the absolute power of chiefs and witch-doctors. Their lives, their possessions and their souls belonged to the witch-doctor. Without education as a basis, one could build any kind of facade on backward Africa, but once the scaffolding was taken down, nothing would hold.

No cultural tradition predisposed the Black man for education. Hundreds of languages, without written literatures, stood in the way of any large-scale educational system. Children and parents resisted instruction, passively or in an openly hostile way. The White man broke through this shell, this fundamental obstruction to further civilization, and the missionaries played an important role in this daily, fundamental struggle to give the African the necessary entrance ticket to the twentieth century. The Whites blame themselves, and are blamed, for not having done more. But a few years ago their first pioneer schoolteachers were still being massacred in the bush.

Today, 15 per cent of the total population of Africa south of the Sahara have received some kind of education. A complete account of this White contribution to civilization in Africa cannot be given in this book. It was the White man who brought the radio, cinema, museums, scientific research, applied science and the Press to Africa. The Press has played and will continue to play a very important role in the political education of the masses, and it is unthinkingly being turned against the White man who brought it.

The White man has opened up the economic potential in Africa to effective exploitation.

Africa has a prodigious capacity for production, to a large degree still unexploited. She possesses 52 per cent of the hydro-electric reserves in the world, and most of its mineral resources. The White man has exploited these riches to his benefit. By doing so, he also taught the Black man the technical know-how and stimulated in him the needs he can now satisfy. This period of colonial transition came to an end after the Second World War. The short-lived and monstrous hegemony of Hitler had one single happy consequence, at least for Africa: it gave the finishing blow to even the legitimate and the most necessary guardianship of one people by another, and it brought the idea of immediate and unconditional independence. The development of the African countries, for the benefit of the African countries, has replaced the doctrine of exploitation by a metropolitan power.

It is in the economic field that the White man has given most to Africa.

When he arrived, Bantu economy consisted solely of agriculture and cattle-breeding—a subsistence economy at a very low level. Characteristically, it was the White man who introduced to the agriculture of the Blacks most of the crops which are thought to be indigenous to Africa, and which are, in fact, imported. The Portuguese brought corn, manioc, sweet potatoes and tobacco. The Portuguese vie with the Arabs and the Indonesians with regard to the honour of having imported from the West Indies, in the fifteenth century, the banana tree, the palm tree and the coconut tree, which in any case are not indigenous to the continent they symbolize! Sisal was brought to Africa by a German botanist, Hindorf. Where would Africa be without these species which form the basis of her agricultural production?

The White man has, above all, through his struggle against soil erosion, termites and the tsetse fly, and through his cattle-vaccination, transformed a subsistence economy into a classical economy, which allows the producer to buy and sell. He introduced the great plantations, giving an economic physiognomy to the territories which possess them: sugar-cane in Natal, cocoa in Ghana, rubber in Liberia—the life-blood of this country—palm trees and coconut trees in Nigeria, sisal in Tanganyika, and the countless industrial plantations of timber, coffee, and cotton in Central Africa.

The White man created industry in Africa. He dug the mines which exploit the mineral riches of the continent: but the great mass of these riches are still unexploited; the territories and the colonies which are achieving independence are masters of vast untapped treasures. The copper-belts in Katanga and Rhodesia are examples: their annual production is worth £200 million! The Congo produces 75 per cent of the industrial diamonds in the world. Aluminium, gold, uranium, zinc, iron and manganese are all to be found there.

The mines have given the Black African his "birth certificate" in industrial technique. The mines led to electrification. Out of a world reserve of 472 million H.P. in hydro-electric resources, Africa possesses 243 million, that is to say 52.3 per cent of the total. The Owen, Jinja and Sheley falls, the rapids cutting through the great African rivers, the Zambezi, the Nile, the Congo, the Niger, the Gambia and the Senegal are the easiest to exploit. The hydro-electric power stations on the falls of the Nile, the Kariba Dam on the Zambezi, the dam on the Kouilou River, the dam planned on the Volta River in Ghana are just a beginning. The mines were the initial cause of the African transport network, especially of the railways. The pattern of the African railways network corresponds to the location of the mineral riches and their markets. The inhospitable coasts of the continent were tamed for the same reason in Dakar, Abidjan, Monrovia, Accra, Lagos, Boma, Lobito, Lourenco Marques, Dar Es Salaam, Mombasa, etc. The mines led to urban concentration, and, consequently, to an increased demand for agricultural products. They stimulated the whole economy. In addition, the largely unvaried production of most African countries, which only possess one or two principal exports, brings with it a semi-dependency on European markets. Ninety-seven per cent of the exports from Gambia consist of ground nuts, and 50 per cent of Ghana's exports are made up of cocoa. But has not Europe given Africa, which has the monopoly of certain products (some of which even have strategic value), the possibility of exerting pressure on the world markets, and not simply depending on it?

Finally, in the political field, the contribution of the White man is fundamental. The Black man does not realize his ambitions by revolting against the philosophies taught by his former masters. The contrary is true. The White man not only created the cultural, social, and economic basis of independence: he taught the Black man to ask for it and to practise it. Six European powers participated in the colonization of Africa: Great Britain, France, Portugal, Belgium, Germany and Italy. Despite the different political systems, despite abuses and excesses, the colonial policies of these powers had one thing in common: the creation of conditions of peace and order necessary to the establishment of a system of Western administration. Great Britain had the guiding rule of "creative abdication", guardianship leading to restoration of the colonial territories to the chiefs or to their successors, so that the natives can govern themselves. France and Portugal aimed at the integration of the colonial territory with the metropolitan power, as a progressive political assimilation of the metropolitan and African populations. These two doctrines none the less contributed to the political development of the African masses, and to their initiation into the European systems of administration and government. The pace of initiation varied according to place and time; but it remains a truth to observe and to proclaim, proudly if necessary, that the political development of the Black peoples of Africa was the work of the White man.

Generally speaking, on all levels, technical, social and political, Africa as we see her today, sometimes a little shaky, sometimes threatening, sometimes attentive in the attitude of the enlightened disciple watching and listening, is a creation of Europe, of Europe alone, and Africa owes to Europe her rapid and brilliant emancipation.

Africa has a long tradition of borrowing from outside civilizations . . . Two thousand years ago, she imported her hatchets and daggers, traded for ivory and palm oil. In 1597, a Portuguese navigator noted in his diary how the natives in Natal treasured glass pearls. Livingstone, in the nineteenth century, found loin-cloths, in the heart of Africa, made of Lancashire cloth, brought over six hundred miles, through bush and jungle, from the East African "slave coast".

III

A great South African, General Smuts, wrote: "For better or for worse, the old Africa has gone, and the White man must face the new situation which he himself created."

Facing the new situation—does that mean stiffening in a gesture of defiance, abdicating, or continuing to claim his share of the "heavy burden", that is to say, continuing to serve the Black man in his youthful ascent?

The White man has abdicated nowhere. He continues to claim his share. People continue to ask for his services: in Ghana, where White technicians are more numerous than before independence; in the Congo, where his expulsion and the rape of his women brought about the collapse of the state; in the former French colonies, where his know-how, his experience, his money are used as before. And all this happens without any false shame, and for the happiness of everyone, without any grandiloquent declarations which would prevent the White technicians from going about their business and the Black students from continuing their studies. The work of the White man is going on. And his work is perhaps more important than before decolonization.

What is his work? What are the great contributions the White man is called upon to render to his former pupils?

Europe is a good conductor. She can and must prevent the new Black republics, the former British, French and Italian colonies (perhaps, tomorrow, the former Portuguese . . .) from coming to add their "wailings"—as Max Olivier Lecamp wrote in the *Figaro* of July 11, 1960—"to what was formerly called the concert of nations."

"In the midst of the folk dances," he adds, "and the joyous cries, the explosions of crackers and the rolling of the drums, shining new flags are raised before ambassadors who have come from all parts of the world to be saluted by national anthems which have never been heard before; more or less magnificent celebrations take place, and they are often very good and always moving, because they are held in the spirit of a friendship preserved—or found again—between those who were colonized, and who bear no grudges, and those who colonized and who have no bitterness. Once the fairy lights have gone out and the envoys extraordinary and plenipotentiary have left for another baptism, everyday life starts again, without any collapse of the machinery of the state which has just been formally handed over, and without the former masters being massacred, chased away or molested.

"Unfortunately this was not the case in the Belgian Congo, whose achievement of independence seems much more like the death of a colony than the birth of a republic."

This is because the worst kind of independence is pseudo-independence. Independence implies more duties than rights. Superficial nationalism leads to the elevation of a rebel who kills the President of a Council in Damas, Cairo, or Tunis to the status of a spiritual descendent of Garibaldi or Jefferson. Many leaders of young nations are haunted by the external, institutional vision of national liberation. Everything is subordinated to the flag, to the name of the currency, to the constitution and to the national Parliament, in short, the forms and outer symbols of sovereignty. Yet, the new currency very often has the backing of only a foreign subsidy, the flag has the support of only one of the two big Powers who are trying to share the world, the constitution does not guarantee any rights to the citizen, and Members sit in Parliament only at the command or sufferance of a dictator. People and nations who have had longer experience of national life, know that once the external forms have been acquired or the domination of a foreign power has been rejected, a nation, in order really to *exist*, must solve the problems of the individuals who form it and the problems of the orderly membership of the society of civilized nations. The name "nation" is nothing but the symbol of a capacity to solve collective problems in international terms. The awakenings and the disappointments, and sometimes the definite failures, occur at these cross-roads. The colonial power has been expelled. The national flag is flying from the poles. But age-old poverty and exploitation persist in the same way, and sometimes worse. The colonialist yoke had, until then, been held responsible: national independence has not changed anything. A man, a people, can be politically free, and yet the quintessence of this freedom remains inextricably entangled in the evils that beset it: hunger, endemic disease and police interference. An institutional victory is not enough. Although it remains the unique expression of victorious nationalism, it is a threat for the liberated people and for their neighbours. Liberty reigns in a country, and peace at its frontiers, only when the national movement has learned to love true independence, which consists in setting positive aims for the culture of the people and their resources. Even parliamentary democracy is nothing. What matters are the parliamentary democrats.

But few men in Africa know this. Europe, who knows a little more about it, must help Africa not to fall into pseudo-independence. In several African countries, the pure and simple retreat of the White man could lead to chaos. A former governor-general of the former Belgian Congo thought that the jungle would soon grow again over the edifice he had left in Africa.

"It will take a few years, because we built well, but the forest will come back, sir, it will come back."

I do not know whether events will justify the pessimistic prediction of this former governor; but it is certain that if rulers like Lumumba were to gain power in Africa, the thickest jungle will inevitably cover up the civilizing influence of the White man. And the worst kind of jungle is not the luxuriant vegetation of the tropics. The worst kind of jungle is the spiritual jungle, the flowering of wonderful projects, of grandiloquent plans which claim to solve, forever, problems which they merely mask. The world is full of sports stadiums which were abandoned after the foundation-stone had been laid, empty theatres, dry dams, big irrigation canals which do not irrigate anything, highways which lead nowhere, and many other projects which only got to the paper stage. One government ousted another, and set up its own great projects rather than realize those of its predecessor. Let us pray that Africa will be protected from this kind of greatness, and that she will be modest! The modesty of good administration, good transport, good teachers, laboratories manned with scientists, hospitals, doctors and nurses with the spirit of missionaries.

Let us pray that Africa will find the vocation to take part in the "concert of nations". This Europe can teach her . . .

An African full of humour and wisdom once said: "You can play a tune of sorts on the white keys, and you can play a tune of sorts on the black keys, but to achieve harmony you must use both the black and white keys." It is more difficult, but more beautiful.

IV

Today, the West is bidding against the East for the soul of Africa.

This is a pity, and in the end it will be Africa that will suffer most.

We see Africa, in degrees which vary according to the countries concerned, sliding into the temptation of positive neutralism. It means eating out of every manger, promising to the highest bidder what the lowest bidder soon buys back with an outrageously high bid. This inflation of the values to be sold (which are not really worth so much) produces apathy, the feeling that there is no urgent need to develop the essential values of culture and political maturity, since one is accepted as mature by the greatest Powers and praised to the skies because of their gratitude and their intrigues.

This illusion is dangerous. Africa's favours are sought precisely because she is the contrary of what she has been made to think she is: a minor, with a new and attractive body; plasticine which is easy to shape, and which people want to mould into a definite shape to suit their selfish purposes. The strategic need for Africa today could

255

easily disappear tomorrow. Both the West and the East could be satisfied elsewhere. Africa, courted with such tender care, is running the same risk as the "Arab world" which is being cultivated today for its oil, but which will be dropped back again into the dark when its oil will have been replaced by nuclear energy: it will be dropped without any consideration for the moral trauma inflicted upon it. The sooner Africa learns this, the better it will be, for her.

In this respect, Europe can perhaps play the important role of helping Africa to be true to herself, and not to be a pawn changing hands between the Powers. To succeed, Europe must inculcate in Africa the conviction that in years to come a series of North-South problems and North-South alliances could take the place of the East-West problems and conflicts which today divide the world. In Asia where everything will come from, the great movement of the mass of continental China might be towards the Soviet Far East, and the unpopulated solitudes of the Southern Pacific, rather than towards Asia and Africa. If this were to happen, a Russo-American pact might bring an end to the current Russo-American conflict. In Europe the success of a great Common Market might mean to the independent countries of West and Central Africa the opportunity of economic integration into a great economic Third Power on which they would be dependent. From a more limited geo-political viewpoint: the idea of the Maghreb having been realized and its disastrous ties with Egypt broken, North Africa might find itself again in a state of independence, and, with the respect of independence, linked to its European destiny. Egypt herself, freed from her Pan-Arab dreams (which cannot lead to anything, because the rich oil countries in the Middle East will always reject the hegemony of the poorer Nile valley) might be able to discover a peaceful, constructive and logical destiny, by investing her dynamism in a huge internal development scheme for the Sudan and for co-operation with Ethiopia, and by the exploitation, together with Israel, of the Sinai Desert. Rhodesia, which has so many prospects in common with the Republic of South Africa, might find in union with this other Europe the consolidation of a destiny which today seems to be an illusion. If Africa—all the states of Africa which have some political status and are fairly mature—understood that they have in the North, whence light traditionally came to them, a great chance against the might of Asia, then the growing-pains which today turn them against their former masters might suddenly change into an awareness of their own maturity, of their equality with the master who will have clearly succeeded in bringing them up to his level.

V

What I have said here about the heavy burden of the White man in Africa and about the future I would like to see for the Black man, vitally concerns South Africa. Europe and South Africa are really two Europes which hold the continent between their two magnetic poles. For political reasons which are known to us, these poles, which used to nourish the continent, have deviated for a time from their natural destiny. I believe that South Africa, when it has been partitioned and South Africa consists only of the Transvaal, the Cape, the Orange Free State and a part of Natal, will once again become a Western country, a country of Whites and Coloureds. I think that the Bantustans will have inherited from the mother country, through their long osmosis, a degree of political maturity equal or superior to that of many other independent countries in the world.

I believe that when this comes to pass, South Africa will have to play an important role. Whatever Europe can provide, South Africa can provide too, not only in the form of guidance to her former internal colonies, but in a great fraternal gesture to the benefit of all her neighbours. Europe and South Africa can help every nation in Africa, provided that it is concerned with true independence, and not with the ecstasy of pseudo-independence.

This must be understood in Pretoria—not only understood, but felt as an obligation towards the whole of Africa. South Africa must cut the Gordian knots of indifference, apathy, routine. It must also be understood and approved in Accra, in Bamako, in Leopoldville, in London, at Lake Success.

I pray to God that this book may contribute its share to this end. If it has made one single heart beat in warmer friendship, if it has opened the eyes of one individual to another approach of South Africa's problems and their possible solutions, it will not have been written in vain on the very brink of a precipice and on the verge of political ruin.

Pretoria-Paris . August 1960—June 1961

257

DATE DUE